More praise for *Survivors in Mexico*:

"West portrays an intricate ancient culture with compelling authority and dazzling wit. Her luminous, heretofore unpublished meditation on Mexico—its landscape, its history, its politics—is a gift from the twentieth century to the twenty-first, a magical masterpiece."—Sandra M. Gilbert, coauthor of *Madwoman in the Attic* and *No Man's Land*

"[West's] book is so interesting because she can encompass the beauty and the genius of the place and its artifacts while turning her always beady eye on the malefactors who despoiled one of the world's greatest, and aesthetically most distinguished, ancient civilizations for private gain. . . . *Survivors in Mexico* belongs on the same shelf as those other classics on the subject, Graham Greene's *The Lawless Roads* and D. H. Lawrence's *Mornings In Mexico*."—Tom Rosenthal, *Daily Mail*

"Too smart to be a specialist, too engaged to study history for history lessons or art for art's sake, West endeavors to understand Mexico as a whole: military history, agricultural advances, everyday life, revolutionary politics, and pseudo-revolutionary art included. . . . West's bold strokes make for compelling writing. . . . Note the relentless emphasis here on greatness, which is what West gets from Mexico, and what she gives to it."—Jori Finkel, *Village Voice Literary Supplement*

Survivors in Mexico

Rebecca West

Edited and introduced

by Bernard Schweizer

Yale Nota Bene

Yale University Press

New Haven & London

First published as a Yale Nota Bene book in 2004.
First published by Yale University Press in 2003.

For information about this and other Yale University Press publications,
please contact:

U.S. office	sales.press@yale.edu
Europe office	sales@yaleup.co.uk

Printed in the United States of America.

Library of Congress Control Number: 2004110108

ISBN 0-300-10521-5 (pbk.)

A catalogue record for this book is available from the British Library.

10 9 8 7 6 5 4 3 2 1

To
Lori Curtis
and the
McFarlin Special Collections Library
at the University of Tulsa

Contents

Acknowledgments

I am grateful to the Committee for Promoting Young Scholars at the University of Zurich and to Peter Hughes and Allen Reddick from the English department of the University of Zurich, for providing financial aid and institutional support to pursue this edition. I am further indebted to Lori Curtis, head of special collections at the McFarlin Library in Tulsa, Oklahoma, for meeting all my scholarly needs and for providing a stimulating research environment. Thanks are also due to Milissa Burkart and Lisa Inman at the McFarlin Special Collections Library for their prompt and expert research support. I am grateful that the literary estate of Rebecca West gave me permission to publish this edition of *Survivors in Mexico*, and I would like to acknowledge Diane Stainforth's prior transcription of a number of West's holograph manuscripts. Carl Rollyson has earned my gratitude for his apt scholarly advice and for introducing me to Kit Wright, who has shared her reminiscences about Rebecca West with me in her beautiful home in Greenwich, Connecticut. Next, I want to thank Mario Chamorro for contacting the Mexican authorities on my behalf. In the final stages of this project, John Kulka from Yale University Press has stepped in as a flawless, energetic, critical, and enthusiastic editor—thanks so much! My wife and daughter, the sine qua non of my life and work, deserve the deepest gratitude of all.

Last, but not least, I would like to thank Greenwood Press for permission to reprint in the Introduction a version of the table that first appeared in my monograph *Rebecca West: Heroism, Rebellion, and the Female Epic* (2002).

Introduction

Survivors in Mexico sums up Rebecca West's mature views on politics, philosophy, religion, psychology, and culture. For a work of such epic aspiration, it had a surprisingly modest beginning. In 1966, West accepted a commission from the *New Yorker* to write an article on Leon Trotsky's grandson, Seva, who was then still living in his grandfather's house in Mexico City. West, who had always wanted to visit Mexico, had recently finished reading Isaac Deutscher's enormous three-volume biography of Leon Trotsky and was fascinated by the prospect of talking to Trotsky's nearest surviving relative. A brief encounter with Seva did take place in Mexico City, but the planned article for the *New Yorker* never materialised. Instead, West began to perceive the potential for a much larger project, a cultural anatomy along the lines of *Black Lamb and Grey Falcon* that would pick up where she had left off in the earlier book. There would be poignant discussions of humanity's obsession with violence, guilt, and sacrifice, as well as meditations on the redemptive function of art. But the book was to transcend these perennial concerns of West's to include other aspects of the human struggle, as evidenced in her sustained reflections on anarchism, determinism, and metaphysical rebellion. Moreover, the word "survivors" in West's working title indicates that she intended to document the ultimate triumph of human strength over worldly as well as cosmic forms of adversity.

Indeed, West's eponymous survivors include such models of resilience as Seva Trotsky, Mexico's Indian population, and West herself; but in a larger sense, she was invoking the very life force itself. West saw evidence of this prodigious force everywhere in Mexico, notably in the bustle and life of Mexico City's crowded streets and parks, in the colourful bounty of the Indian markets, and in the revival of the Aztec heritage in modern-day Mexico. In one of her diary entries for November 1966, she remarked on the collective aspect of this cultural revival, noting that "Mexicans do not ever stand up for themselves. They are standing up for a process, for the Indians, for the 'tradition' or 'innovation.'"

West's notion of process, which is an integral dimension of the life force, had already been invoked in *Black Lamb and Grey Falcon*, her book on Yugoslavia published in 1941. But there it had been overshadowed by its very antithesis, namely the destructive cycle of sacrifice and victimisation as personified in the figures of Gerda and Tsar Lazar. A similar sense of doom and apprehension is evidenced in West's writings about South Africa in 1960. In one of her dispatches for the *Sunday Times*, she stressed that "the racial problem erodes everything in this country, invites vain sacrifice and penalises merit." West's four articles about South Africa built a powerful case against apartheid by documenting its noxious social effects, its legalistic inconsistencies, and its inhuman logic. Writing to her husband, Henry Andrews, West let her journalistic guard down to exclaim: "I regard Apartheid with contempt as pure idiocy and provocative of endless suffering."

In Mexico, quite a different political, racial, and cultural dynamic was in evidence, and it pleased West that mestizos not only constituted the majority of the population but were treated on an equal footing with their white fellow countrymen: "Here, if a white man and a man of mixed blood quarrel, it is simply as if a dark man has fallen out with his brother who takes after the other side of the family and is fair: no more than that." Of course, West was well aware of the inequities suffered by the nation's pure-blooded Indians, and she explored their tragic predicament at length. But she was swayed by the omnipresence of cultural and racial mixing, as she saw it evidenced in the streets, the museums, and the recreation parks of Mexico. She even compared the skin tone of the people thronging Mexico City's sidewalks to the colour of her favourite beverage, a blend of coffee, milk, and cocoa. West's notion of process, then, becomes intertwined with the forces that drive the multicultural, multiethnic, and multiracial society of Mexico—forces which she saw as springing from the ongoing dialectic of past and present and from a frank physical attraction between the races.

In spite of her enthusiasm for the country, West's stay in Mexico was not devoid of setbacks. She was often irritated by Mexican incompetence on an official level, once fuming in her diary: "The near impossibility of getting my gloves back from the Hilton. 'There's no need to get excited.' This from a Mexican." West also came to believe that she was the victim of a plot to withhold information from her, and she suspected her Mexican liaisons of subterfuge. It was not the first time that West felt her local contacts were sabotaging her investigations. Writing from South Africa in 1960 she had complained that "the secretary of the Treason Defence Fund . . . is obviously a Red. I have asked again and again for particulars of the treason trial and how I can read certain passages—and got nothing out of her." In her own account, West ran into similar difficulties in Mexico. Kate Robinson Schubart, an American journalist who had provided West with introductions to Mexican government officials, remembers that "she came back and at some point told us that the government people with whom I had connected her had foiled her attempts to travel and/or to contact people she wanted to talk with. She was convinced it wasn't incompetence, but malicious intent. At the time I felt this was evidence of Rebecca West's paranoia, though I suppose it's possible the government didn't want her to contact some of the people she was interested in."

The substance of West's suspicion about the uncooperative behaviour of Mexican officials is now hard to verify, but because she did not speak Spanish the language barrier seems to have exacerbated whatever animosity existed between West and her contacts. She describes in her diary, for instance, a "mysterious incident at the Palace of Bellas Artes. Hernandez had told us to look out for a secretary at the main entrance. We recognised him by his markings. . . . We told him in French and English that we were Madame Hernandez's guests—he said we must get tickets—he went in and [after] refusing to admit us suddenly he gave in, we could not think why he had rejected us, he had the slip in his hands." To an external observer, this surely looks more like befuddlement than conspiracy.

Her real or imagined tangles with Mexican officials aside, West managed to fulfil an ambitious visitor's programme, travelling to Puebla, Chulela, Oaxaca, Mitla, Cuernavaca, and Teotihuacán. But although she was charmed by the rural villages and was impressed by the ecclesiastical architecture of Puebla and Oaxaca, she felt most at home in metropolitan Mexico City. Here her intellectual faculties found innumerable opportunities for exercise, as culture, history, and society fused in an exhilarating fabric. When visiting the Anthropological Museum or the museum of Diego Rivera, she was enchanted as much by the museum-goers as by the exhibits themselves: "They have a reverence for objects," she wrote approvingly in her diary. "They stand in museums." What struck her about Mexicans' interest in their own culture, both past and present, was that it had not been jaded by cynicism. She once elaborated on this notion, writing: "It came to me that Mexico has escaped the age of the snigger. You can tell that by the sculpture. The sculptors weren't afraid of being naive in [the] extreme. The New York sculptors (Park Avenue) are not afraid of being extreme but they are afraid of being naive. The whole thing would stop if Mexicans began to snigger and fear the snigger." Lest this be taken as evidence of a latent primitivism on her part, let me juxtapose this statement with another comment from her diary. After cancelling a planned trip to see an Indian village mystic on the Day of the Dead, she recorded wryly: "I could only have D. H. Lawrenced that." Instead of celebrating and mystifying the nation's Indian roots, West had something else in mind—to explore the process by which Mexico's past had made the present and to find out in what ways the history and culture of Mexico were typical (or indeed symptomatic) of the larger human predicament.

Upon returning to England in December 1966, West began to read voraciously about Mexico and its history, and she soon produced a long, sustained draft detailing her stay in Mexico City, reflecting on Aztec civilisation, and narrating the history of Mexico's conquest by Hernán Cortés. But then the work began to sputter. One major distraction was the progressive illness of her husband, Henry Andrews, who had moreover discouraged her from writing the Mexican book to begin with. West confessed in a letter to a friend: "I just had to put my Mexican book away. Henry didn't approve of it and his disapproval is pervasive like a London fog. It suffocated that book." It seems that after her husband's death in the fall of 1968, West took up her Mexican project intermittently for another year. But she still struggled with alternate beginnings, and her second journey to Mexico, in October 1969, must have been an attempt to revive the ailing work. Apart from a brief journey down to Villahermosa and Yucatán, she spent most of her time in Cuernavaca enjoying the hospitality of her old friend Kit

Wright. But now her Mexican project began to evolve into a biography of her late husband, and even that remained incomplete.

To West's biographer Carl Rollyson, these are indications of West's advanced age, leading to a lack of writerly stamina and a terminal loss of vision. Rollyson explained the matter this way: "She began her book at the age of seventy-four; it would have taken at least five years to finish at a time when she also wanted to complete *Cousin Rosamund*, her fictional sage of the century, and to write short stories. It was an enormous, astonishing pyramid of a book to consider scaling at this late state in her career. It is not surprising that she did not complete it; what is remarkable is that some of the sixty-thousand plus words she produced approach the level of *Black Lamb and Grey Falcon*." Although Rollyson's account makes perfect sense in its own right, he actually hints at another explanation that might be just as relevant to her inability to conclude the book. By comparing what he calls the "Mayan ruin" of *Survivors in Mexico* with her earlier book, *Black Lamb and Grey Falcon*, Rollyson identifies an important clue. It is just as plausible that West was consciously (or unconsciously) measuring her progress on the new book against her towering achievement of twenty-five years before, trying to live up to her efforts on a work that had already become a classic of twentieth-century literature. It would be a tall order under any circumstances.

That West was indeed reckoning with *Black Lamb and Grey Falcon* while composing *Survivors in Mexico* is evident from numerous cross-references, topical allusions, and ideological similarities between the two works. In fact, the anti-Turkish rhetoric of the opening passage links the book ideologically with *Black Lamb and Grey Falcon*, just as the first sentence establishes the continuity on a geographical and chronological level: "Thirty years ago, in the Macedonian province of Yugoslavia, I knew one of the last pashas." This is a clear enough indication that *Survivors in Mexico* was planned as a sequel to *Black Lamb and Grey Falcon*. Although the fragmented and unfinished nature of *Survivors in Mexico* obviously makes this the smaller achievement, the book need not fear comparison with its illustrious predecessor. *Survivors in Mexico* parallels the conceptual precision, the intellectual audacity, and the figurative subtlety of West's most sophisticated nonfiction writings. The fact that West told one of the most frequently rehearsed stories in world history, the conquest of Mexico by Cortés, does not detract from the interest of her narrative. As in *Black Lamb and Grey Falcon*, West brings her conventional historical material to life with brilliant interpretations and creative narrative extrapolations. She embellishes Bernal Díaz's stolid account of Cortés's first interview with Montezuma, for instance, so ingeniously as to shed a revealingly new, personal light on this fateful encounter.

West's emblematic approach to Mexico indicates another area of similarity between *Survivors in Mexico* and *Black Lamb and Grey Falcon*. Just like Yugoslavia before, Mexico now served West as a foil to throw into relief her own society's political, social, and cultural condition. She repeatedly compares the Aztec system of taxation, for instance, with the demands made by Britain's Inland Revenue, and she considers the social policy of the Aztecs as a form of the welfare state; sometimes, too, she equates the status of wealthy Aztec traders with the social standing of affluent members of the middle class in England. West even admits that "looking at the Aztec society is, with the exception of one grim feature, like looking into a mirror." Of course, this one grim feature is human sacrifice, and West significantly shied away from a full-scale engagement with the subject. As I have shown elsewhere, West takes the story of the conquest of Mexico by Hernán Cortés up to the point where the practice of human sacrifice needs to be dealt with—only to become evasive and start on another footing, with a different topic. West must have felt that she had said all that needed to be said about humanity's twin infatuations with sacrifice and victimisation; at the same time, however, she sensed that this problem still haunted her, all but defying a rational explanation.

Other parallels to *Black Lamb and Grey Falcon* come to mind when reading *Survivors in Mexico*. In both books West develops a historical double vision that encompasses both the conventional historical approach of "great deeds by great men" and the perspective of "peripheral" participants to the historical process, notably underprivileged and forgotten segments of society. Thus, not only does she cast her conceptual nets very wide (in this case covering the conquest of Mexico, the Mexican Revolution, the European sources of Mexican radicalism, the Mexican mural movement, race relations, and contemporary Mexican life), but the mesh is fine enough to catch the small as well as the bigger fish. Although she dwells at length on the deeds of Cortés, Montezuma, and Trotsky, she also discusses the life of slaves and peasants in Aztec society. West's revisionist historical impulse is further evidenced in her resuscitation of two half-forgotten political thinkers of the nineteenth century, Elie and Elisée Reclus, and in her focus on a little-known Mexican radical artist called Dr. Atl. Although Atl had slipped into obscurity by the second half of the twentieth century, he had actually played a crucial role in Mexico's political development and in its art history. He can be credited with having discovered and promoted the talent of Diego Rivera and for having initiated the artists' association called Centro Artístico in 1910, which gave the Mexican muralists a collective voice and political mission. Moreover, he helped Venustiano Carranza oust Victoriano Huerta from the presidency and had a hand in the writing of the Mexican constitution of 1917. Most contemporary histories of Mexico mention Dr. Atl only in passing, but this was not always so. MacKinley Helm's seminal study *Mexican Painters*, published in 1941, opens with an entire chapter on Dr. Atl. West recognised the centrality of this now "peripheral" figure and intended to place Dr. Atl squarely in the thick of twentieth-century Mexican history.

Part of West's interest in Mexican artists stems, paradoxically, from her fascination with French and Spanish painters and revolutionaries during the nineteenth and early twentieth centuries. She knew that several Mexican painters, including Francisco Goitia, Dr. Atl, Diego Rivera, Frida Kahlo, and David Alfaro Siqueiros had all been to Spain and France at some point in their artistic careers, honing their artistic skills while undergoing a parallel education in political radicalism. West was highly sensitive to this side of Mexico's cultural history, and she was pleased to bring into play her deep knowledge of continental political and aesthetic history. But Mexico held a number of other fascinations for her, including an epic clash of civilisations in the sixteenth century, a pioneering decolonisation movement, a foiled attempt to extend the Habsburg monarchy, and a heroic gesture of national pride—the nationalisation of foreign petroleum companies by President Lázaro Cárdenas in 1938. Moreover, West was attracted to the figure of Leon Trotsky, the arch-rebel who had found his final exile and eventual death in Mexico. She applies her trademark personal approach to all of these topics, following the public manifestations of historical agency all the way back to their origins, to the inner lives and subjective impulses of such personalities as Cortés, the Reclus brothers, Diego Rivera, Dr. Atl, Leon Trotsky, and even Benito Mussolini. This approach recalls Michel de Montaigne, who stressed in one of his essays "'tis not all the understanding has to do, simply to judge us by our outward actions; it must penetrate the very soul, and there discover by what springs the motion is guided." West, who admired Montaigne, cast her historical approach in this very mould and patterned her discourse similarly on the ruminating, associative, and introspective model pioneered by the sixteenth-century Frenchman.

Readers of *Survivors in Mexico* may find passages dealing with peasant life and slavery most congenial to West's customary championing of the weak and downtrodden. But it is important to note that her sympathetic attitude is not exclusively marshalled in favour of the poor and disenfranchised members of society. Anybody who is a victim of prejudice, including wealthy members of the bourgeoisie, can count on her compassion. She recounts the story of Jacques Coeur, for instance, the medieval merchant prince of France who had been wrongfully tried and imprisoned because his extraordinary worldly successes had aroused the king's jealousy. West cites this incident to make a comment on the moral and philosophical roots of antibourgeois sentiments in all cultures and at all times. In such instances, West acts on an impulse to expose hypocrisy, duplicity, and error in any form, whether its victims be women, peasants, merchants, or even kings and conquerors. In most instances, such moral pragmaticism is persuasive. One can hardly take issue with her view that peasants, instead of being despised, should be credited for replenishing the nation's food supply; that miners, instead of being driven like mules, should receive thanks for filling the state coffers with gold and silver; and that tax collectors, instead of being treated like lepers, should be honoured for helping the government to balance its national books.

But West does not stop there. She argues that even colonial invaders, having introduced technical and agricultural improvements, should be given credit for such contributions. Here West comes close to endorsing the myth of the colonising mission, an impression which is strengthened by her apparent approval of the colonial paternalism of Hernán

Cortés. Moreover, West insists that he "was victorious simply because of his courage," which gave him the edge over Montezuma's passive defeatism. Of course, West was not blind to the dark side of Cortés's endeavour. She repeatedly stresses that "a more thoroughly fallen man than Cortés, and one determined to fall as often as possible, can hardly be imagined. . . . He could be merciless. He hacked off the hands of the Indian spies who infiltrated his camp. . . . Also Cortés let Cuauhtémoc be put to the torture when Tenochtitlán had fallen." But having said this, West adds a startling rationalisation for Cortés's behaviour: "Always when Cortés committed such deeds as these it was for the sake of self-preservation, never to derive disgusting pleasure from inflicting pain." At this point it is hard to stifle an outcry of moral indignation; moreover, one feels compelled to question the reliability of West's presumed knowledge of Cortés's inner motivation. Also, didn't Cortés willingly place himself in situations where he *had* to be cruel in order to fulfil his essentially grasping, self-serving intentions?

Why was West so partial to a champion of imperial conquest? One explanation suggests itself readily: Cortés was, after all, a zealous crusader against the Aztec practice of human sacrifice, and anybody who opposed sacrifice can count on West's support. Moreover, West considered the Aztecs in the same light as she did the Turks: both cultures were pervaded by a martial spirit, and both plundered their subject territories to finance an opulent courtly culture. Indeed, West's Montezuma comes across as an incarnation of the "last pasha" invoked in her opening lines, as the placeholder of a declining culture of decadence. West even compares Montezuma's extravagant living quarters to a "Moslem paradise." Her point is that the Turks, then a mighty seafaring power, might have found the Aztecs to their liking and pressed them into the service of a pan-American Islamic colonisation: "If Ferdinand and Isabella had not thought quickly and cleverly and boldly, I should have been looking across the stone square not at the Basilica of Our Lady of Guadalupe, but at a mosque, and the women about me would have been veiled and have had not faces but black snouts . . . and the fashion might have been running up all over North America." West believed the Spanish conquistadors might have transferred their allegiance to the (supposedly less scrupulous) Moslems, had their brutal colonisation of the Americas been impeded by moral considerations.

Thus, judged from an anti-Islamic perspective, Cortés was merely the lesser of two possible evils.

But West's anti-Turkish bias is not the only reason for her surprisingly lenient attitude towards Cortés. Although West rarely missed an opportunity to denounce what she called "masculine obsessions," meaning selfish, sexist, male-chauvinistic behaviour, she was enamoured of masculine heroism. One cannot better Carl Rollyson's description of this attitude: "Although West excoriates men for usurping positions of power, and she is nearly as severe on women who allow themselves to be exploited, she is obviously attracted to powerful males and often presents them in her fiction and nonfiction as alluring figures. A good part of her finds the idea of kingship emotionally satisfying." Similarly, West was attracted to the daredevil conqueror Cortés, who single-handedly subjected a rival empire to his will. Although West abhorred Cortés as the genocidal nemesis of the Aztecs, she also revered him as the embodiment of pure vitality and the herald of much positive change. West puts it this way: "For the first hundred years of the Spanish occupation of Mexico, the Indian population drained away at the rate of about 9 percent a decade. . . . Yet the Spaniards did much for Mexico. Indeed, their gifts are beyond counting."

The existence of such paradoxes is nothing new to readers of West. A significant part of her worldview was based on the recognition that the universe was constituted by contradictory (sometimes mutually opposing, sometimes dialectical) principles. In this regard, too, *Survivors in Mexico* resembles Montaigne's *Essays*, which display a similar concern with the incoherencies of human nature and behaviour. Like Montaigne, whose anti-dogmatism and Epicurean morality surely appealed to her, West ranges over a vast terrain of institutions, customs, opinions, and ideas in *Survivors in Mexico*, to reveal that human aspirations are haunted by incomprehensible and conflicting motives. This sensibility undergirds West's discussion of the mixed admiration and hatred which all successful businessmen elicit, it dominates her analysis of the incomprehensible reactions to the China Poblana costume, and it shows in her presentation of a Mexican official's simultaneous denial and advocacy of the Aztec cultural heritage. Although paradoxes also appear in *Black Lamb and Grey Falcon*, there they were often defused by an appeal to the vague notion of "mystery." In Mexico, West no longer invoked mysticism to shield herself (or her readers) from the troubling knowledge that human and cosmic matters are not ordered coherently. This lack of syncopation, symmetry, and synthesis in human affairs led West to state sceptically that "we develop by misunderstanding," a conclusion she had formulated similarly in one of her short stories published in *The Harsh Voice* (1935): "There is no such thing as conversation. It is an illusion. There are intersecting monologues, that is all."

In a world rife with paradox, misunderstanding, and contradiction, magic would seem to offer a panacea against such confusion. Indeed, West alleges that the Aztecs were driven into the open arms of sorcerers and magicians because they had "too obstinate a determination to make the universe consistent." But although West abhorred magic and denounced its power over the rational mind at every opportunity, she did not simply blame its prominence in Mexico on the "pagan" mindset of the Aztecs. Instead, she argues that magic was a legitimate way for the Aztecs to communicate with their gods. Since the Aztecs had done away with the pretence that the gods were anything but vindictive, irrational powers, they responded to them in kind, with equally irrational and violent means. To West, the gist of Aztec sculpture reveals "an honest recognition that human beings are often made hideous by what the gods do to them, and that it is therefore probable that the gods are hideous." Such views, however, are not limited to the peculiarities of Aztec religion. Indeed, West arrives at the troubling conclusion that "the case against religion is the responsibility of God for the sufferings of mankind, which makes it impossible to believe the good things said about Him in the Bible, and consequently to believe anything it says about Him."

Although it has gone virtually unnoticed to date, West's work is pervaded by an undercurrent of what Albert Camus termed "metaphysical rebellion," a spiritual insurrection against the perceived tyranny of God. With the exception of a phase of quite conventional Christian piety (lasting from about 1940 to 1960), West's overt rebellion against God weaves through her writings like a motif. As early as 1917 she fulminated that "God who blessed the merciful has let mercy and kindness be driven out from the world. God who made Heaven and Earth lets Earth be swallowed up in Hell. God who is Love has given the world as food to Hate." And in 1926, West protested against God as follows:

"That a father should invent the laws of a game knowing that they must be broken, force people to play it, sentence the players to punishment for breaking them, and accept the agony of his son as a substitute for the punishment, was credible enough to people who believed that hate might be the ultimate law of life." This anti-theistic principle finds arguably its most sustained and forceful expression in *Survivors in Mexico*, where West pursued her doubts about divine benevolence to their logical conclusion.

But such spiritual rebellion reverses a more familiar pattern of British responses to Mexico. I am referring to the country's appeal as a topos of spiritual and religious renewal. In D. H. Lawrence's novel *The Plumed Serpent* (1926), for instance, the British protagonist Kate Leslie celebrates the "primitive" vitality of pagan myths associated with the revived worship of Quetzalcoatl; she even agrees to become the new religion's manifestation of the rain goddess. For the Catholic writers Graham Greene and Evelyn Waugh (both visiting Mexico in 1938), the country held a different religious significance. They saw in Mexican Catholicism a bulwark against the godlessness of anti-clerical left-wing politics. While Waugh highlighted the civilising mission of the Church in his travel book *Robbery Under Law: The Mexican Object Lesson* (1939), Greene's novel *The Power and the Glory* (1939), set in southern Mexico, is a Christian allegory of unconditional faith and a celebration of martyrdom in the face of religious persecution. West defied such precedents. Although writing about a deeply religious culture, she eschewed reassuring spiritual certainties, be they Christian or pagan; instead, she questioned the very premises of religious faith. This is a heroic gesture of humanistic scepticism, demonstrating once again that West never flinched at going against the grain or taking on hallowed master narratives, no matter their political, literary, or religious pre-eminence.

Her writing is inherently appealing, for it is filled with vitality and insight, but *Survivors in Mexico* is also important for a larger understanding of Rebecca West as a thinker and writer. *Selected Letters of Rebecca West*, edited by Bonnie Kime Scott and published by Yale University Press in 2000, was invaluable for bringing West's radical views, which she often expressed in private communications, to the attention of a wider audience. Moreover, Scott's inclusion of many letters from the later part of West's life sheds a revealing light on this previously understudied period of her creative and intellectual development. *Survivors in Mexico* is equally indispensable for a thorough assessment of West's world of ideas, and it holds the key to her final pronouncements on political, cultural, and spiritual matters. Interestingly, though, some of her most extreme arguments reflect the young rather than the middle-aged Rebecca West. Thus, readers familiar with her youthful work will register a conspicuous return of her rebellious theology and her interest in anarchism. After all, it is in *Survivors in Mexico* that West gives the fullest treatment of her father's relationship with one of Europe's leading anarchist theorisers, Elie Reclus; and it is here that West confesses, "my father was in part Elie Reclus all his life long . . . [and] since my father was so largely Elie Reclus, so am I." She further states: "Anarchist doctrine had, indeed, certain compelling attractions. We must all concede, it would without question be the most convenient way of ordering life, if there were only a small number of human beings in the world." Of course, the proviso "only a small number" is crucial here, as West had no doubts about the utopian basis of philosophical anarchism, although she gave it credit as a respectable system of political theory. This does not imply the slightest sympathy for what Mikhail Bakunin had called "propaganda by the deed," or terrorism. In fact, West is out of temper on that score with her two most cherished anarchist philosophers, Elisée and Elie Reclus. "The mildest of men, they could not bring themselves to denounce terrorism, even when it took the form of senseless bomb-throwing at crowds," she writes here. West had good reason to distance herself from the Reclus brothers in that regard, because she shared much else with them.

In addition to this revival of West's anarchist leanings, many passages in *Survivors in Mexico* are reminiscent of the polemical, acerbic, and unabashedly opinionated discourse that had characterised her early journalism in the 1910s and 1920s. But although *Survivors in Mexico* contains ample evidence of West's satirical wit, it is also pervaded by a deeply humanistic attitude. In other words, this text practises precisely what West had preached in *The Strange Necessity* (1928), namely, that great art is evidence as much of analysis as of synthesis. One could perhaps say that West started her writing career heavily on the analytical side, giving the impression to readers that she had a "tongue like broken glass, fierce, mocking, inhuman." But with the wealth of accumulated experience and an ever deepening fund of philosophical and historical erudition at her disposal, West's acerbic, analytical style was tempered by a more humane, mellow attitude. *Survivors in Mexico* is pervaded by an entirely winning humour which amuses without being bitter or demeaning.

This tendency is reflected in her argumentative style as well. Instead of being polemically categorical, her critical approach is now self-consciously dialectical. When discussing the relationship between the coloniser and the colonised in Mexico, for instance, West initially gives the conventional imperialist argument a chance, that argument being that "they were conferring benefits on the native populations by inviting them to participate in international trade." But immediately the dubiousness of this line of argument is exposed, because "unfortunately they also felt compelled to confiscate both the accumulated wealth of the native populations and their natural resources, so far as these were mineral." The dialectic continues with the admission that "this is not altogether the plain peculation that it appears, for they had an ingenuous belief that, as the native populations had no monetary system, these [metals] were wasted on them." West then gives her argument another twist by insisting that "these predators were actually conferring a huge benefit on another part of the world, on the Old World, by relieving its currency famine." At the end of this dialectical train of thought comes the shocking conclusion: "This is not a moral universe," a statement which defers any clear-cut moral judgement.

If nothing else, this procedure is an applied example of process on the intellectual and rhetorical levels. In an essay dated 1939, West had called the attitude which supposes that "all is now known" as the "lie of lies." Against such mental stasis, which West always saw as a function of "masculine obsessions," she posited the female preference for process. In *The Fountain Overflows*, West had linked Clare Aubrey's supreme musical talent with the expression of a truth "not yet fully revealed but in the course of revelation." Clare's musical propensity for process could serve as an analogy for the intellectual principle guiding West's own argumentative procedure in *Survivors in Mexico:* she takes a proposition, turns it around in her mind, considers alternative interpretations, and then takes it one step further.

This inquisitive, dialectical, and probing attitude makes *Survivors in Mexico* a valuable contribution to the philosophy of history. But the book also gives an insightful account of Mexican social and cultural conditions at the end of the 1960s. West was not only a perceptive observer of contemporary affairs but a sensitive barometer of future trends as well. Her analysis of the relationship between Mexico's Indian and non-Indian populations, for instance, aptly foreshadows the revolt of the neo-Zapatistas in Chiapas during the 1990s, and her focus on overpopulation contains an uncanny prediction of Mexico City's explosive growth and its discontents. Although *Survivors in Mexico* does not climax in a well-orchestrated ending, the work is internally unified by symbols, leitmotivs, and coordinated thematic developments which had been put into place in the hope of constructing a sequel worthy of *Black Lamb and Grey Falcon*. In weaving together the rich tapestry of cultural and historical observations that make up this edition of *Survivors in Mexico*, I have tried to let the stark beauty of West's vision of humanity reveal itself clearly and uncompromisingly.

Editing *Survivors in Mexico*

My attention was first drawn to West's work on Mexico by Carl Rollyson's description of it in *Rebecca West: A Life*, published in 1996. Rollyson said that West's "truncated Mexican epic is even more fascinating than her published work, because its multiple drafts reveal how hard she worked at achieving her autobiographical/historical/psychological effects." This remark led me to study the textual evolution of *Survivors in Mexico* from the perspective of "critique génétique," a textual approach developed by French critics in the 1980s to track the psychological, intellectual, and ideological ramifications of the creative process. At the same time, I became inspired by the potential of the text for publication. Indeed, I came to realise that West's views on the noxious ethic of sacrifice and victimisation were more meaningful than ever. The beauty of her language, her relentless pursuit of justice, and the strength of her faith in survival revealed that art really does hold an answer to the destructive element.

These fine qualities of West's work, however, were sadly dispersed over a multitude of documents including one substantial fair copy,

I	II	III
Pasha	Pasha/Kosovo	Pasha
Coffee and chocolate	Coffee and chocolate	Coffee and chocolate
Sunset	Sunset	Sunset
Mexico City	Mexico City	Mexico City
Unstable ground	Unstable ground	Unstable ground
Taxi driver	Taxi driver	Taxi driver
West's Law	Mestizos	West's Law
Aztec past	Xenophobia	Wild architecture
Shifting soil	Exploitation	Mestizos
Wild architecture	Joyfulness	Poor Indians
Mestizos	**Village market**	Fallen civilizations
Cortés/Montezuma		Dr. Atl
Poor Indians		Anarchism
Fallen civilizations		Reclus brothers
Schizophrenia		Elie & Fairfield
Village market		Misunderstanding
Swooping Eagle		Nudism
Paradox past/present		Elie-father-West
Reasons to come		Volcanoes
Dr. Atl		Paris Commune
Anarchism		Revolution & artist
et cetera		*et cetera*

many corrected typescripts, assorted carbon copies, and several handwritten notebooks. Therefore, my first task at the McFarlin Special Collections Library in Tulsa, where these papers are housed, was to systematise all the constituent parts of *Survivors in Mexico*. To this end, I kept track of the progression of discrete topical elements in each of the drafts that I read. Once a number of such topic strings had been entered on a large poster board, I could trace the thematic transformations of individual drafts and determine the precise point where separate manuscript versions overlapped or diverged. The result was a detailed and complex map of textual relationships that resembled a genealogical family tree.

The accompanying table illustrates this approach with some examples of several topic strings from the beginning of six different draft versions. What it shows is how Rebecca West frequently rearranged her

IV	V	VI (fragment)
Pasha	Pasha	
Coffee and chocolate	Coffee and chocolate	
Sunset	Sunset	
Mexico City	Mexico City	
Unstable ground	Unstable ground	
Taxi driver	Taxi driver	
West's Law	West's Law	
Wild architecture	Wild architecture	
Mestizos	Mestizos	
Poor Indians	Poor Indians	Poor Indians
Village market	Technical college	Technical college
Armando	**Village market**	Schizophrenia
Restaurant clients	Mexican Revolution	**Village market**
Indian vs. bourgeois	Aztec past	Frost
Special justice	Swooping Eagle	Indian King Lear
Aztec past	Chapultepec Park	Genocidal sin
Swooping Eagle	Anthropolog. Museum	Grow maize
Chapultepec Park	Aztec poem	Prof. Hutchinson
Fountains	Fountains	
Balloon sellers	Balloon sellers	
Anthropolog. Museum	Atl & Mexican artists	
et cetera	*et cetera*	

sequence of topics, and modified or omitted certain topics, from one draft to another. Her gorgeous description of the "village market," for instance, is preceded in drafts I and VI by a discussion of racial "schizophrenia," whereas in draft II it is preceded by a description of Mexican "joyfulness," in draft IV by the plight of "poor Indians," and in draft V by the history of a "technical college" for Mexicans. The "village market" scene, moreover, is followed by different topics in four of the drafts. This observation makes the village market episode a likely place to switch from one draft to another. In editing *Survivors in Mexico*, I kept looking for such topical overlaps, linking the drafts with one another at the precise point of verbal convergence. This was rather like assembling a jigsaw puzzle, making the resulting text as much a mosaic of interlocking pieces as it is a narrative.

Such a synthetic, reconstructive editorial approach resembles what

Faith Evans did in editing Rebecca West's autobiographical essays titled *Family Memories*, published by Virago in 1987. Evans regrouped the available draft materials to ensure coherence, trimmed repetitive passages, changed the paragraphing, and introduced chapter divisions and notes, all of which is similar to what I have done here. Such editorial handling can be intrusive, but if done judiciously and tactfully it alone can reveal the inherent quality of an unfinished work. The alternative approach, namely to leave gaps between fragments and to let inconsistencies stand, perhaps with editorial interpolations on the text's surface, is evidenced in Antonia Till's edition of West's unfinished novel *The Only Poet*, which was published in 1992 by Virago. I believe that Rebecca West's own preference in the matter would have been to reject this technique, and that putting in print textual fragments of a larger project would constitute a greater infringement on her intentions than shaping the existing parts of an unpublished work into a coherent whole.

In the case of this book, the method described here can even be said to come with authorial sanction. In one draft version of *Survivors in Mexico* (not included in this edition), West wrote about her writing process as follows:

> By habit I sit down after breakfast at a desk in a second-storey window which looks down on a cedar Lebanon, and through its horizontal branches at a Chinese landscape. The valley below is brimful to the hilltops with morning mists, and the sun has to rise quite high before it can disperse them, so the trees on the slopes come up slowly as black brush-strokes posed on a paper-white background, following lines as inevitable as if an artist had determined them, for they trace the contours of the land. It is a pattern of order which can be used as a guide, and it is then that the section one wrote the day before appears in its full repulsiveness, but this unfolding of a masterpiece persuades one that it can be set right, that if one takes the four units which make up the middle passage and puts C after A and fuses B with D and adds a new one, E, the meaning will be plain.

The process that West described here is the same approach I have used in rearranging and coordinating the disordered fragments of *Survivors in Mexico* to form a coherent text. Although it is impossible to know exactly how she herself would have linked her own textual fragments, I have tried to reflect as faithfully as possible the way West's ideas aggregated and evolved during the writing of *Survivors in Mexico*.

This edition is based on the four most developed, annotated typescripts of *Survivors in Mexico* (identified above as drafts I, III, IV, and V), one long handwritten manuscript (not represented in the table), and some shorter fragments (such as drafts II and VI). Among these manuscripts, all of which are undated, the handwritten draft detailing Leon Trotsky's fate had to be edited quite heavily for content because of repetition, poor readability, and derivative passages; but for the most part West's corrected drafts are thoroughly considered and stylistically accomplished. Some passages exist in as many as ten different versions, which complicated the editorial process; yet in another respect this textual plurality proved extremely helpful. In fact, a close analysis of West's cumulative stylistic changes of identical passages enabled me to infer the relative chronology of composition. In most cases, the latest version of a given scene is stylistically the most sophisticated one. Therefore, when there were several drafts of the same scene, I generally gave preference to the most recent one.

Although my primary goal was to preserve Rebecca West's own unmistakable style and to remain faithful to her overall vision, minor alterations in the text were unavoidable. Notably, I have silently corrected obvious grammatical mistakes, rectified factual errors, and introduced more consistent punctuation. I have further added accent marks to reflect contemporary spelling of Spanish names: Zummaraga is spelled Zummáraga, for instance, Cortes is Cortés, and so on. For the names of Aztec gods and places, I have followed the Nahuatl spelling used by Warwick Bray in *Everyday Life of the Aztecs* (1968), which by and large corresponds to the spelling in *Merriam Webster's Collegiate Dictionary*.

Aside from such minor corrections, however, all other alterations of the original manuscripts are delineated in the notes that appear at the end of the text. The editorial operations I performed were of four types, and each is identified in the notes by type. First, the word "Correction" marks a change where West obviously mistyped a word or made a factual error, such as a wrong date. Second, because of overlap and duplication among different drafts, certain passages had to be cut, an operation identified in the notes as "Excision." In these cases the note begins with the last three words before the omission, followed by a slash (/) indicating the place of the excision, followed by the first three words after the omission, and then by West's unabridged language. If only a few words were omitted within a sentence, the original sentence is simply given in its entirety. Third, "Modification" indicates each instance where words have been interpolated, either because West left a blank in the manuscript (intending to do the necessary research later but then not getting around to doing so) or because of stylistic, syntactical, or grammatical infelicities. In such cases, a note gives the first three words of the changed sentence, followed by the term "Modification" and West's original language. Fourth, sometimes both an alteration and an omission were simultaneously called for, which is identified by "Modification/excision," followed by the original language of the manuscript. In transcribing West's original language for these purposes, there are occasional handwritten words in the manuscript that can't be made out, and these are indicated in the notes by a question mark enclosed in angle brackets; she also occasionally left blanks to be filled in later, which is indicated by the word "blank" enclosed in angle brackets.

Besides endnotes dealing with such textual matters, I have included two kinds of contextual notes. One kind provides biographical data and brief commentaries on the many artists and historical figures that West refers to in passing, except in the case of obvious references to a person so well known that it would be superfluous, such as Charles de Gaulle. While I have chosen to err on the side of thoroughness in this regard, my tracking of West's allusions serves to highlight the amazing range and depth of her erudition. In the other type of contextual notes, I either elaborate on selected cultural and historical topics that are controversial by nature, or comment critically on issues that are treated rather idiosyncratically by West.

Survivors in Mexico

Mexico City I

Thirty years ago, in the Macedonian province of Yugoslavia, I knew one of the last pashas who were stranded there after the Turkish Empire had been driven out of the Balkans. Such Turks were in sad straits. Five hundred years before, their ancestors had been settled there by the sultans to colonise the territories their armies had conquered, and now the Christians had turned on them, and they were amazed, as exploiters always are when the exploited turn and bite the hand which has not fed them. There was nowhere for these obsolete pro-consuls to retreat from this revenge, for they were strict Moslems, the women wore the veil and the men the fez, and they knew that if they went back to Turkey they would find that by order of the Atatürk the Turkish females' faces were naked and Turkish males had adopted infidel bowlers.

Therefore the old pasha, like several of his kind, lingered on in Macedonia, living in the crumbling villa-palace of his ancestors, with only the few acres round it that he had been allowed to keep when the rest was cut up into peasant holdings under the land reforms of King Alexander. The one place in his home where his poverty did not show, where there were no cracked tiles on the floor and no plaster dust fallen from the wedding-cake vaults above, was a second-storey balcony, which the old lilac trees in the garden had long overtopped. Sitting there, one could stretch out an arm into the branches and stir up the purple flowers and set the scent rising in clouds. There we used to pass the summer evenings, up among the lilacs, drinking a mixture of coffee and chocolate, not thick Turkish coffee, but the thin Western brew, laced with sweet chocolate beaten to a foam. "This," the pasha told me every time we drank it, "is how they serve coffee in Mexico." That was the only thing about Mexico I was sure I knew when I went there.

It is in line with life as I know it that when I got to Mexico nobody had ever heard of mixing coffee and chocolate. But my misapprehension worked out well, for Mexican waiters always took an interest in my husband and myself after we had ordered this bizarre beverage, saying, "Chk, chk, do they drink that in England?" and when we said, to save ourselves trouble, "Yes, all the time, all the time," they nodded tolerantly, feeling that as foreigners we had to be wrong about something, and this was error in an innocent field. So they bore with us every afternoon, round about six, when we went up to the bar on the top floor, though that was the hour they liked to doze; and while they stretched themselves on the plush benches round the walls, we sat undisturbed by the huge west window and watched the sunset make a cavalry charge on the sky and beat the daylights out of it and then itself get beaten by the night.

The conflict might go this way: above Mexico City the November skies were pearl grey, not luminous as might be expected at the height of seven thousand feet, not trembling brightly as they do over Johannesburg and Saint Moritz, for the reason that here they are thickened and sobered by industrial pollution contained within the walls of the wide basin in which the city spreads. These pearl-grey skies became a honey-coloured vagueness, a primrose glow, an amber fire, orange flames, and it is no use objecting that this process happens everywhere at that hour. Only here does it seem that the skies go on fire as solid objects do, as if their ashes might rain down on the spectators. Then the mountains were black against crimson, and the crimson marched on and on until it was overhead, and then purple clouds rushed from horizon to horizon, fusing with the crimson and dissolving to rose veils floating on a mulberry firmament, which then was bleached, but brightly, into a greenish crystal arch traversed by white phantoms of mist through which shone stars larger than they had been last week in New York. Lights twinkled up at them from the city below, and it was full night. The operation had taken twenty-five minutes.

The lights that twinkle back from Mexico City are sparse. Over Washington and New York and other urban complexes in the States there stand in the night other shining, immaterial cities, created by profligate use of electricity: a lovely form of waste. But Mexico is huge and poor and profligate only in fields indicated by its political soul, which acts (like even the best of governments) half out of a genuine desire to promote the happiness of the people and half to catch votes.

The Federal District of Mexico contains 6 million people who have to be kept happy, not including the half-million provincials camping in the dust-flats outside the city limits, waiting for jobs they have imagined—which is not so hopeless a state as might appear. Mexicans have a creative imagination. They might imagine prosperity into being. They have imagined themselves into the present United States of Mexico against all probability; they have imagined the huge solidity stretching for miles below the glass window where we sat, a solidity which at that hour was dense not only where there were houses, but in between. A seventh of the national population lives within the Federal District; to take a larger unit, nearly half that population is to be found in the 14 percent of the national territory contained in the wide basin of the Valley of Mexico. As my husband and I sat looking at the sunset, most of that half were trying to get home. Below us was a traffic congestion startling even to those who know New York and London and Paris.

There has only just been built the beginnings of a subway in Mexico City, and the reason for this—like the reason for everything that happens in these parts—is historical. In 1521 the Spanish conqueror Cortés destroyed the Aztec capital, Tenochtitlán, which was another Venice, poised on silt in a lake, and he built Mexico City on the ravaged site. In the process he rashly drained channels which should have been left alone, and the water table shifted and has never been quite itself again, so solid earth round here is not so solid. Many old buildings have a heavy list, often with ironic effect. Surely the offices of the Congregation for the Propagation of Faith ought not, with its influential connections, to be sinking into the ground at an angle of twenty degrees. So it happens that no engineer was eager to build a subway anywhere near Mexico City, and till now there has been no public transport except buses and two kinds of taxis, one the kind for hire by a single passenger or acquainted group of passengers, the others who take a mixed bag and drop them in turn. The drivers of this latter sort show what they are by putting one hand out of the window when they have room for another passenger, and it becomes a folk gesture peculiarly appropriate to the town.

They are Mexican hands, more often beautiful than not. (It is only we Europeans who have ugly hands, with thick fingers, broad palms, heavy wrists, and an alarming liability to go uglier still in age. No wonder we have had to excuse ourselves by technological activity.) Mexican taxi drivers' hands, like everything else Mexican, are involved in history. By day they are asking for more passengers, and avidly, for there is poverty here, but they are also pointing out the scenes on which their national drama has played itself. Listen to one of the drivers who can speak a foreign language and ferries tourists to whom that language is native: he will not be difficult to hear, he will be giving forth that open-mouthed shout which in all countries is the voice of nationalism: "That marble colonnade is a memorial to OUR GREAT STATESMAN JUÁREZ—he was NOT A SPANIARD—he was an INDIAN—an INDIAN—a PURE INDIAN—a ZAPOTEC INDIAN—he came from OAXACA—are you listening, Ma'am? THE PARK BEHIND IS ONE OF OUR MANY BEAUTIFUL PARKS—it is called the Alameda—the Poplar Park. HERE THE AZTECS HAD A GREAT MARKET—where they sold everything, Neiman-Marcus nothing—THEY SOLD GOLD AND JADE AND CLOTH MADE OF FEATHERS—and CHOCOLATE and VANILLA—but when the Spaniards came they STOLE it all—and the merchants they KILLED—and when the Dominicans came they turned it into the CREMATORIUM Square—there they BURNED ALL THE VICTIMS OF THE INQUISITION—human sacrifices they said the Indians made—but human sacrifices they were few, they were nearly nothing—BUT THE INQUISITION IT BURNED AND BURNED AND BURNED." The substance of the polemic is slightly surprising to the foreigner, because the speaker is unlikely to be a pure Indian. Of the 40 million Mexicans alive today only 29 percent are Indian, and most of them live in the country. Of the remainder 15 percent are white, 1 percent negro, and no less than 55 percent mestizos, of mixed blood. The man is not denouncing some monstrous invader of his people's lands, as Poles might denounce the Nazi Germans; he is denouncing some of his ancestors for maltreating other of his ancestors, which, as he is both, must lead to schizophrenia. Yet he glows with health. He is a strong swimmer swimming with the tide which is gathering momentum. Never did the Indians, during their centuries of subjection to the Spanish, lose their pride of race; but probably these taxi drivers' grandfathers could not have delivered these crowded and coherent impromptu lectures, for lack of substance. That was delivered to their sons and grandsons in superbly assimilable form by, they think, just one person. "But you will read ALL OUR GLORIOUS

HISTORY in the murals of DIEGO RIVERA. You have seen them? IN OUR NATIONAL PALACE. IN CUERNAVACA. IN THE MINISTRY OF EDUCATION. He was OUR GREAT MAN, Diego RIVERA." There is an enchanting paradox here. Because Rivera was a member of the Internationalist Communist Party he became the most persuasive nationalist propagandist ever known. If Hitler had had such a painter on his side I and millions of others would not be alive today.

Diego Rivera and Frida Kahlo

Nobody ever worked harder than Diego Rivera to give the Mexican people a seed bed for their pride by reconstituting the Indian past, and he succeeded because his patriotism was a real passion. All his life he collected works of art produced by the pre-Columbian peoples of Mexico, and he set a large part of his personal fortune aside to found a museum in which these could be exhibited after his death. To this museum we were taken by our driver one Sunday morning, and it was for him a religious experience. "Did you ever hear," he asked me, "that President de Gaulle is the Joan of Arc of today?" I did not wish to discuss the comparison, which always reminds me of how much I dislike female impersonators, but I admitted that I had heard it made. "Well," said the driver, "that is wrong. The French have no right to say that President de Gaulle is like Joan of Arc. But we have a right to call Diego Rivera our Joan of Arc. De Gaulle is a tyrant, but Joan of Arc was a great revolutionary who loved her country, and Diego Rivera was a great revolutionary who loved Mexico." These remarks betrayed no ignorance at all. Our driver had been well taught at school and he was widely read. He was simply using the word "revolutionary" in its Mexican sense, which denotes any person who initiates against opposition any action or course of actions beneficial to his people. It must be added to this definition that the initiation must be performed with a certain fervour. A revolutionary must have overthrown the stoney idols of the heart.

Certainly, Rivera's museum was the work of a sincere revolutionary. He sought to restore in it the Mexican's pride in his Indian past, as he had restored it in his murals. But it is built to a plan that has no real relationship with the Aztec Empire. To the eye of a Londoner it suggests a section cut out of Wandsworth Jail, and a New Yorker would see it as the offspring of Grant's Tomb and one of the Arsenals. Grey blocks of stone have been piled up by an architect who had the Aztec pyramids in mind, but not as they were in the days of what was probably the most highly coloured (to use the word in its literal sense) civilisation the world has ever seen, but as they are in their ruined state, after having been stripped of the gorgeousness they were designed to display by the Spaniards and rough-housed by four hundred and fifty years of neglect and weather and a century of archaeological research. Around this bleak edifice is a garden laid out with an austere air of serving a high purpose which need not necessarily be enjoyable, and it was the one public place where we saw no balloon-sellers and no hawkers of "pig's crackling." As we approached it, there issued from its funerary portals a party of people whose faces were stiff with a sense that the visit was not yet over, but only slightly stiff, for it was nearly over. They were members of a provincial branch of the Communist Party, who had come by bus which was even then starting up its engine to take them on to places where the sellers of balloons and pig's crackling were of good heart, and they could enjoy the Indian heritage of laughter and colour that had given Rivera his joy and his genius, but which was strangely absent from his museum.

For within were grey stone steps and corridors which certainly reproduced the interior of the pyramids, but those which would have been visited by Aztec plumbers and engineers, rather than by their priests or artists, for they led to no painted shrine. Against this monotone background the beautiful sculptures and pottery, which were also grey and black, went for nothing because they had been designed to stand in bright light or against bright colours; and since the intention of many of them was comic, they were as disconcerting as Rowlandson drawings would be hanging in a crematorium. Only in the centre was a room, free of melancholy, large and light; and the most conspicuous object was Rivera's last picture, an unfinished portrait of a pretty Mexican woman of an insipidity not at all distressing, because it showed such good will, it simply put forward the proposition that it would have been agreeable if women were roses, people precious objects, the world a candy. Its insensibility was balanced by another sort of sensibility, which recalled the statue of the Prince of the Flowers in the museum, smiling indifferently but urgently up at the sun, or it might have been the rain. From hooks high up on the wall dangled two giants made of stuffed basketwork, the figures of Judases as are burned at the fiesta of

Gloria every year; and it came home to one that the huge, rip-roaring man who was responsible for all these murals, for this exquisite collection of sculptures, the massive and generous error of this museum, was now nowhere, not as much of him was left as these two straw men. An Aztec poem quoted by Soustelle had something to say about that:

> Does one take flowers along to the land of the dead?
> Flowers are only lent to us, the truth is that we go.
> We leave flowers and songs and the earth.
> The truth is that we go.

The Aztec poet went on to say that this being so, we should get all the enjoyment out of flowers and singing while we can, but though every literature does the best it can with that sensible consideration it does not drown the wail of the wind down the chimney.

In further rooms were objects of popular art which were also related to mortality, the sugar skulls and painted plaster fruits and loaves used in the Celebration of the Feast of the Day of the Dead, looking shy as such objects do when they are abstracted from the peasant world which made them for temporary use and preserved in places in which they would never have appeared spontaneously; and as it was only a day or so after the Day of the Dead, some marigolds had been set here and there as a message to Rivera. By now they were faded, and they made him seem more dead than ever and the grey museum a reminder that he had been only lent to us. The atmosphere was the unhappier because the custodians were evidently proud (and such pride was justified) in guarding this monument to Mexico and a great Mexican, and they held themselves as if the museum might at any moment be attacked, and the visitors were light-minded if they had not grasped this danger and resolved to stand shoulder to shoulder with them. One found oneself showing sympathy for this likeable attitude by scowling at the Aztec exhibits, even at the jolly little dogs.

"Now you have done this," said the driver, "we must go to the other museum given us by Rivera, who gave and gave and gave without stint. It is in the house of Frida Kahlo, who was his wife, who also was a painter, who also was a great, great revolutionary." I could remember nothing about Frida Kahlo except that she was either Rivera's second or third wife; that she was the conventionally beautiful woman, with raven hair and regular features, who appears in several of Rivera's murals, once at least with a sister; and that, like Rivera, she was of mixed origin, being the child of a Spanish Mexican lady and a Hungarian Jew who had emigrated from Germany to Mexico and there made a name for himself as a pioneer of modern photography; and beyond that a vague recollection that the marriage had had its ups and downs, even to the hole in the road of divorce and remarriage, but had lasted many years and had ended only with Frida's death in the middle fifties. I also had seen one of her pictures in the Museum of Modern Art in Chapultepec Park. She was a surrealist, and therefore it was only to be expected that it treated a subject extreme in its fantasy by a glossy and matter-of-fact and strictly academic technique, though there are signs that she had learned from Matisse. The woman recalls his odalisques. It is called *The Two Fridas*, and it represents the artist as two women sitting side by side with hands clasped, while a nightmare version of blood transfusion joins their two hearts by tubes. It has been described as a confession of her own schizophrenia and her resentment at her psychiatrist's attempt to abolish it. I have also heard the subject identified as the Yin and Yang, but a description which can be applied to at least two-thirds of all works of art in which there are two objects ceases to be a description at all. It has also been alleged that Frida Kahlo showed a neurotic's narcissism in this self-portrait, because she represents the two women as very beautiful; but the testimony of photographs and of those who knew her testifies that she was in fact very beautiful, and it is difficult to see how a beautiful woman who was also an honest artist could paint herself as other than a beauty. I had formed the impression that she must have been a rather silly woman, to have cluttered up her artistic life by joining a school, which meant that her work invited discussion of a psychological nature, usually bogus; for the picture is a good solid piece of painting.

We then drove across the suburbs of Mexico, but I have no idea for how long. It is odd that the evolution of our species never implanted a clock in our brains which would have been most serviceable; but perhaps Teilhard de Chardin could have proved that this omission showed a divine care for the populations of Switzerland and Waterbury, Connecticut. As it is, we become incapable of judging the passage of time when we are very much interested or greatly bored. But it cannot have been long before we found ourselves in a grid of pleasant tree-lined streets, where the broader ones are cut at right angles by side streets narrower, but not mean. The district had evidently been developed during one generation, for the main avenues were called by the names of European capitals, London and Berlin and Brussels and Vienna, and it could be assumed that only the man who had first conceived the joke would care to carry it on so long; and the properties had originally all been of one type. It was not quite easy to see this at first, for the district had become a victim to the congestion which is the incurable disease of Mexico City. Here and there a house, or even two or three, were crammed into what had evidently been the garden of the older house next door, and there were some small apartment houses, and a garage or two. There is a curious atmosphere as if the district itself was trying to make up its books and balance the satisfactions that the old houses and the new houses gave their occupants, in fear that the whole business is coming to an end, at least in any recognisable form. Forty years ago, a corner of Staten Island gave just such an impression of anxious accountancy, rather more elegiac than hopeful, on the part of timber yards and pavements and trees and gardens; and today it can be found in many parts of North and South London.

Suddenly we were looking at a blaze of blue slashed with scarlet. The houses on the corners of the streets were built to abut on the pavement of the side streets, and the walls of this one had been encrusted with paint so bright that the weather had not denatured the colours, they were still blue as gentians, red as poppies, though perhaps as these look at the first moment of twilight, when there seems a sudden liquefaction of all things growing low on the earth, while against the sky the leaves of the trees become hard as metal. "This is the Frida Kahlo Museum," said the driver, "and how horrible, it is closed for repairs. But please get out, we can look through this window, it is not curtained, you will see something." I was not greatly concerned that we could not get in, for it seemed to me that nothing about this house could be as remarkable as the red and blue outer walls. "Did Rivera paint the walls these colours?" I asked, getting out of the car. "No, no, Frida Kahlo painted them, this was her house, it was her family house, all in it was hers, and it is very strange inside, but it has all to do with the revolution, it has all to do with the Mexican people." I thought the red and blue paint on the walls might probably also have something to do with the Russian ballet and the designs of Bakst and Benois, for *The Two Fridas* had shown signs of several European influences. But when I put my hands on the iron bars which protected this as every Mexican window and peered through the reflections on the glass, I saw nothing any ballet had ever known. I looked into a room, which seemed a bedroom with furniture set about it and through an open door through another window beyond it. The interior walls of the garden beyond were also painted this deep, singing blue, slightly keyed down by distance and perhaps not so recently renewed; and in this blue world stood trees, with down-stretched branches and upstretched creepers, in a profusion that gardeners would normally have cut away, not just because it was unhealthy but simply because it was too much, much too much. "And in the garden are many of our people's gods," said the driver. "Let me shade the glass, so that you can see what is hanging on the wall. Look, it is one of our people's dresses, it would be one of the dresses Frida Kahlo used to wear, she wore the peasant dresses because she had to hide her leg."

"Why did she have to hide her leg?" I asked. I had assumed that every part of Frida Kahlo would be as perfect as her face.

"Why did she have to hide her leg?" the driver repeated, his voice rising, "because the poor woman had it not. She was in an accident, and her foot was crushed and she had to have her leg amputated from the ankle."

I felt ashamed and embarrassed as one does when a woman comes to one's house and one treats her on the level of one's usual relationship with her, and afterwards one finds out she had suffered a tragic loss of which nobody has told one. I had known that Frida Kahlo had died in early middle age, but I am old enough to know that that is as likely to be an escape from misfortune as a misfortune. In fact, the driver's version of her misery was incomplete. When she was seventeen, and was a first-year medical student, she sustained injuries in an automobile accident, which were infected by an organism causing gangrene to spread gradually through her body. It was true her foot had been amputated, but this was only one of a number of operations to which she had to submit, and it caused the death at birth of her only child. As time went on, her continued agony made her fantastically minded, and it is said that a visit to the museum is more disquieting than enjoyable, for the inner side of the house, which was originally as traditional as the outside, was recast in the same Puritan neo-Aztec mould as the Rivera Museum, and all over the grimness of its grey stone and all over the garden, where the vegetation seemed not so much growing as reeling, a superb collection of sculpture was disposed with such a troubled inconsequence that the curator might have been Ophelia. It testifies to the greatness of Frida Kahlo that all her life long not only Diego Rivera but many friends, both men and women, loved her as usually only the lucky are loved.

"Look, now I hold my hand, so you can see the dress better," said the driver. "It is sure to be a China Poblana dress, that was what she wore nearly all the time." Of this preference I knew already, for it is mentioned in the memoirs of General Salazar, a former chief of the Mexican Secret Service, but I had then not known how curious a choice it was. The China Poblana who invented this dress is one of the ingredients that make the glory of the city of Puebla, which served God but would not have it that there should be no more cakes and ale. Her name was Mirra, and she is said to have been a Chinese princess, who for some reason was involved with the Great Mogul; in any case she was an Asiatic of high rank who was sent on a sea voyage and was captured by pirates, who brought her to Mexico and sold her in the slave market in the year 1650. An army officer living in Puebla bought her, and when he took her home, his wife and he found themselves abashed by the sweet and patient quality of her grief. In everything she was gentle, and since they had had a right to buy her, she did not try to punish them by proud disobedience. She was converted to Christianity and was baptised under the name of Catalina of St. John. None of this was done to win an easy life in captivity. She did not marry, which she could easily have done in that multiracial society, but devoted herself to the service of the sick and the poor. One can imagine her, treading the streets of Puebla, her wimple white against her jasmin skin, her strong feet so comically narrow under her trailing black habit, lowering her eyelids like the petals of a flower closing at evening when she passed any plumed young men in velvet, since she had taken her vows and such imagination would be wholly wrong. Such were her works of charity that it is today the firm belief of many inhabitants of Puebla that she is a canonised saint. But she did not become a nun, and she devised for herself one of the most alluring and gaudy dresses ever worn by woman: a wide red skirt with a green hem embroidered with flowers, a cream lawn blouse, also embroidered with flowers, and necklaces and bracelets of coral and pearls, a translation of Oriental and European Renaissance luxury into the materials which were accessible to her. When she died, the women of the district took her dress as a uniform. This was to express the grief they felt at losing her, but they cannot have been wholly unmoved by the consideration that it is one of the most becoming dresses ever devised. The Chinese princess would not have been disturbed by this, or she would have been unable to design the dress.

Yet there is an odd passage in the memoirs of Fanny Calderón de la Barca, the clever Scottish girl who married a Spanish diplomat and accompanied him when he went to represent his country in Mexico in 1839, three years after Spain had made its long delayed admission of Mexican independence. She was invited to a fancy dress ball held for charity in the middle of January 1840 and as a compliment to Mexico chose to go in the China Poblana costume. On January 4, which was a set day for paying calls after mass, it being the first Sunday after the New Year, the house of the Spanish minister was thronged with visitors, all of whom, to Fanny's surprise, seemed intensely anxious to know whether she was really going to wear the China Poblana costume. Among them appeared two people whom she described as "young ladies or women of Puebla," who came to offer their help in getting her costume correct and even dressed the hair of one of her servants in the Pueblan manner. When they left they expressed such pleasure at her having chosen this dress that Fanny was bewildered.

At twelve o'clock the president of the Mexican Republic paid a curiously formal visit. Wearing full uniform and accompanied by his aide-de-camp, he stayed for half an hour. A couple of hours later, when the Calderón family were going in to dinner, they were informed that the secretary of state, the ministers of war and of the interior, and other important persons were in the drawing-room. The inopportune guests had come, they informed the Calderóns, to beg Fanny to abandon her intention of attending the charity ball in the China Poblana costume.

For what reason? Because, it was feebly suggested, the Poblana dress was often worn by women of so little consequence that they wore no stockings. Fanny had her costume brought in to demonstrate its propriety, but it was of no avail. As a diplomat's wife, Fanny surrendered, and they left. As soon as the door had closed on them, a Mexican gentleman arrived charged with a message from several ladies prominent in the society of the town, whom the Calderóns had not even met but who felt compelled to urge the same mysterious prohibition. Even then the ministerial family was not allowed to sit down to dinner, for there was delivered at their house a letter from an old gentleman, a local social dictator, declaring that Fanny's intention was unthinkable, because "the lady of the Spanish minister is a lady in every sense of the word." What is remarkable is that he too was a stranger to them.

Possibly the solution of the riddle is to be found in Fanny's description of the gorgeous crowd that walked in the Zócalo at Easter. "Above all," Fanny wrote, there was "here and there a flashing Poblana, with a dress of real value and much taste, and often with a face and figure of extraordinary beauty, especially the figure; large and yet *élancée*, with a bold coquettish eye, and a beautiful brown foot, shown off by the white satin shoe; the petticoat of her dress frequently fringed and embroidered in real massive gold, and a rebozo either shot with gold, or a bright-coloured China crepe shawl, coquettishly thrown over her head." The whole thing costing, Fanny guessed, not less than five hundred dollars. The combination of a bold coquettish eye, the sum of five hundred dollars, and the strong reaction of Fanny's well-wishers suggests that perhaps the China Poblana had been adopted as the uniform by successful prostitutes. That would be extraordinary. The year was 1840 and the China Poblana had died not a century and a quarter before; and today, in 1966, she is still being revered as a saint.

In Puebla, the Company of Jesuits built a church joined to a seminary, which is now a state university, eighteenth-century baroque and very fierce and businesslike, with towers that might be computers designed to be used by large, angry angels calculating rewards and punishments as vast as their own power: it would be natural to find on the tracery of the façade the initials ADMG and IBM. The interior is competently ornate but nothing more, and the only strong attraction is in the sacristy where an austere tablet marks the tomb of the China

Poblana. Before it, when we went there, stood an old Indian couple, who presented a heartrending sight peculiar to Mexico. Their clothes were falling to rags and were ritually clean. The man's grey shirt and blue trousers were several sorts of grey and blue, because of the many patches, but they had all faded to much the same phantasmic colour, and his feet showed brown through the holes in his white canvas shoes; and all were luminous with years of scrubbing. The shawl about the woman's head had the pleasant surface of newly washed wool, but was strange in texture, because it was a complex of darns. Both man and woman smelt of some herb or spice they had been eating but not of dirt. They were worshipping. The man bent his head, she bent her knees, almost to the floor, they crossed themselves and mumbled. This was not a golden altar with supernaturally beaming or agonised holy people, all that was before them was a white tablet with black letters on it. They must have known of the China Poblana to seek her out and find her.

So, Frida Kahlo wore the dress of an alien saint, which was perhaps all the uniform of successful prostitutes; which was in either case a boast of beauty, and an insistent demand that, though beauty is only lent to us, the loan should be laid out to the best advantage before the merciless lender takes it back. Afterwards, a friend showed me a photograph of Frida and Rivera standing near one of the most idiosyncratic features of her frenzied garden, a thatched pyramid protecting a four-tiered altar on which idols are staked in a congestion which, granted the fiery nature of Aztec gods, should have led to seismic disturbances. Rivera and Frida are looking at each other with that look of slow pneumatic expansion always displayed by lovers in opera, which suggests that, like balloons, they have to be subjected to a certain degree of inflation before they can get off the ground. It is an unbecoming convention; indeed Rivera is so plain that it seems certain they are together only because they made contact. But nothing can blunt Frida Kahlo's beauty, and it is enhanced by the dress she is wearing which, a magnifying glass discloses, is the China Poblana costume with the wide hem. But even then the beauty which had been lent to her was being withdrawn, inch by inch, and diminished not by the normal technique of aging or death, but by a creeping corruption. Yet her brows were smooth.

The driver was saying, "She was so good, so kind. Think of what she and her husband did for Trotsky. They were artists, they were quite different from people like us. Therefore they lived in different houses, though they loved each other very much. She lived here in the Blue House, Rivera lived in his studio over at San Angel. But when Trotsky came to Mexico, Frida Kahlo moved out of this house and went to live with Rivera, so that Trotsky and his wife came here."

"But this wasn't the house where Trotsky was murdered, it doesn't look like the photographs."

"No, this is the first house he lived in when he got here. He was murdered in the house he went to when he left here, it is just a few blocks away."

"But I thought he died in Coyoacán."

"We are in Coyoacán."

I looked about me in astonishment. I had made a picture of Coyoacán which had entirely convinced me. When Cortés's administrators had shifted for good and all to Mexico City, the town had become a centre of the sugar-cane industry, which is a proof of the damage involuntarily inflicted on Mexico by the Spanish exploitation of its resources. Nobody could grow sugar-cane in this area now, it is not hot enough in the season when the plant needs heat, nor rainy enough when it needs moisture. Since the seventeenth century, Lake Texcoco and many waters in the Valley of Mexico had been drained, and huge tracts of woodland had been felled, so that climate had changed. I had imagined that the place had remained static for at least the last hundred and fifty years. I knew the beautiful square with Cortés's palace on one side and the cathedral on the other, and I had been to Dolores del Rio's old house beyond the square, which is the only possible frame that could be appropriate for her, where a sober, restrained house was magically so proportioned that the effect was extravagant, and in the patio the trees drop great flowers which in the night did not disclose their colour, but were big as a clenched fist and smelt more like honey than a honeycomb. I had considered it as a core of glorious old houses used by the rich as summer or suburban houses, surrounded by a desert. This was perhaps because Isaac Deutscher, in his biography of Trotsky, describes him as finding his last home in a street which was "empty, stony, and dusty, with only a few *campesino* hovels scattered on either side," which he used to penetrate in order "to find out how people lived there and what they thought of the land reform." The recollection astounded me, though I did not regard as typical the blue and red house in front of us, which recalled not only what an imaginative child will do with its paint-box on a wet afternoon, but also the more extravagant works of Matisse, Maeterlinck, and Edgar Allan Poe, as he is interpreted by the Latin races; though indeed it was not so much an isolated phenomenon as I supposed at that moment, for Coyoacán has been the home of a group of avant-garde painters after the First World War. But the neighbourhood was so happily bourgeois, such an armchair, such a mattress, so well protected from the draughts.

Leon Trotsky

I was glad that Frida Kahlo had been so kind to Trotsky, leading him to this haven in the tenth year of his exile. Anybody who had been kind to Trotsky is surely agreeable, though he belonged to a class which is surely not often attractive. The men who excite adoration, who are what is called natural leaders (which means really that people feel an unnatural readiness to follow them) are usually empty. Human beings need hollow containers in which they can place their fantasies and admire them, just as they need flower vases if they are to decorate their homes with flowers. Almost everything that Napoleon did was interesting, but he gave no outward signs of having any private thoughts or feelings that would give the slightest pleasure to any stranger who became aware of it. One can imagine that the most interesting aspects of Napoleon, say the geographical genius he shows in his political and military plans, and the nose for abstract aspects of political science manifest in the constitution he gave to Switzerland, could be reproduced by a computer; his decisive error, the invasion of Russia, was the sort of thing one might expect from a computer which had been improperly programmed. But Trotsky was one of the great men within whom there was something resembling the inner vexations suffered by us lesser animals; who could say to us, "I am a great man. Hath not a great man eyes? Hath not a great man hands, organs, dimensions, senses, affections, passions, is fed with the same food, hurt with the same weapons, subject to the same diseases, heal'd by the same means, warm'd by and cool'd by the same winter and summer, as a little man is? If you prick us, do we not bleed? If you tickle us, do we not laugh? If you poison us, do we not die?" It has been given to only a few that they should utter this plea with conviction, but certainly Trotsky was one of them.

Think of what he did that made us all know his name, not only during his glory and during his disgrace, but now, when he has been dead a quarter of a century. All his adult life he had been telling one thing to every human being whom he could persuade to read his articles or come to listen to him in a lecture hall: that the people who were exercising power did not know their job, and he and his friends could do it better. Intellectuals had been doing this same thing ever since the first scratching beneath the surface of appearances by Greek philosophers, but most of them had been lucky. They had been told to drink hemlock, or they got burned at the stake, or were hanged, or had their heads cut off with a simple ax or by the guillotine; or nobody noticed them, and they lived out their lives like their less articulate brethren. There was one unfortunate episode in 1789 when the escape hatch, the French Revolution, made it appear as if intellectuals who had said they discovered the secret art of government would find themselves compelled to exercise it, and they were only able to get themselves out of this embarrassing situation by guillotining each other. Thus they left a power vacuum, which was filled by Napoleon. Until his destruction by faulty programming, he saw to it that this embarrassment did not recur, and though it raised its head again later, it never had made a very long stay. For the greater part of the nineteenth century, the intellectuals limited themselves to their proper and glorious business of working out principles of political science which contemporary legislators and administrators could apply to the problems of the age, only occasionally becoming themselves involved in the application. But when the Russian Revolution broke out, the intellectuals who belonged to the Russian revolutionary parties were compelled to provide both theory and practice for the government it set up.

Thus they were offered the opportunity of governing their country in circumstances which made refusal impossible. The offer was made publicly and in foreign countries. Not to accept it would have meant abandoning their professions and even to lose their identities. When the call came, Trotsky was earning his living in New York as a writer and lecturer within the circle of the faithful, and Lenin ran a Bolshevik paper in Switzerland. In both cases their friends and supporters would have withheld their support and their money had they known that their leaders could have gone back to Russia and have abstained. Trotsky had to board the *Christianiafjord* in New York harbour, Lenin had to get into the train that took him across Europe. Once they arrived in Russia, they either had to seize power or relinquish it to other parties or, again, lose their identities, become nobodies; and very few professional revolutionaries could turn to another trade. They could not turn round and go back, for by this time many countries would not receive them, and there would have been the question of earning a living after they had forfeited their prestige.

How magnificent it was, Trotsky's handling of this predicament! Plainly he never let the risk of ruin affect him for one instant. Simply he grasped the opportunity that had been offered him with it and ran away with it never minding that he thereby became a comic figure, like the man in the old funny films, who had a baby dumped on him, has nowhere to take it, cannot ask anybody to help him, and has an obligation to hold on to it and prevent it being snatched from him by the Keystone Kops, who were chasing him, their moustaches waggling as fiercely as his own. With his Jack-in-a-box figure and his tousled macaw head, he could have been as funny as Harold Lloyd. But the baby in his arms was power. It was natural enough that the Keystone Kops should be pursuing him as a kidnapper, for he had absolutely no title to power except his genius, which he had not yet proved to any but a small group, themselves unproved. But as he scuttled along, the baby grew into a child, it dropped from his arms, it ran beside him, a man with invincible weapons. Trotsky became the chosen companion of power wherever he went, taking on himself the guilt of power and knowing it was guilt, but seeing no way of casting off the burden. He felt no shame. The guilt had been imposed on him by necessity.

Nevertheless, he felt he had done things which must logically bring down on him punishment of one sort or another, though his admissions are tortuous. There is a unique passage in his diary which shows us his mind as it twists and turns in the indigestion caused by this sin-eating. When Lenin was dead and Stalin showed his strength and ruin descended on Trotsky, he was falling into a state of apprehension about the safety of his own family. He had two daughters by a marriage of his youth, who were consumptive, but they had husbands who were healthy enough for deportation, a fate which befell them both in 1928. Some time later, when Trotsky had been thrown out of Russia and had found temporary lodgment in France, when Kirov, the head of the Politburo, was assassinated and Stalin started a purge, Trotsky began to fear for the younger son of his second and enduring marriage, Sergei, or Serinzha, to give him his little name. This was a charmer who had won Trotsky's affection the cruellest way, by refusing to down his natural weapons because of the ties of blood. He had always avowed that he found politics boring and that his mother was more to him than his father. As an adolescent he had run away to join a circus, had earned his living as an acrobat and had had a love affair with a trapeze artist, then come home and suddenly changed his ways and took a science degree, working so well that he became a lecturer at the Higher Technological Institute in Moscow. But this alienation had been maintained to a degree when it must have been acutely painful to Trotsky. For the past five years, though Trotsky had been suffering disgrace and exile, Serinzha had written only to his mother, and it appeared possible that his attitude to his family was not a manifestation of the general rebellion of youth against age, but that he was stung by a particular grievance. It might be that he saw his father's career simply as a wildly imprudent persistence in associating with a group of merciless men who were dragging his whole family into hardship and danger. This view may be justly considered as limited, but not as inaccurate. For, after Serinzha had written to his mother stating that his situation was very grave, he disappeared and was never seen or heard of again.

In the diary Trotsky kept at this time there are many entries expressing his anxiety about his son, and suddenly there appears among them, "seemingly out of context," as Isaac Deutscher notes, a passage describing and discussing the murder of the tsar and his wife and children in the cellar of Ekaterinburg. Nobody can be at a loss to imagine why he should think of the murder of these children at that time. But most of us, if we had had the misfortune to be in his position and had to think that thought, would not give it more power over us by writing it down. He tries to weaken it by recording that he had not given the order for their murder. The responsibility for that lay on Lenin; the particulars he gives to establish that are interesting, for it was long pretended that the victims had been shot by their Hungarian guards, acting on their own initiative. But though Trotsky is careful to absolve himself, he brings no charge against Lenin, for the murder was necessary for the safety of the revolution. So long as the tsar or the tsarina or one of the daughters or their son were alive, the enemies of Communism had what Trotsky called "a living standard" to place upon the throne if ever the Bolshevik government weakened. He writes, "the Tsar's children fell victim to that principle which constitutes the axis of monarchy; dynastic succession." So it was right they should have been killed. But, of course, when he wrote that he meant much more. He meant that he knew that Serinzha had been killed. For when a revolution is successful, the revolutionaries who made it must suffer the defeat of themselves becoming effectively royal. Trotsky had founded a dynasty, and his children were falling the victims of the principle of dynastic succession, for it was not only Serinzha whose situation was grave. Trotsky's first wife and the husbands of both his daughters had been deported. And he could not say the precautionary murder was unjust. He had not said it was unjust when the murders were done at Ekaterinburg. The message is tortuously composed but its meaning cannot be misread: Trotsky said, "I am part of a system which is sacred and to protect it I have assented in a crime. The crime was necessary. But it was a crime." He would not have been human had he not thought he should be punished and that through Serinzha he was now being punished. The next entry announces, quite crazily, that his anxiety about Serinzha is dying down. As an attempt to cancel the preceding entry, it is quite inadequate.

A man of such intense awareness, who chose to be aware of such terrible things, and who had so much less ability for self-deceit than most of us, he must be an object of compassion, no matter whether some of the terror was his own work. When Frida Kahlo opened the door for him, Trotsky was famined for kindness. He had been an exile for eight years, and an accident-prone exile. His house in Prinkipo was largely destroyed by fire and with it some of his manuscripts. When he arrived in France, ill with fever, and went to a hotel, it burst into flames within an hour. Then he was expelled from France and went to Norway, and natural catastrophe was replaced by the man-made article. The Norwegian government that had granted him a visa changed their minds and harried him to leave. This attitude was reasonable enough. Stalin had long had his bayonets in Norway's back, and the Nazi movement had many adherents in their country under the leadership of a Major Quisling. The Norwegian Fascists actually broke into Trotsky's home in order to steal documents which should show that he was breaking his promise not to take part in political activities while he was in Norway, for the purpose of using it in a coming election. This was only two years before the outbreak of the Second World War, and the government would have been wildly imprudent had it not determined to rid itself of its dangerous guest. Trotsky should have understood their attitude, since it had been his creed that the sole criterion by which any action should be judged was its usefulness in preserving the sort of state of which one approved. But his fatigue made him want to rest a while in Norway. He would not accept that the Norwegians had a right to save the sort of state of which they approved. He brought into play his power of presenting and pointing up the events of his life so that they appeared as episodes in a work of art, and he made this seem as if it were a companion piece to Ibsen's *Enemy of the People*.

The Trotskys were put on a tanker, which was virtually a prison ship, and on January 9, 1936, they reached the oil harbour of Tampico, Mexico. It was ideologically splendid that this should be his landing place. The climax was being reached in the long war between Mexican nationalists and the international petroleum interests, who had been doing too well. True, they had introduced modern technological methods, and they had brought oil production up from ten thousand barrels a year to 47 million in 1937. But Mexican economists drew up a balance sheet showing that in that time foreign investors had drawn in profits ten times greater than their investments. This is unlikely to be as true as the statement that two and two make four, since economists are like Aeolian harps, and the sounds that issue from them are determined by the winds that blow; but there was in the propaganda conducted by the great oil corporations and carried on for the next few years, with the object of scaring foreign capital away from Mexico, the particular indignation felt by people who have lost a very great deal which they had no right to have in the first place. The crucial battle was still being fought, and it was more than a year before President Cárdenas was to sign the decree of expropriation. As a flourish, President Cárdenas arranged for the great revolutionary to land in the great oil harbour and sent out a general with a group of officials to fetch him and his wife, Natalya, off the Norwegian tanker and bring them to a pier, which was crowded with waving and cheering Trotskyites, some specially invited from the United States. Among them was Frida Kahlo, to tell them that they were her guests. The train stopped at a station outside Mexico City, and there Diego Rivera was waiting. He and Frida took them to the Blue House, beside which my husband and I stood with our driver that Sunday morning.

The Trotskys stayed there for two years. It must have been an ambiguous experience. At first they were intoxicated by Mexico. The austere Mr. Deutscher records with surprise that Trotsky's letters expressed delight with his new country, "even with its fruit and vegetables." Why not, indeed? In no other place I have ever been are the peppers flashing green like emeralds, or the tomatoes red as coral but brighter. Impermanent jewels, and the impermanence does not matter, there are so many high piles of them on the tables before the Indian women sitting quietly in the markets. Also the taste is often new. But it was Trotsky's nature not to dwell on such pleasures, though he was capable of recognising them; he was like a camera which rejects colour films and insists on photographing in black and white. For that very reason, the new phase of his exile must soon have struck him as not at all the proper, classic thing.

It cannot be exaggerated how blue the Blue House is. It is a theatrical set, designed for the performance of some such play as Maeterlinck's *Blue Bird* or a nineteenth-century ballet about a nymph who lives in the "Blue Grotto." The distinctive characteristic of this theatrical set is that it is littered with objects, organic and inorganic. It was as if the woman who had made this house, having been born perfect in form and lost that perfection by gross surgical assaults, tried to put back her lost perfection into her life by assembling as many beautiful works of art as possible around her. But Trotsky also had his chosen theatrical set, and its distinctive characteristic was that it was so far as possible destitute of objects. There he was following a European convention of long standing. It has to be remembered that Trotsky was not brought up in poverty. His father, though he was a farmer, was not a simple peasant but a member of an urban middle-class family, who was so successful that he could give his children a good education and was able to help his son by supporting his first wife and their two daughters. When members of the middle class formed a left-wing movement, they often felt an obligation to furnish their houses as sparsely as possible. This was in some cases due to a reaction against the taste of the

Victorian bourgeoisie, which loved to lumber up its homes with sofas and ottomans, display cabinets, ormolu tables, heavy draperies, bronzes, and porcelain on pedestals. In the home of Beatrice and Sidney Webb, chairs and tables stood far apart with an air of having just managed to pass gruelling tests as to the fulfilment of utilitarian purposes and no other; and it is said that in the mansion owned by Beatrice Webb's father, a nineteenth-century railway magnate, there was an unparalleled density of furniture. But long after that Victorian fashion had passed, middle-class radicals obeyed this convention of the bare attack, and it seems to have been due to their belief that the homes of the proletariat are similarly deprived. So they are, if the proletariat is doing badly, but if the proletariat is doing well, then the first things it goes for, after it has given itself enough food and clothing, is furniture. As the only members of the proletariat likely to join a radical movement are those who are doing well, this had led to many painful encounters. Even in England today many a trade unionist couple has accepted an invitation to Sunday supper with a middle-class co-religionist of superior social status and returned to their cheaply and competently furnished house in a state of bewilderment. Had their hosts been moving in or moving out? Or were they quite simply daft? Trotsky obeyed this convention to a degree which delighted those that followed it and disconcerted those to whom lowly birth had given the privilege of being as comfortable as if they had not been saved. His houses were always Saharas. His theatrical set was designed to serve a bleaker performance than has yet been seen. It could not even have sufficed a Beckett play. Three dustbins? Trotsky and his wife would have insisted there should be only one.

In the wrong scenery, mimosa blossom drooping over him in uncontrollable and overscented luxury and tickling his neck, Indian ceramics and Aztec idols of terrible frangibility hemming him in, Trotsky faced less material and more complicated hardships. The sword of his power rusted in him. President Cárdenas had given him the freedom of Mexico for several reasons. The first was that the Mexican people, in a very gentlemanly way, would automatically be hospitable towards a true revolutionary, a man who had pledged himself to overthrow a tyranny, particularly if he was out of luck. The second was that by receiving Trotsky, the enemy of Stalin, Cárdenas could send a message to

Stalin that he did not appreciate Stalinist influence in the Confederation of Mexican Workers and was not going to surrender to it. But that message was for the Soviet Union. He had another one for internal consumption. He did not want to irritate the Stalinists in the Confederation of Mexican Workers to the point that they would refuse to cooperate with him when he was expropriating the American and European exploiters of industry. Thus it happened that Cárdenas and Trotsky never met. The president simply exacted from Trotsky a pledge not to interfere in Mexican politics and let him be. The Stalinists shook their fists at him, but it was all quite handsomely tolerant. The president set police guards all around the Blue House. This, however, was very small beer for Trotsky. When he was at Prinkipo, the Turkish authorities also gave him full hospitality, but he had the Soviet Union breathing down the back of his neck over the frontier, and he was able to take a trip to Denmark and have difficulties when he got there and more at a Belgian port and more at Marseilles; and when he was in France, he and his wife were chased from refuge to refuge, until they left to avoid forcible deportation, and in Norway he had had a running fight, not only with the Norwegian Fascists, but with the government itself, in the distinguished person of Trygve Lie, and this had ended in his internment and expulsion. Now there was nothing but flat tolerance.

There was a temporary diversion in the countertrial of Trotsky, which Cárdenas very handsomely allowed to take place in Mexico. This was a curious enterprise, designed to meet the charges of conspiracy with Trotsky that had been levelled against Kamenev, Zinoviev, Bukharin, Pyatakov, and other old Party men in the trials which had been going on at intervals since Stalin came to power. It was possible to disprove these charges, because they were specific and false. Pyatakov, for instance, gave evidence that he had flown from Berlin to Oslo in December 1935 and had seen Trotsky and taken instruction from him regarding sabotage to be committed within the Soviet Union. The Norwegian Government, anxious to prove that they had done no harm in giving asylum to Trotsky, readily provided proof that no plane had flown from Berlin to Oslo in December 1935 or for some weeks before or after. (It is odd to realise that only thirty years ago winter flights in cold climates were often not feasible.) Others of these charges did not even require to be disproved, for they were inherently impossible. Trotsky could not have entered into a conspiracy with Hitler to disrupt the Soviet Union, even if he had wanted to do so, for Hitler could not have accepted an ally so widely known to be Jewish. A tribunal could easily make mincemeat of these charges; and that is what was done by the commission that sat in Coyoacán under the presidency of the aged philosopher, John Dewey; but it is to be doubted whether these proceedings were valuable according to Dewey's own belief that the outcome of the operations that are guided by a hypothesis is the only context in which the truth of the hypothesis can be decided or is of importance.

Trotsky had not then learned the bitter knowledge which comes to all people who are victims of a lying campaign: that all the world loves a liar. There is a sort of sanctity about a lie. If a man says of another that he is guilty of meanness, dishonesty, sexual depravity or cruelty, even of murder, it does not matter how worthless the accuser may be, the accusation will be joyfully believed by a large number of people, provided it be false. If the accusation should be true, they will be inclined to disbelieve it, and if belief is forced on them, they will not enjoy it. To take an example from recent English scandals: the British public took great pleasure in falsely believing that Mr. Galbraith had had homosexual relations with the spy Vassall and felt disappointment at having to admit in the face of overwhelming evidence that he was innocent. But they took almost no pleasure in believing the allegation that Mr. Profumo had been guilty of improper relations with Christine Keeler, which was perfectly true. They did get pleasure, however, in believing that the authorities had had discreditable reasons for prosecuting Stephen Ward, who was Christine Keeler's procurer, though this was not the case. So strong is this love of the lie that those who are falsely accused get little or no sympathy. They say to their friends, "So-and-so has accused me of doing this or that, of embezzling this or that, and I could not have done it, for no such sum exists," and their friends' eyes remain dead. The explanation is perhaps that the lie tampers with fact and produces an illusion that we live in a universe which is not rigid, which can be adjusted to suit our needs.

It was Trotsky's lot to afford the world this form of gratification, and it really did not matter how his innocence was established by Otto Rühle, Liebknecht's old colleague, and the rest of the assembled radicals, gathered so incongruously in the romantic scene of the Blue House. Trotsky's situation was summed up better by certain of the objects set down between the cacti under the lowered branches of the trees and shrubs by the beautiful woman who wandered among them in the fancy dress of the China Poblana, which she wore partly because she was Ophelianish, partly to hide her surgical boot. Among them were the idols which the Aztecs had made to embody the forces which shape human destiny; many of them hideous, frenzied, unreasonable.

Trotsky had to bear another affliction not generally recognised. The air in the Blue House must have been as heavy as it used to be in Emma Goldman's little house in the South of France, or in her flat in London, when she had left the Soviet Union in a mood of disillusionment, had married a Welsh miner and thereby acquired a British passport and could come and go about Europe as she liked. All her life she had been harried by the police and in defying them had had constant opportunities to assert and reassert her value by demonstrating her courage and her resourcefulness. The kind of person who desires power and fails to achieve it can find a satisfactory substitute in challenging power; and he does not make himself ridiculous by using this alternative outlet, for very often power needs to be challenged. Now that Emma was deprived of this relief, to visit her was often a labour, warm and affectionate though she was, because her undischarged dynamic force was like a thundercloud before the storm breaks it. Trotsky had been exercising power or had been challenging it continuously through all his adult life. Now that he was so far from Europe, he could not exercise the faintest pressure on events, and it was not possible to challenge a power that amiably supplied a police guard and watch dogs. He must have been like a smouldering volcano.

Of course, he had his wife, for whom he felt the enduring love that clever men often feel for women who are devoted to them and whose conversation is of an incoherence which, though candid, serves the same purpose as lying, in that it suggests that reality is not rigid. Others she often startled, particularly when she spoke of politics. Once, when Trotsky had been outlining to a visitor the creed of the Mensheviks, in order that he might realise its damnable inferiority to Bolshevism, Natalya Sedova nodded brightly and said smiling, "Yes, this is the faith that has inspired both Lenin and my husband." She herself describes a morning conversation with her husband, when he said that he was feeling very well, and that was perhaps because he had taken a double dose of sleeping-powder the night before; and she pointed out that it was not the sleeping-powder which did him good but the deep sleep which gave him complete rest. Trotsky remarked with the restraint of real love, "Evidently." He was loving wisely, for Natalya was magnificently courageous, had a passion for domestic cleanliness, and never lost a certain delicate, fluttering prettiness. A letter quoted by Deutscher suggests that at some time during their life in Mexico Natalya suspected her husband of having fallen in love with another woman, and it was probably Frida Kahlo of whom she was jealous. But there she was almost certainly wrong. Trotsky arrived in Mexico in 1936. In 1939 Rivera went to the United States and he and Frida were divorced. Among the objects in the Blue House is a ceramic clock painted with the names "Diego" and "Frida," and Frida had added to them the date 1939 and the words "The hour stands still"; and there is another ceramic clock, also with the names "Diego" and "Frida" on it, and the date of their remarriage and the words, "The hour strikes again." Frida was sick in body and sick with love; and for Trotsky, too, it would have been too late. He was thinking a great deal about death.

Vehemently but without real vigour he formed the Fourth International, which was to replace the Second (a Socialist) and the Third (a Communist) International. It is still a force in the Miners and Metal Workers' Association and with a certain federation of students and teachers. He was on a vast fine drawn web of correspondence. Wherever his followers were, his letters to them must have taken a long time to reach their destination, and he must have waited a long time to get their answers. The substance of these letters became more and more academic. He started a debate between him and some American Trotskyites on the subject of the bureaucratisation of the Soviet Union, which was in part a recognition of a serious difficulty in the establishment of a Marxist state, that it was hard to make it a worker's state, because modern industry called for a managerial class which were bound to seize privileges because their skill was so essential and who must become privileged to the point of tyranny if they were not only managers but state officials. But many of Trotsky's correspondents and visitors followed a mysterious pattern which recalled another, connected with

Frida Kahlo, drifting about the congested garden which she had made, which she lent to her friends.

When Fanny Calderón de la Barca had desired to wear the China Poblana dress at a fancy dress ball, her house became thronged by visitors who gave her praise, which she found quite incomprehensible for the intention, and by others who begged her in a panic, which she found equally incomprehensible, not to commit what was evidently to them a supreme solecism. The Trotskyites who argued with Trotsky that, because of this bureaucratic tendency in the Soviet Union, they could not in any way defend it a moment longer had a point, and so had Trotsky when he said, let us not despair, but see if this danger can be eliminated by an insistence on the part of the proletariat that the government be kept in the hands of workers' councils. But many of his correspondents were as cryptic as Fanny Calderón de la Barca's Mexican friends when they did her servant's hair to show how she must appear when she attended the fancy dress ball in her sacred costume, or told her that her intention to do so was unthinkable because in her position she should be a lady "in every sense of the word."

A certain number of Trotsky's visitors not only showed veneration for him, which indeed they were bound to feel for his gifts and his courage, but also treated him as if he knew the secret of establishing the kingdom of heaven on earth, and that he did not. For one thing, he had insufficient information about the earth. Bolsheviks were so busy caring for their baby, the revolution, that they suffered that isolation from affairs which young mothers often deplore. He was an inveterate novel-reader, and his associates refer to his reading of English and French novels. He might have learned a great deal about life this way; Beatrice and Sidney Webb approved of fiction on the ground that it was "applied sociology." But from his diary of his exile it is obvious that he was quite out of touch with the European literature of his time. When he was living in France, where one is never far from a bookshop, at a time when bookshops were crammed with interesting French books and translations of English and American books, he had a secretary to do his shopping for him. The youngest writer he read was Jules Romains, who was then sixty, and he could not understand Romains's dominant idea, which was unanimism, an attempt to give modern society by conscious effort the sense of unity which came naturally to smaller communities, to make an art of brotherhood, as the best of young people engaged in the civil rights wish to do. This means that he had no real sense of the psychological problem raised by the growth of population in the twentieth century. He only once mentions a writer who was to dominate the present and a good part of the future. He refers to François Mauriac as "a French novelist I do not know" and adds "an Academician, which is a poor recommendation." This is quite untrue. The French tradition does not include rebellion, the British tradition does, but it is unique. We have Byron, Shelley, Blake. But within a very wide range of conformity the Academy has had the best.

There was not the slightest hope that Trotsky could present a solution to the problem which was 1939. Nor was there any fear that he would make that problem more difficult to solve. He was becoming more and more concentrated on private anxieties. He was obsessed by the fear of death. Not for himself. At four o'clock in the morning of May 24, 1940, the police were called to the house in Coyoacán because there had been an armed attack on the household. Twenty men in police and army uniforms had overcome the sentries without firing a shot, and the only gate had been opened by one of the secretary-bodyguards, a young man from New York called Robert Sheldon Harte. The intruders machine-gunned the Trotskys' bedroom, keeping up a crossfire through the door and windows. Seventy bullet holes were found in the walls. Meanwhile, Trotsky and Natalya lay silent under the bed. Then they heard a cry, "Grandpa!" from Seva, Trotsky's orphaned grandson who had come to live with them the year before, followed by an explosion. The intruders had set his room on fire, and after firing another volley at the Trotskys' empty bed, they left. If Seva's elders did not go to his help, they cannot be blamed. They dared not. Had they shown they were alive, they would have been killed and taken from him. It was the child's fate that he was surrounded by adults so troubled that it was beyond their power to protect him from his own troubles. "We felt the stillness of the night, like the stillness of the grave, of death itself." There was the noise of starting cars. The raiders got away in two cars that Trotsky always kept. Then they heard the child's voice, but outside the house, out in the garden. "Alfred! Marguerite!" He was calling to the French Communists who had brought him to Mexico, but not in panic. He had been wounded in the foot and wanted to be bandaged.

The chief of the Mexican Secret Police was roused from his bed and came quickly enough to the house in the Calle Viena. When he went through the garden with one of the secretaries, he was halted by the sight of Seva sitting in the early morning light on a flight of steps that led up to his room, seriously engaged in whittling a piece of wood. His left foot was bandaged. The chief said to the secretary, "What has happened to him?" and the secretary answered, "Oh, he was grazed by a bullet. Happily, it's nothing serious." The child looked up for an instant and then went on whittling the wood. He was behaving according to the pattern of the household. Trotsky and his wife greeted the police so calmly that the police chief thought for some time that the whole incident had been a hoax that they had planned to bolster up their stories of persecution by Stalin. His suspicions were furthered by the conduct of the secretary-bodyguards, who were surprisingly reticent and answered all questions with "yes" or "no," and who seemed to have behaved with remarkable pusillanimity during the raid. It was also remarked that Robert Sheldon Harte, who had certainly allowed the assailants to enter, had been taken away by them; and it was thought by some who had seen his departure that he was offering no resistance whatsoever, the conclusion being that he was a Stalinist traitor, though Trotsky himself would not believe this and thought he was a silly fellow, who had been gulled into opening the door. Harte's body was later found buried under the kitchen floor in a farm outside Mexico City, covered in a chemical that made it resemble a bronze statue. He had been seen by neighbours moving round the farmhouse and going for walks about the countryside, and it had to be assumed that he had been a Stalinist agent killed by his comrades in case he was taken by the police and talked about the attack. This discovery was made a month and a day after the midnight attack.

Eight weeks after that, Trotsky was murdered by a man calling himself Jacson Mornard, whom the boy must have known as a visitor in the house. Trotsky had by now lost all sense of self-preservation and had admitted Jacson Mornard to his household without due care. He had been introduced to the house by a girl from New York, Sylvia Agelof, a graduate of Columbia who was a Trotskyite courier. She was a good-hearted girl but quite noticeably silly and gullible, and she had reason to be gulled by him, for though she was not very sexually attractive (and why should she have been? It is not a demand made of men; but in all accounts of the Trotsky murder the writers take time off to comment on her lack of obvious sensuous appeal) Jacson Mornard had been her lover, giving her the classic pleasure of seducing her in Paris, not in spring, but at least in summer. But Trotsky and his friends had no reason for letting him into the house, for he was a curiously witless conspirator, whose chief qualification for the job seemed to have been that he had been educated in Belgium, so could speak Spanish perfectly in Mexico but pass himself off as a Frenchman. As it turned out afterwards, he never seems to have been primed with a satisfactory cover story, or if he had, he had forgotten it. He told a story of being the son of a Belgian diplomat whom the most superficial enquiry could have revealed as a mythical character. Even Sylvia noticed that his account of himself had holes in it. By this time Trotsky should have been watching his household with the utmost care. His wife and his grandson were now the only members of his family who had not either been subjected to penal deportation or died tragically or disappeared without trace; and no fewer than eight of his secretaries had died in mysterious circumstances, the corpse of one being found mutilated in the Seine. But it was a curious thing that the more he became intellectually convinced that Stalin was planning to murder him, and with resources which made it impossible he should escape, the more he became emotionally free of any such fear.

In the early part of 1940, he wrote a last testament in which he dwelt on the disquiet he felt at his failing health, which was a delusion. He was only sixty-one, and quite fit for that, with no symptoms to justify his conviction that he was nearing death by arteriosclerosis. He added a special postscript to explain that he and Natalya had agreed that they would commit suicide if they felt senility was creeping up on them. In this state of euphoria, they ignored the long-term reasons for feeling suspicious of Jacson Mornard and his peculiar behaviour on the seventeenth of August. In the afternoon of that day, he arrived at the house in Coyoacán green in the face, carrying a hat and raincoat, though he never wore either, and in a peculiar way, which became explicable afterwards, when it was realised that this was a dress rehearsal, and concealed under the coat he was carrying the ice axe with which he was going to kill Trotsky three days later. He went into Trotsky's study and showed him the draft of an article he had written against a figure who today plays a part in New York in the discussion of political theory, James Burnham, who was then heading a splinter movement of Trotskyites against Trotsky. Trotsky was disconcerted, most of all because of the crudity and confusion of the draft, and then by Jacson Mornard's odd behaviour. He did not take off his hat when he came into the house, and when Trotsky sat down at his writing table to read the manuscript, instead of drawing up a chair beside him, Jacson Mornard perched himself on the writing table looking down at his astonished host, still wearing his hat and clutching his raincoat. Trotsky mentioned this incident to Natalya, who had been out of the house at the time of the unwelcome visit, with uneasiness and distaste. But neither he nor she gave orders that the guards should refuse him entrance. The only explanation can be that the faithful included so many odd fish that they were used to them.

Three days later, on August 20, in the late afternoon, Natalya went out into the garden and saw that her husband was feeding the rabbits, and Jacson was standing beside him. Again, he was wearing a hat and clutching his raincoat, though the day was fine. She offered him tea, but he asked for a glass of water, saying he felt ill, and she noticed that his face was green and he looked distraught. Jacson had brought the fair copy of his manuscript, and Trotsky, with evident reluctance, for he enjoyed attending to his rabbits and had no desire to read the article, closed the hutch and took Jacson into the study, and Natalya went into the next room. In a few moments she heard a cry from the study, and when she rushed out she found Trotsky standing at the doorway that led out on to the balcony. His glasses were broken, and his face covered with blood, through which his intensely blue eyes shone very brightly. The roof of the house was being repaired, and at first Natalya thought some heavy object had fallen on him through the ceiling. Trotsky never realised he had been stabbed and believed till he died that he had been shot. Natalya helped him as he slumped down to the floor, and he told her that he loved her and then said, "Seva must be kept out of all this." This could hardly be hoped. Trotsky was taken to the general hospital, operated on for extensive head injuries, and died twenty-four hours after the attack. Two days later his body was placed on a hearse and borne down the main thoroughfares of Mexico City and the working-class suburbs, and for five days his body lay in state, and three hundred thousand men and women filed past the coffin. Thereafter, Seva and his grandmother were alone together in the house on the Calle Viena and were obliged to remain there, for Trotsky's body was cremated and the ashes brought back and interred in the garden. Now the fortress had become a mausoleum, and it was not for the only two survivors of the dead man to desert it. Natalya lived there for the next twenty years, until her death in 1960.

I would have liked to ask her grandson, Seva, whom I caught sight of standing at his garage door, how much of that time he had lived with her, whether his presence there on that Sunday morning meant merely that he still owned the property and took advantage of the weekend to see it was in order, or if he had never freed himself from it and was still its prisoner. But I could not say anything to him at all except that I had respected Trotsky as a very great man and that I would like to see his grave. To know as much about a stranger as I did about this man is an impertinence, and I did not want to betray my knowledge, particularly as he at once bade me a gentle welcome and stood back, kind and incugarious, for us to come past him into the garage and through to the garden. Once we were inside, the place was even more horrible than it had looked from the outside, though the garden was very pleasant, with several tall trees. It was such a house as one has seen in Austrian and Baltic and Balkan towns. The house, which had been built at the beginning of the century and was of the one-storeyed romantic, Florentine type fashionable at that time, ran at a level height along one of the outside walls and less regularly along an adjacent one which, in Trotsky's time, must have looked towards the river. We had seen from the outside that it had had added to it some machine-gun towers, with lookouts, which went ill with it; but it was even more sinister that on the inner walls there were two more concrete crow's nests. The Trotsky family had expected that the outer guards might be overpowered, and that Trotsky might have to have the hand-to-hand struggle in which he did in fact meet his death. They had lived in the extremity of fear, like rats whose ratholes had been stopped up, and their fear had been realised.

Then I caught sight of the tombstone in the middle of the garden. It was a tall, narrow slab of stone, which stood with a slightly nautical tilt, and from each of its two upper corners there grew a cactus. It bore the name "Leon Trotsky," and underneath was engraved the emblem of the surpassing obstinacy that had wiped out all the dead man's limitation and left him great. Trotsky's widow had had carved below her husband's name the hammer and sickle, and it cannot be doubted that she was following her husband's wishes. He had been exiled by the Soviet Union, traduced by it, murdered by it, but he was loyal to it. For twenty-two years before his death he had lived in hell, not more than the hell he had brought on many other people but still hell, and he could have ended it with a word of submission. For most of those twenty-two years he had been overshadowed by the dread of being killed, and that too he could have brought to an end with a word of submission, and been given permission to die in his bed. The thing was fatuous. It could have been avoided. None of these disputes mattered. Mexico was doing it a different way. But it was glorious. The value of human life depends on people having the capacity to do such things, though it also depends on their having the sense to do them as rarely as possible.

Behind us Seva Trotsky and the driver were talking.

"I came here when your grandfather was alive. I came here often. With another boy. To bring the meat for the dogs."

"Ah, yes, the dogs."

"But I'm not sure I remember you. There wasn't anybody of our age living here. But there was a boy, quite a young boy, younger than we were—"

"Well, how old are you? Forty-one. I'm thirty-eight."

"Yes, that makes it right, you must have been the young boy. Oh, you were quite small—eleven, twelve—"

"Not so young they didn't try to kill me. There was an earlier attack on the house, you know, before the one that did the work. That time they nearly killed me."

His voice twanged like a harp. Probably he did not want to think any more about his grandfather, very probably he had an engagement for Sunday lunch. I would have liked to look about me for a certain relic. Trotsky had never admitted that Robert Sheldon Harte was a Stalinist agent and insisted on putting up a marble plaque to his memory in the garden. I wondered if it was still there. But I really could not ask. We shook hands with him and bade him goodbye.

He said, "Have you read Deutscher's book on him?"

I said I had.

He said, smiling beautifully, "We think it very good. Do you?"

I feel horror of all Isaac Deutscher's writings on the Russian Revolution and, indeed, on any other subject, because he believes that life is predictable, that the practice of politics must be rigidly determined by theory, and that the theoretician had a right to fire to the wall the man who works by another guide than theory. He was the enemy of everything I liked in Mexico, everything that had made Mexico give what should have been a safe house to Trotsky. But I could not have explained this to Trotsky's grandson except in a way that would have taken about twenty-four hours. I knew that his reason for liking Deutscher's biography of Trotsky was that he loved his grandfather, and that love was sacred. Also, I knew that the thing that made Deutscher's million or so words of pedantry enjoyable if not approvable was that he, too, loved Trotsky, and I therefore said "Yes, I like it very much" and at once was overcome by a wave of primitive feeling. I should tell lies in the presence of the dead.

Mexico City II

A boulevard called the Paseo de la Reforma runs through Mexico City for three and a half miles, which brings nostalgic tears to the elderly, for along those three and a half miles there survive fragments of what the Avenue of the Champs Elysées was before the rag shops and the chromium cafés leaked down its sides. In between the skyscrapers and the clumsily romantic Edwardian shops and houses are those white villas with louvre shutters, square but elegantly proportioned, which all the characters in the stories of Paul Bourget and Maupassant and Marcel Prevost called their own. One expects the doors to open and emit tall women with serpentine figures, feather boas running tangentially down their curves, and men with moustaches and beards and very high top hats and suits closely moulded with an air of satisfaction with the way God made man, on their way to fine-wheeled carriages drawn by horses shining as if varnished. There must have been a great deal of that sort of thing going on here in the nineteenth century, when Mexico was a power vacuum which European nature was eager to fill and France particularly eager. But by night the boulevard loses its past. The roadway is solid from sidewalk to sidewalk with a demonstration of what, were I a professor of social sciences, would be known as West's Law: once man has invented the internal combustion engine and succeeded in making automobiles at a price which makes it possible for enough of the community to purchase them for the manufacturer to earn a reasonable profit, then at all times when the purchasers of such vehicles feel the need to use their automobiles they will be unable to proceed at a speed as great as that attained by vehicles before the internal combustion engine was invented. The Mexican Indians had a genius for running. They still have. In certain districts they hunt the deer on foot. But today a tortoise could race a Mexican in his automobile at the rush hour.

It is difficult to get home in Mexico City and difficult to have a home to get to. Mexico has built its capital under grave handicaps. There is the insubstantiality of its soil and a network of intractable lava; but also it is only fifty years since the Republic rose into peace from a century of unrest rarely steering quite clear of civil war or the risk of civil war. This really is a new country, as the United States keeps on saying they are, though they have not been that for quite a long time. In consequence, Mexico had fifty years ago an illiteracy of 75 percent, which meant a shortage of foremen and clerks and all white-collar workers, recruits for managerial positions, and civil servants. Now the illiteracy is down to 35 percent, which is better but not satisfactory, and anyway any state which tried to keep a roof over the head of a population certain to double itself every thirty years is trying to practise white magic, however many foremen it has.

Mercifully, Mexicans are rather good at white magic. They have let stand in the city and round it many of the old houses built on the Latin plan, such as one sees by the mile in Spain and Italy, private little places, as there have been since Greek and Roman times. They turn towards the highway windows hooded by outward bulging cages of wrought iron, set in incommunicative walls. But here these walls are painted colours that are special to Mexico, touching variants of periwinkle blue, a faded acid pink, the terracotta one has seen on Greek vases, a tear-stained elegiac green. They have also reared in the upper air municipal apartment houses, some of which have, like their kind all over the world, the dated look of Corbusier, but are redeemed by that element in Mexican art which might be described as romanticism, were it not that it lacks the softness and arbitrary quality associated with the romantic in other cultures. Up, up, up come the skyscrapers, homes, and office buildings. One is uniquely lovely: a tall thin triangle, definitely ingenious in that from every aspect it looks just that—a tall thin triangle printed grey on space. But obviously apartment houses offer some problems here, since they cannot be ideal for families of ten children (and that seems to be the dream of the moderate Mexican) if only because of the strain on the elevator system; and therefore many Mexicans build houses, even if it has to be on snippets of sites. The scale, however, does not deprive them of imaginative scope. In Mexico City there is in street after street of tiny houses an architectural carnival. Here a small balconied reference to Venice is squeezed up against a neoclassical edifice rubbing its minuscule colonnade against the product of what someone remembers about the Bauhaus from an article seen in a dentist's waiting-room. It is an architectural lark, but the cramped measurements appal. How does one make love here without being congratulated by the neighbours in the morning? How can one groan as one dies without making public one's private death, like a poor lost French king? How does one have diarrhoea and go to the bathroom in the night without virtually nationalising one's intestines?

Privacy can be bought in this city only by the rich rich. The merely rich can afford a lot, but not that. We went to a house which had roughcast white walls, blue louvre-shutters, a red-tiled roof, and ample room inside for father, mother, five children, guests and servants, and believed the owner when he told us that he had copied it from his London stockbroker's home at Huntercombe, where there is a moneyed golf course. By rights there should have been in front of it a lawn with the children's tortoise crawling through croquet hoops and to the left a tennis court and a swimming pool and to the right a kitchen garden and an orchard and somewhere a paddock for the horses, but there were none of these things. Instead, within touching distance were three other substantial houses, one slightly Florentine, one modern Swiss, and another Nurembergish, all set at quarrelsome angles, so that the occupants need not look into each other's windows. But at least those houses were rectangular, as they had been put up on a site of some size cleared all at one time. But where an owner has sold off his land piecemeal, and in a delirium of excitement has chopped it up into smaller pieces every time he made a fresh sale, probably having to dodge the zigzag of a laval vein, then the householder may find himself living in rooms which form the shapes mathematicians coldly call "Monstrosities." We complimented some friends on the picturesqueness of their six-sided living-room and were irritably told that they had had to live in this area for family reasons and had had to buy the only site they were offered and had had to call in architect after architect before they could get a plausible ground-plan. This growth of Mexico City presents a grave problem, but it is characteristic that its solution looks gay and prettily surrealist in a jigsaw way.

Race Relations I

No doubt the Mexicans will solve this problem, since they have solved another, which everywhere else I have been had seemed insoluble. It is a triumph which I would have witnessed had I gone anywhere in Latin America, but it was here in Mexico I saw it. The proof of the triumph was in the traffic which every night clogged the city below the glass windows where my husband and I were drinking our coffee and chocolate. It was an eight to one chance that the passengers in any bus or taxi or automobile in the traffic block would be something like the colour of what we were drinking: coffee, chocolate, chocolate and milk, coffee and milk, beige, copper, cinnamon, fawn, dark cream, but always brown, brown with a definiteness that in some communities would invoke both insult and injury, and in most communities would bring them at least some risk of insult. For why? Not because angel's blood runs in the veins of white Mexicans, not because some heavenly gospel has been preached here in a more convincing accent than preachers have commanded elsewhere, but because the brown are in a majority. That can hardly be the whole answer, though, for the black and the brown form the majority of the population in many countries where the standard attitude to them is poisoned with varying degrees of insult.

Looking at the Mexican brown majority, it appears possible that it is immune from insult and injury because, to use a Shakespearean phrase, there was good sport at its making. It is a matter of history that when Cortés conquered the Aztecs the daughters of the Emperor Montezuma were so beautiful and charming that it proved not difficult at all to marry them off to the Spanish nobility, and today the ancient families of the Andradas and the Canos and the Sotelos and the Miravalles are all proud to be their descendants. Don Jose Sarmiento Valladares was the thirty-first of the sixty-one viceroys who governed Mexico while it was a Spanish dependency, and he was one of the clan. It took time for them to gain actual power, but they stayed there. These successes were not exceptional or fictions, contrived for political purposes. All these brown people in the Mexican streets are there because throughout the centuries Indians were physically and mentally delectable. It must be remembered that very soon after the conquest of Mexico Spanish colonisation was so well developed that a white man or woman could easily find a spouse of the same colour without going back to Spain, and such a marriage must inevitably have been what white society, if only out of vanity, had preferred. But innumerable dark women must have been so delightful, and so resourcefully and wisely delightful, that white men, though mobile as the male is in an undeveloped country, decided that by these dark charmers was where they wanted to be; and somewhat later innumerable white women must have said to themselves, "It would have been pleasant to marry into a Castilian family, but this dark young man is the husband I want."

The emotions must have been of the dignified sort that engender a sense of responsibility, for the mestizos of today have not just come to the surface from waifdom, their stock has not been starved. There has never been great plenty in this place of fierce geological faults and climatic crisis, but what there has been must have been spread out to cover thoroughly, though thinly, the ancestors of these quick-moving, well-coordinated people. No doubt there are countless hundreds and thousands and even millions of dead Mexicans who died of malnutrition and left no descendants; but there were millions who got food and care, and their children are prospering, in body and soul, and doing us a favour. For it is wonderful to find oneself in a country where the population is black and white and see that though they are subject to rage (even specially so) there is not among them the disgusting bickering of master and slave, which never can come to agreement because slavery lies athwart the argument, blocking the road to solution. Here, if a white man and a man of mixed blood quarrel, it is simply as if a dark man has fallen out with his brother who takes after the other side of the family and is fair: no more than that.

This is so with the mestizos, but not with the Indians. In the modern Mexican consciousness there is passionate love for the Indian and pity for his martyrdom, a sense that nothing can now be done to him to compensate him for that violation of his rights, but the situation has needled Mexicans into two kinds of prickly ambivalence regarding the pure Indian. He is horribly poor, and all over the world poverty is so painful that a man who has escaped falling into its abyss feels terrified lest someone else who has gone over the edge will claw at him and drag both down together. Sometimes one will see this panic acted out as in a charade, in the heart of Mexico City. A party of Indians who have come in by truck from a remote village will join a queue at a bus stop, and their outsiderishness, their ignorance of what the modern world buys will show itself in their attire. A headdress handsomely shaped by memories of the Spanish mantilla may be made out of a cast-off clout from a gringo kitchen, printed in faded red letters with the inscription "Glass Cloth"; and a skirt may be made (with some elegance) from still identifiable pillow-slips. The town-dwellers in front of them and behind them behave correctly and do not break their ranks, but on their faces is dread. I recognise the situation: people have bad dreams when they see the very poor, as if they feared that through this proximity to deprivation their appropriate clothes may become misty filaments and float away, and that, even if the buses did not cease to run and they could get home, they would find that no light came when they turned on the switches, no water came out of the taps, and the new cooker had gone. The reason why I recognise the situation is that I was the youngest daughter of a penniless widow. We asked nothing of our relatives, being natural optimists and sure that things would work out well, which, so far as money was concerned, they did. But our relatives regarded us as if we were come to tell them their money was to go the way of ours, by a sort of malignant miracle, against which they could do nothing; and even when we had ceased to be poor, when, in fact, we had become as prosperous as they were, they still did not regard us as their ordinary flesh-and-blood kin, but rather as if we were Lazaruses returned from the tomb.

The Indian arouses such fear in his white and mestizo fellow citizens in an embittered form, since they feel responsible for his poverty. This is an uncomfortable position which perpetuates the Indian grievance, since it is a characteristic of human nature that people feel hostile towards those whom they are conscious of having injured. The Mexican is taught, and the lesson never stops, that the Spaniards caused the Indians' poverty and the colour-bar, which both accentuates the poverty and is accentuated by it, and the lesson will be learned. But it is doubtful whether the hatred of the poor can be removed by pedagogic means quite so briskly. The result must therefore be a certain degree of schizophrenia. To feel guilt about the past ill-treatment of people whom one wants to ill-treat in the present and the future: that is too complicated for true mental health.

Schizophrenic too is the other attitude towards Indians which strikes the foreigner. The faith by which modern Mexico lives calls for Mexicans to abandon the instinctive life and accept all the disciplines necessary to make them good technicians, industrialists, scientists, artists, lawyers, doctors, politicians, civil servants, for the sake of the national prosperity and the national glory, which they quite rightly identify. Not until they get their welfare state working can they afford to turn up their noses at affluence. This duty weighs heavily on some individuals, and these are apt to think enviously of the Indians as having opted out. This is an unfair view, for every year more and more Indians become modern Mexicans. All the same, quite a number remain where fate and the Spaniards pushed them. The Aztecs had no monetary medium except a system of arrangements for giving change when bartered goods were disparate, in little packets of chocolate or gold-dust in quills. It is said that in parts of the country there are still Indians who have never succeeded in getting on to the currency system. There they are, almost as helpless before drought and frost and hurricane and flood as the coyotes and the deer, but getting their responses sharp-edged, their senses unblunted by the disease of responsibility, unbullied by the beckoning future.

There is something in that view of them. When my husband and I went to the village markets, particularly the ones that are held indoors, in high and bright halls, we were enchanted. The fruit shone brightly as if they were in a poem by Keats, some, like the one with the pale gold husk curling back from garnet-red pulp, were formal like jewellery. The unleavened bread lay in amber sheets. There were bunches of tiny bananas like casts of children's hands in soft gold. I have seen a pile of straw hats which exploited their unpromising form as ingeniously as I had seen it done in a drawing by Braque. Behind the benches laden with this exquisitely presented and exquisite merchandise sat the small-boned people, all looking as if they would make good ballet material (and so they do, the Mexican Ballet Company and the independent groups use any number of Indian boys and girls). They seemed not to see us until we wanted something from them, then they smiled distantly and spoke softly and gave us what we needed, even when we did not know what to ask for. But as the moments flowed delightfully by in this place, which was truly a super-market, something above any market we had ever known, we suspected, then recognised, then deplored that to the Indians we were appearing as characters out of the Forsyte Saga, say old Jolyon and Aunt Juley. Old and thick-blooded and dreamless creatures, able to deal with the cash nexus but no good for anything else.

Well, really, we were not that. We might have been, were it not that all our generation had had its experience by a historical crisis which we could quite decently compare to the Spanish conquest. We had seen a vicious political theory find its incarnation in slaughtering hordes that had altered our continent, we had had bombs dropped on us. It is quite a serious education in its way. But there is a breakdown in communication between the country Indians and the rest of the world which must cause some considerable political irritation. We had a revelation of that when we had got over the first mountain range on our way down by road to Oaxaca, and we stopped at a great sixteenth-century Dominican monastery that rides like a moored ship among the foothills, overlooking a wide plain. There were some old Indians sitting on a bench at the foot of the splendid march and countermarch of stone stairways and platforms which led up to the church, and our driver halted and talked to them while we looked round at the landscape. It was very like parts of Greece and Macedonia, though the hillsides were clawed by the fiercer climate into deeper gullies of erosion. Here and there were plateaux engineered into terraces where corn was growing. Though this was not as high as Mexico City, the altitude was still considerable. My husband said just what anybody with any knowledge of farming would say, "On the flat and very high, my God, what frost they must get," and I exclaimed sympathetically. All the way corn had been signalling to us piteous messages about the poverty of the people: high, high up on a stoney slope covered with scrub an Indian had discovered a few flat yards, and there the leggy stuff was drying off, not to autumnal gold but to the yellow of jaundice. Our driver repeated what we had said about the frost to the Indians sitting on the bench and their faces changed. They had been half-smiling to us with the uninsistent cordiality of hosts faced with guests who are not going to stay long or come back, but now they showed real curiosity. The driver interpreted their answer: "Yes, the frost here is terrible, sometimes they lose all the crop. But they wonder, how do you know?"

We stared back at expressions which we could interpret for ourselves. What the Indians were asking was how it happened that somebody foreign travelling about the country in an automobile could make a sensible remark. They were doing us and our kind an injustice. It was true that my husband and I have a sharpened sympathy with farmers because we had to redeem land we owned, which had been long set aside for grazing horses, and turn it back into a food-producing farm during the last war. But anyway, all our sort of people knew all about frost and how it is nearly as destructive as fire. Who did I mean by "our sort of people"? The people in our village. The houses run along the street which follows the backbone of a ridge, and I ticked them off one by one and was sure that all the occupants would know about frost, for where they had nothing to do with agriculture they still had their gardens. In the neighbouring industrial town and in many districts in London, they would not know anything about frost, and even those of us who have the knowledge do not know the full horror of it that was revealed to these Indians. In 1784 there was a great freeze which killed three hundred thousand people, and though this is the record there have been great flower-blackening, flesh-bluing slaughters since. But are the Indians right in despising the people who do not know of them? Does it really matter? There are now 3,706 million human beings who are weaving fantasies of interchange between their bodies and what they find on the terrestrial surface of 57 million square miles. One cannot hope to be informed about more than an infinitesimal fraction of those fantasies; and what the Indians (and indeed all of us) have a right to insist upon is that the thinkers of the world should work out general principles likely to lessen pain and enjoyment, even when specialist knowledge is not available. That, indeed, was the aim of Jewish and Christian ethics.

But the foreigners, or the Mexicans who look at Indians with foreigners' eyes because they are town-dwellers, are applying what they believe to be sound general principles. They think it possible the Indians could be saved by some simple governmental action, such as distribution of more land, and by greater efficiency on their own part. But this becomes doubtful if one watches an old Indian against his background. He looks like a neat small-boned Lear, and it is the violent skies above him and the violent earth behind him which are his Regan and his Goneril. Mexico is as beautiful as Greece, but it is more perversely anti-human than even that barren land. In the far backward of time, the isthmus was wrecked by an explosion in its basement, which sent up a line of volcanoes, some now extinct, some still in practice, and three at least of marvellous beauty. There are the docile, serviceable lands round Cuernavaca and Oaxaca to show what a paradise was then riven down the middle; but riven it was, and there are huge areas where the surface is broken up into blocks, varying in size from acres to feet, set at angles to each other. Most of the rivers in such districts run at the bottom of deep gullies, hundreds or even thousands of feet in depth, and elsewhere there is a superficial layer of limestone through which the water runs as if it were a sieve, to be tapped only by wells. Where the hurricanes come in from the Caribbean they produce violent winds which can blow people and mules off roads, or rains which wash the soil off the rocks and force it down to the valleybeds where it forms a sponge unkind to plant life.

All this has been worsened because man is given mobility long before he has acquired the information which would enable him to avoid genocidal sin. This lack of syncopation has often accounted for the guilt of colonialism. First the Romans and then the Venetians wanted Dalmatia to prosper, for it was theirs by conquest, but they cut down its forests, never thinking that they were thereby giving the soil the signal to slip down the coastal slopes into the Mediterranean and dooming all Dalmatians not sailors and shipowners to poverty. In the same way the Spaniards, though anxious to gain favour with their king by turning Mexico into a profitable investment, cut down the Mexican forests and cut them down again as soon as the new wood was standing, and that again and again, till the mountains were bald-headed and the sun-consumed plains were deserts. Between nature and uninstructed man, Mexico shows a lot of land which could not get cultivated except in small plots: give a peasant too much of it and you would break his heart. It also shows a lot of land which could not be cultivated except on a large scale which demands ample capital. On the mountain highways one sometimes passes Indians waiting on the verges for the truck which will pick up the sacks of produce beside them, which look more real than they do, for their cotton suits are always spectre-colour, white or pale grey or pale blue or a breath of coffee brown. Behind them is a magnificent landscape of shining ranges cleft with deep gorges, which is also a map of their poverty.

There is no chance of cutting short the argument by pretending that the Indian was doomed to poverty by his own deficiencies. When he was conquered by Cortés he showed every sign of picking himself up after the defeat and coming into the Western system of civilisation at a high level. Some years ago, one of the imaginative presences who are shaping Mexico City (I never found out who they are, nobody was interested in telling me) bethought himself that under some railway yards and slums there was the site of the great market of Tlatelolco, which was the trading centre outside Tenochtitlán, the Aztec capital, which was probably one of the most gorgeous fantasias on the theme of trade that the human race has produced, on a par with the bazaars of Constantinople and Baghdad, much, much more glorious than anything we know today. The site was cleared, and they found among the tenements a seventeenth-century church and a superb cloistered building and, when they grubbed under the earth, an Aztec temple. Now the steps of the Aztec temple are uncovered, and behind it, as if it were a substitute for the temple building, is a new technical college, which is a masterpiece of practicality and is also strangely beautiful, lying along the ground like a huge glittering snake; and alongside, the seventeenth-century church has been cavalierly gutted of decoration inferior to its general design and stands in almost Romanesque beauty, while the cloistered building is being repaired by workmen who all know its story and are aware of its implications. It was a college founded after the conquest by an enlightened Spanish bishop for the higher education of the sons of the Aztec nobles. The young Aztecs showed such aptitude for their studies, particularly Latin and theology, that after the first decade or so, the college staffed itself with its own graduates and furnished tutors for many of the sons of the Spanish colonists. But deliberately, because the inferior kind of colonials wanted the Indians to be a source of cheap labour and nothing else, the college was first turned into a primary school and then closed. Nothing is more certain than that when the building is repaired and opened as a museum this story will be forcibly injected into the mind of every visitor as a sting, it will not just be blandly introduced.

Chapultepec I

But to see how unconquered the Aztecs are one must go to one of the chief glories of Mexico City, Chapultepec, or Grasshopper Hill. That is where He-who-gets-angry-like-a-Lord had his summer palace. Then it was an island rising from the salt lake of Texcoco, which was to Tenochtitlán what the lagoons are to Venice, and which Cortés drained. Then the place must have been an earthly paradise, a pious offering to pleasure, like the Palace Domain at Peking. It is now a uniquely delicious park, splendidly various, like an amalgam of all the parks in Paris, with Hyde Park and Kensington Gardens and a bit of Epping Forest thrown in, and more besides. There is a romantic castle on a high porphyritic cliff, where the Mexicans put Maximilian, the spare Habsburg wished on them in the 1860s as a king by the idiot, Louis Napoleon. In that castle they allowed Maximilian to remain till they thought it time he died, when power was taken over and the matter seen to by the Zapotec Indian, Juárez. The story is heart-breaking because the young man, who had a golden beard cascading from his chin which would have been more in place covering Godiva, was endlessly sentimental and loved beauty, and in particular the beauty of Mexico.

There are also on Grasshopper Hill a zoo, pleasant as zoos are in the lower latitudes, with not an animal in it looking as if it were feeling the cold; two lakes, one wild like a New England or Canadian lake, with the clean rock running sharply down through the scrub to the winding water, the other open and bland in the Chinese way, with people traversing it in brightly painted pedalos and boats, very slowly, as if their mandarin employers had given them a day off; an amusement, which has a mad ethereal Chagall look to it; a polo-ground where beautiful rich young men, who ought to be odalisques if women had their right, ride ponies still more beautiful; a garden full of signalling cactus; an auditorium which is a complex of theatres; a most imaginatively constructed restaurant with walls like half-furled wings and a trick to it all that makes it not easy to understand how one room melts into another. Make no mistake, whatever we have in London or New York, they have it in this capital of a poor country, and they have it in a way that is more fun: at least two art galleries, which is surely unique in a public park, two battlefields of national importance, and the Anthropological Museum, which is its supreme glory.

Anthropological Museum I

There are many museums which are beautiful like the Louvre or the Museum of Oriental Art in Zurich, because the premises were once palaces or the residences of the rich. But this must be by far the most beautiful museum built as a museum. Its substance is exquisite. The walls are made from stone bricks of subtle colours, pale grey, storm grey, violet-grey, violet, grey-blue, blue, rose-grey, rose, and they shimmer as if alive and breathing. Its proportions handle space as if it were a delicious drink and the architect was pouring it out for a world of guests. To go into the vestibule, to look at the fountain that is like a huge tree, to cross the courtyard with the pools is like emptying a glass, a glass of something better than wine. Then comes the shock, the revelation. The halls contain a huge collection of works of art produced in the first sixteen hundred years of the Christian era by about eight indigenous Mexican civilisations. These are the expressions of Indian genius in its purity, unaffected by Europe, with which it had no traffic until Cortés came. True, there is one mystery. According to Mr. Burland of the British Museum, in his *Gods of Ancient Mexico*, there have been found under the sealed floors of a ninth-century house in Central Mexico some fragments of pottery, figurines, certainly made in Rome during the first or second century. But this is a true mystery, such as Charles Fort chronicled in *Lo!*: comparable to the showers of frogs, of ice blocks, of money, which he reports as having been dropped like the gentle dew from heaven. In all Mexico there is not another trace of Europe: not a mill of the European kind, not a loom, not a fingerprint of our kind of craftsmanship, not a European character inscribed on a stone nor painted on leather, not a scruple of iron, nor a grain of wheat, not a planked boat. And indeed when the foreigner looks at these works of art, he knows that his kind had nothing to do with them.

First of all, there is from his point of view an enormous imbalance. There is too much caricature, too much ridicule of the human body, too much mockery of the mind's hopes. Consider how European art would appal, if 90 percent of all European artists had followed the line that runs between Hieronymus Bosch and Daumier, how European literature would appal, if 90 percent of all its writers were wry-penned like Jonathan Swift. But this is not a superficial grimace. It is an honest recognition that human beings are often made hideous by what the gods do to them, and that it is therefore probable that the gods are hideous. They knew what beauty was. They would have preferred it to be the predominant element in life.

There was a high military order in the Aztec Empire, one of the two highest, called The Eagle Knights, whose helmets were eagles' heads and who were the soldiers of the Sun, of the Creator, the great god. In the museum there is a head of an Eagle Knight which is a defence of the human species, an account of it which rebuts every hostile and derogatory argument, which speaks the best for youth and courage and virility. There are also Mayan figures which have that trick of proportion performed by the greatest sculpture. One is greatly impressed, one takes home a photograph, looking at it one cannot remember if they were large or small. If they could lie on one's palm or had to be left in the open because no building was high enough to house them. Their dolls have faces smooth as some of the statues in these galleries, yet as one pauses to say, "So this is Olmec" or "This is Mayan," the words sound extraordinary, for this smoothness speaks of the experience of everyone, everywhere, in any age. The smooth heads that nevertheless speak of all human anatomy are tilted at angles which suggest comprehended suffering, on bodies which brace themselves against a downward force, which is perhaps simply heavy rain or meridian sunlight but might be sober apprehension. There are gods resembling all the impersonations indulged in by destiny, gods who look like babies with open wet exorbitant mouths, like prairie foxes wrapped in ceremonial feather vestments, like disturbed moose who snuff up news of weather unfriendly to the herd. There is the Lord of the Flowers, patron of love and dancing and games, sitting cross-legged and beautiful as Cassius Clay, and as bitchy about his beauty, but also an angel. Intimations of reality as remote as float on Rilke's lines are here made concrete.

These might not be exhibits in a museum, this might not be a museum. It might be the palace of a sorcerer king who had turned away suddenly and left his treasures forever, and as they were tools of magic they naturally radiated force through the solid but shimmering walls. It is not only Indian art which archaeologists have, very suddenly, unloaded on the modern Mexican mind, it is the knowledge of an Indian civilisation which was dynamic and impressive and had not decayed but been annihilated by an act of aggression against which it was not able to prepare. Paradoxically, one of the most enthusiastic celebrants of the pre-Columbian tradition who walked among the Toltec and Zapotec and Mayan and Aztec objects in the Anthropological Museum, as if he were a pious Catholic following his devotions at the Stations of the Cross in a church, was the son of parents both born in France, and of Polish-Jewish origins. It is not easy to trace the ins and outs of this alien involvement in the local tradition. I went to see an official of pure Spanish blood who, when I spoke of the Anthropological Museum and my admiration for the pre-Columbian objects it displayed, responded with only moderate enthusiasm, and pointed out that the idea of founding a museum to commemorate Indian civilisation was first proposed by a Spanish viceroy at the end of the eighteenth century; and that it had taken a hundred and fifty years for the Mexico which had thrown off the Spanish yoke to get round to building it. He also discounted the idea that patriotism had had anything to do with the speed with which the museum had been built. Very reasonably he pointed out that it would be difficult for a modern Mexican to feel any real affinity with the Aztecs; but less reasonably, I thought, asserted that this was because the Aztec civilisation had become a dead stop. It had been carried on by an elite, and the Spanish had destroyed the elite. So nothing could have remained to pass on the tradition. But would not the elite have imprinted the tradition on the masses? No, the masses were nothing, they had received nothing, they had preserved nothing, they were transmitting nothing.

Later that day I met another Mexican of pure Spanish descent and told him how odd I found it that a government so intent on linking modern Mexico with the Aztec tradition should have appointed to an important office a man who was so anti-Aztec.

The astonished answer was "But he's not anti-Aztec and anti-Indian," followed by, "Oh, but I see what happened. You might get that impression from an attitude of his, which is really quite natural and does not mean what you suppose."

He explained that this official belonged to one of the Spanish families which left Mexico when it detached itself from the Spanish Empire, but which later returned. They might be likened to many English whose forebears have worked in India and are returning now to India, not so much from economic need as from homesickness, but with the difference that though such English usually go to India to work and come back to England when they retire, these Spanish families made their permanent homes in Mexico. Such Spanish families were usually contemptuous of the indigenous Mexican civilisation and the mixed population, but members of this family had dissented from their view, and this man had been very forcible in his dissent, going into conflict with his own kind again and again.

"Therefore," explained my Mexican friend, "for the sake of his integrity, he would want to give you the impression he did."

"For the sake of his integrity," I said in despair, "he would want me to believe he held opinions which are the opposite of those he really holds?"

"For the sake of his integrity," repeated the Mexican, "because there is much to be said on both sides." There was some sense in that.

"I see that," I agreed, "and after all it all happened a long time ago."

"No, it is still happening all the time, the issues are constantly arising which relate to it, that is why we must keep ourselves ready to admit the truth."

The thing, when it was spread out on the dissecting table in front of one, was valid enough. For many parts of the world the past is so complicated that it is practically impossible to make a clear statement about the present which is not more or less fictitious. The past is the great intoxicant of nations. The Serbs could never have driven the Turks out of their country had they not remembered that in the fourteenth century their king was as mighty a monarch as any in Europe. And what makes the Mexican find the knowledge of Aztec civilisation as intoxicating as pulque and mescal is that not only does it show them they were once great, it shows them they were great in the same way as the powers which have the most prestige today and use it or have used it to bully Mexico.

Aztec Society

The society which the Spaniards destroyed is best described in Jacques Soustelle's obsessed little volume *The Daily Life of the Aztecs*. There was a league of three Indian states: Mexico, where the Aztecs lived, Texcoco, and the little kingdom of Tlacopan, clustering round the lake which is now the dust bowl where Mexico lies. The league was dominated by the city Tenochtitlán, which lay on the water like Venice, and was, in the opinion of those Spanish captains who had seen Rome and Constantinople, not less magnificent than those cities. From this capital there was dispensed a peculiar economy. There was no monetary system, the land was nationalised, the emperor was the only capitalist, it was a welfare state, and the needs of the people in sickness and at times of fire and flood and famine were met by the state. This economy required a vast administrative personnel, and Tenochtitlán must have resembled a Washington that was all Pentagon and a London that was all Whitehall, though the comparison with Washington is the more apt, because the emperor was, like the president of the United States, also the commander-in-chief of the armed forces, as our monarchs are not. The society which he governed was split up into five classes, none of which was a leisure class. Everybody worked, nobody had any resources except their earned income, unless they had inherited what their parents had saved out of their income, but these sources were unlikely to be enough for them to live on, as the cost of the administrative machine meant that taxation was high. This is not at all unlike life in the United States and Britain as it has become since the Second World War or, at least, as it is becoming. True, the land is not nationalised, but all considerable properties are broken up by our death duties, and though fortunes are made out of real estate it is by development and not by mere acquisition. They had no monetary system, but that hardly seems to matter.

The emperor was elected from the members of one dynasty by an electoral college of a hundred eminent persons, and his four principal aides were also elected. Below them were these five classes, who did not go to each other's parties, but were not rigid, for an unworthy person born into a high class might drop to a lower, and merit would reverse the process. The highest was the ruling class, which consisted of civil servants, warriors, priests, and judges. There were no landowners, and as they had no iron, there could be no industrialists. The civil servants were either appointed by the emperor or nominated by districts or cities and passed by a sympathetic central authority. The top level formed a war cabinet, others the treasury; the lesser breed had to guarantee the cleanliness of the streets and the efficiency of the water supply if they worked in the cities, and in the country they had to see that the peasants were cultivating the land properly and settle minor legal disputes. In either case they had to see that the emperor was getting the taxes he had decreed and protect the citizen from over-taxation and keep an eye on the men who would be drafted in case of war. They were given houses and servants by the district where they worked, and the central government gave them food and textiles and general stores, but they were never very well off, for they had to control the inhabitants of their bailiwick so closely that they were always having to receive them in their houses and give them food and drink. So heavy was the burden of this administrative personnel on the country, so much in need of funds was the central government, that special honour was paid to the civil servants who ranged the country and the subjected territory outside the bounds of the empire and collected the grain and merchandise and good-stuffs which was the agreed tax. Their function was not wholly inhumane; if there was famine or a cloudburst they could exempt the district from its duty to furnish tribute and actually open the imperial stores to relieve the distress. But the country must have felt for them as we feel for the Inland Revenue.

Not much trouble can have been given these civil servants by draft evasion. There is no question but that Mexicans enjoyed soldiering. They were conditioned to it, starting their military education at the age of seven, and after they had killed or captured four of the enemy they had a legal right to a share in the loot of the campaign and thereafter could swagger in dyed and embroidered clothes denied to civilians and enjoy the company of the official army corps of courtesans, the *auianime*, the smooth ones, the satisfying ones, trained like geishas to please, and beautifully dressed. They could move on and up through society, getting richer and richer, bedecked with jewellery and wrapped in splendid clothes, not only exempt from the duty of farming their original share of land, but the recipient of other shares, often in conquered territory, cultivated by slaves. If they were able enough, they could in their maturity join the highest ranks of the civil service, they could become the emperor's close advisers. They had, in fact, the prestige that the soldier has had and that the industrialist still has, and for good reason. Without them the Aztec Empire could never have balanced its books.

Its natural resources were poor. They had not enough textiles and not enough protein. All the game in the isthmus had been killed off between 7000 B.C. and 1500 B.C. by a cycle of hot weather, ironically called the Climatic Optimum, which had burned up all the grass; and when they had gone, the smaller, solitary creatures went too. The Aztecs were down to fish taken along the coast and in the streams, wild turkey, partridges, pigeon, quail and duck, with such oddities as a breed of dog that ran to fat and a kind of caviar which floated on lakes and dried into cheese. It is significant that the Aztecs, whose gods were not representations of what they found adorable but recognitions of the forces they knew to determine their lives, had a god of sepsis and deformity, two consequences of malnutrition. Hence they made war on all the tribes round them, simply for the purpose of imposing tribute which would come in edible form, as grain and chocolate; and if there was cotton, so much better. To buy themselves goods and clothing the Aztecs had to pay a proportion of their means to the army, which was as considerable to them as our defence programme is to us.

Torture was common practice in Europe when Cortés came to Mexico, and was not to be abandoned in England till the seventeenth century, and lasted in Germany and Italy and Spain till much later, and has been revived in our lifetimes by the totalitarian governments. The Aztecs would have none of it. Their legal machine was not exercised brutally. Some of their law was warmed by chivalry. There was a certain elegance and even sweetness in Aztec justice. The judges were appointed by the emperor himself, and he looked for them not only in the ruling class, lest the courts should fall under suspicion of favouring the interests of that class. He did not take them from the class immediately below, the *pochteca*, which consisted of merchants who had a monopoly on foreign trade and constantly sent out expeditions from the central valley of Mexico all over the isthmus to the Pacific Ocean and the Gulf of Mexico. They were working too hard in the national interest to be called to the service of the law; if they were young they were often away on these expeditions, which might keep them in the strange lands for years at a time, and they were then working in a double capacity, as traders and as members of the intelligence corps of the army; their elders planned the expeditions and marketed what the expeditions brought back and arranged for the conversion of the raw material to manufactured goods, kept accounts and transacted much legal business, for they had their own courts, in which all commercial cases were tried, as well as all disputes between members of the guilds. But there was another reason why judges were not picked from this class. In a queer way the merchants were without moral authority in Aztec society.

The class below the pochteca was the *tolteca*, the craftsmen, called by that name because the crafts they practised were supposed to have been invented by the Toltecs, a vanished people who had maintained a civilisation far more brilliant than Mexico between A.D. 600 and 1200. Like artists all over the world, these craftsmen lived in happy isolation from the rest of society; and they were also considered as not truly Aztecs, with some reason, for they seem to have been descended from a group of survivors if not from the Toltecs from some other gifted race, who, craftsmen already, had joined the nomad Aztecs, who knew none of these accomplishments when they first settled by the lake.

It was in the class below them, the *maceualli*, that the emperor found his extra judges. These could be called the plebeians but that this name has been darkened by overtones of contempt, while these people were regarded rather with grateful sympathy: the name means those who work and acquire merit. They furnished the judges that were wanted, and it speaks well for them that they could fulfil the requirements. A judge could be dismissed for private drunkenness and killed for public drunkenness and killed also for taking bribes, and he had to be uninfluenced by his personal interests or by his prejudices. Under the control of the judiciary was a huge police force, which would arrest any Aztec except a member of the dynasty, a body of court reporters, who took down all proceedings in picture language, and a host of clerks and attendants and messengers. These must have been immensely numerous, for there were metropolitan and provincial courts, and an appeals court, which, oddly enough, sat not in Mexico but in Texcoco, the capital of the allied kingdom, and consisted of twelve judges under the presidency of the king. The population seems to have been litigious, and it is significant that there was a regulation that no case could drag on longer than eighty days.

The lowest class of Aztec society were the slaves, who were the chattels of their masters. But if they could save money and acquire possessions, good luck to them—their children were born free, even if both parents were slaves. They could not be sold until their master had admonished them three times before witnesses, with proof of dishonesty or refusal to work. There was a picturesque law which seems based on some curious metaphysical conception, akin to our Christian idea of sanctuary: if a slave could escape from the slave market and could make his way into the royal precincts and find the emperor, then he was free. The state of slavery was annulled by the royal presence. Furthermore, any free man who tried to prevent a slave from escaping out of the slave market or entering into the palace, unless he was the slave's master or the master's son, he became a slave himself. This too recalls our society. We remember men like Mr. Justice Holmes or Mr. Justice Learned Hand or Mr. Justice Brandeis with the feeling that they were loyal to a valid common cause. We hate a bad judge as a traitor to that cause. We feel that true justice is mercy, an unfair favouring of the unfortunate. We know that the law has built into it an inherent immorality, for none of us knows enough about another man to feel safe in punishing him, yet our own morality depends on the risk, since we ourselves might not refrain from crime if there was no such punishment.

Looking at the Aztec society is, with the exception of one grim feature, like looking into a mirror. The slaves could rise out of their class, they could be freed by masters grateful for good service or by the emperor himself if they had performed a public duty. The pochteca, the merchants, did not rise to the ruling class and they did not recruit their members from the plebeians. They were a nation within a nation. They married among their own kind, they lived in their own districts, they not only had their own law courts, they had their own priesthood within the priesthood, that served their special gods by a special liturgy and went out with the expeditions. They were very brave, and their work was essential to the natural economy; they exported manufactured goods, cloth made of cotton and rabbit-fur yarn, embroidered clothes, jewellery, and cultivated herbs, and they brought back luxuries such as jade and precious stones, feathers and jaguar and puma pelts. The trade balance was not such as can be imagined pleasing in the sight of God. The Aztecs got their raw materials, their precious metals, and their raw cotton as tribute from the tribes they had conquered and probably would never have conquered had not the expeditions brought them back information about the military and material resources of the tribes and the layout of the country. There was a special section of the pochteca called the "disguised traders" or the like who were James Bonds, who wore the clothes of the tribes and mastered their languages and practised their liturgical forms so that they could infiltrate them.

This predation was conducted in a spirit of exalted patriotism. Some years before the Spanish conquest, an expedition of Aztec traders went down to the Isthmus of Tehuantepec on the Pacific Coast and were surrounded by four tribes of Zapotec Indians, who were pretty fighters. The Aztecs sat it out for four years, then burst forth and slaughtered the besiegers and stripped their territories. On the road home they met an army of their own people sent to relieve them, who turned about and led them back to their emperor, and at his feet the returning traders laid trophies of captured standards and insignia, such as any of their superiors, the warriors, might have been proud to bring back from a campaign. The emperor gave them the odd honorific title of his "uncles" and gave them the right, normally enjoyed only by the ruling class, of wearing jewellery and gold ornaments and feathers. They replied in a speech which the Spanish friar Sahagún took down after the conquest from an Aztec who remembered it.

> We, your uncles, the pochteca who are here, we have risked our heads and our lives, and we have laboured day and night; for although we are called traders, and although we seem to be traders, we are captains and soldiers, who in a disguised fashion go out to conquer.

This sounds like Cecil Rhodes and the early developers of Africa, but in the African case there was at any rate some attempt, due to Jewish and Christian ethics, to give the inhabitants some return for values received. In Britain it was said that trade followed the flag, and it was hoped that the trade would benefit both sides, though it was also hoped that the lion's share of the benefit might accrue to the British, and often even that hope was disappointed. In Mesoamerica the flag followed trade, and once the flag was leaving, the trader came in again, accompanied by the tax collector, and there was no pretence that anybody in the conquering body worried about the prosperity of the annexed territories. But this process was an absolute necessity for the tripartite alliance of Mexico, Texcoco, and Tlacopan, which were not a viable unit. Nothing can make it moral, but the three countries could not have survived without it, and the traders were essential to its operation. But they were despised.

The resultant social situation has a fascinating resemblance to what had happened, was happening, and was to happen on the other side of the world. When Cortés went to Spain, and for long afterwards, Europe could not have met its expenses were it not for the economy set up by its merchants, yet royalty and the landowners and the soldiers held them in contempt and the common people regarded them as morally tainted. Their good will was cultivated, for the rich have never been shunned, but there was hatred. It sprang from sheer envy of those to whom money came easily, any time that they saw the possibility of exploiting a new trade route or a technological invention, much more quickly and lavishly than it came to royalty (except when there was a tricky piece of confiscation) or to landowners or to soldiers. But there was a nobler cause of resentment: a feeling that the feudal period and its imposition of taxes and services had settled what a man who did his public duty was entitled to get as a reward, and that a merchant could take a thievishly high profit from the goods that passed through his hands and hang the good of the people. There was also in Europe the belief that the lending or borrowing of money at interest was always an immoral proceedings, even when the state and the church regulate the rate of interest. But there could be no drastic laws curtailing commerce, because it followed no predictable course, springing up here, there, and everywhere, and anyway there was a sneaking admission of the importance of its function. So the authorities made false charges against merchants with a feeling that in a high sense they were really true. Jacques Coeur, the famous entrepreneur of Bourges, was ruined by a ridiculous charge that he had murdered the king's mistress. The class learned to walk warily and look poorer than it was, sometimes simply to avoid arousing envy and inviting such false charges, sometimes out of genuine moral fear, which showed itself very clearly in such communities as the Quakers, that they should be tempted to let too much of the wealth that passed through their hands stick to their fingers.

Hence there was founded a European tradition that even the richest bankers and industrialists must bear themselves soberly, which grew into a tradition that the best was good enough for a banker and industrialist, provided it were the sober best. But the more exuberant in the class have refused to be curbed by this and lived like princes and nobles and filibusters; but they have been met by a tradition held by other classes that they must sneer at such splendour, even when it takes the form of hospitality and even when the community would charge the merchants with meanness were they not hospitable. A millionaire's party is a classical subject for sniggers, and it imposes something less than the loyal response expected from guests: one such, a ball which lit up a Venetian palace not long ago, was preluded by a number of dinner parties given by the guests, none of whom invited the host to her table, so that he ate alone at a restaurant.

This is fantastically like what happened among the Mesoamericans. The Aztec traders were the object of a contempt which knew it had no right behind it, but went as far as it dared. The trader heroes of Tehuantepec were given the right to wear jewellery and gold ornaments and feathers, but only on their special feast-days, while the ruling class could wear them any time. If a trader became affluent and showed signs of forgetting his place, false charges would be brought against him as they were brought against Jacques Coeur, and he would be disgraced or fined or even killed, and his goods shared out as pensions to elderly members of the ruling class. Therefore the trader went about plainly dressed, and he would assert that the burdened porters behind him were carrying goods belonging not to him but to a friend, and that the boats which travelled by night up the canals to his warehouse were unloading cargo he knew nothing about, because he was simply letting storage space. Occasionally he gave a party, and this was an oddly schizophrenic affair. A great banquet was expected from him, lasting perhaps two days, with a distribution of food to all the inhabitants of the quarter where he lived, but all the guests insulted him as they came in, pulling about his hangings and the furniture and accusing him of having come by them dishonestly, and it was his part to bow in sorrowful acquiescence. This was incongruous, considering that the law recognised his function to the extent of providing that if he died when he was on his expedition, his body was burned and he was supposed to have joined the sun in heaven, just as if he were a warrior killed in battle. Jacques Soustelle suggests that "the class represented the principle of personal capital as opposed to that of income attached to office, of wealth as opposed to renown, of luxury as opposed to austerity." This would give the Aztec community the same excuse for humbugging censoriousness that Europeans derived from the idea that all investment was culpable usury. In both cases it was hard on the man that balanced the books.

The tolteca existed like our own luxury trade: in defiance of the aching fact that a large part of society had not the bare necessities of life. Yet the existence of that trade was not deplored by the Aztecs and is not deplored by our society, because man cannot live by bread alone. The way that the Indians rejoiced in the ornamenting of the churches after the conquest, in splashing on the gold leaf, shows how much they had enjoyed the show put on by their own society before it was conquered. They obeyed that moral imperative so beautifully put by the Swiss poet Gottfried Keller: "Lass die Augen fassen was die Wimpern halten von dem goldnen Ueberfluss der Welt." "Let the eyes hold what the eyelids can contain from the golden overflow of the world." The gold jewellery in the museums at Mexico City and Oaxaca is more arresting, more lyrical, more stimulating than Greek goldwork; and their use of precious stones must have been fabulous. Cortés is said to have wrecked his career at court because the empress was angry at not having received the five emeralds he had kept for his second wife; they had the forms of a rose, a bell, a fish, a trumpet, a cup. This might have been frightful, like the objects the inflamed imagination of the Fabergé family produced in Saint Petersburg, but we have expert testimony to suggest that the Aztec craftsmen satisfied the highest standards. Dürer's work gives the impression that he lived in an attic on cabbage soup, sustained only by the beauties of his faith, but he actually was a Little Brother of the Rich, rosily fortunate, warmed by the sun of two emperors' patronage, and the integrity of his eye is a miracle of the will. In Nuremberg and at Venice and in the Low Countries he had opportunities for seeing as magnificent jewellery as the Renaissance ever created, but in a letter, quoted by Soustelle, he wrote of the presents from Montezuma which Cortés had handed on to Charles V, and explodes in the great praise the great can give to greatness: "In all my life I have never seen anything that rejoiced my heart so much," he wrote, "I have been astonished by the subtle spirit of the men in these strange countries."

Nevertheless, if accounts are what matter, Mexico could not afford this luxury trade, not with the peasants, the maceualli, those who acquire merit by toil, in the state they were. On them rested the whole burden of physical labour. True they were not without their rights: they had their plots of land, which they lost only if they failed to cultivate them; their children went to local schools provided by the state and administered by the civil service and the priesthood; they had (if they were born within the tripartite alliance of Mexico and Texcoco and Tlacopan) their share in the distribution of food and goods and clothing from the imperial store. They could pick their local officials, and their recommendations were rarely rejected by the emperor. If they acquitted themselves well during their military service or showed outstanding ability in civil life, they could arise to the ruling class. But they were taxed. They had to yield a considerable proportion of their crops to the state granaries. This must have been a great hardship in Mexico, where the climate varies unpredictably, where much cultivable land lies in high flat terraces subject to frost. But worse than this, they were subject to innumerable corvées: taxes paid in the form of personal labour. They had to build and maintain the roads, bridges, waterways, and temples, cut and carry timber for imperial and public use, and build the fortifications necessitated by the constant state of warfare throughout the isthmus. These might be movable wooden barricades or walls or cemented stone, which might be three yards high and seven yards wide and run for miles across valley mouths. This work would have to be done at the emperor's pace, to meet military demands, with no regard for the peasants' individual needs.

The maceualli were not so badly off as the landless peasants, the *tlalmaitl,* the lowest class of freemen, the "hand of the earth." These were tenant farmers, who worked on the land of others, paid no taxes and could not be called on for labour, but had no rights and never shared in the imperial distributions of food and clothing. This class should not have existed, in view of the Aztec principle that every member of the tribe had a right to his own arable plot, and it must have edged its way into the community as refugees from some unrecorded historical crisis. We learned in our time what happens to refugees. The maceualli were far better off than they were, but were still in a wretched state. Proof of their wretchedness lies in the remaining class of Aztec society, the slaves.

Soustelle is in love with the Aztecs and puts a good face on slavery, imagining the owners as treating their human property tenderly, and so perhaps they did. The slaves did all the domestic work and all jobs in the cities and on the farms which demanded hard physical labour or was tedious, and the women had as usual to throw in concubinage with the rest of their services; and they were paid simply by their place in their owners' households, which, considering how high the standard of living seems to have been, was probably generous payment. But they had no share in the imperial distributions. They did not exist, except in their relationship with their owner, and in that relationship the slave had no liberty. He could do nothing except what his owner commanded, and he was considered as utterly without public value, nobody respected him. People were not cruel, they simply turned on him faces which were quite blank and assented to the infliction of the most terrible punishment on him if he showed signs of vice. If his master thought him lazy and vicious, he could accuse him of his faults before witnesses, and after he did this three times he put a heavy wooden harness round him and led him to the market; and the slave who had been sold by three masters could be bought by a pious Aztec to be sacrificed to the gods. This might happen to a drunkard or a thief or a mischief-maker, but it might happen to a man or woman who was getting old or was ill or was the object of sexual jealousy or was independent of spirit.

What is horrifying is the identity of these slaves. Some were prisoners of war, some simply enemies captured in battles, others more unpleasantly procured. Certain of the tribes subjected by the empire were obliged to furnish a number of slaves as part of the annual tribute, and they found them not from their own population but by raids on their neighbours. Others were Aztecs who were sentenced to slavery under peculiar laws, which must surely have produced embarrassment. A detected burglar became the slave of the owner of whatever building he was caught burgling; surely no private person or palace would want a butler, no temple an acolyte, recruited on that basis. There was also a most curious law that if a man took another man's slave as his mistress and she should die in childbirth, he was obliged to become the slave of her owner. One looks through history at a face distorted by grief and sexual jealousy and hunger to get a law on the statute book which would punish the worst one, the lecher, the murderer, the defiler. But most of the slaves had simply chosen to be slaves.

They had to be deliberate about it. Four aged and respectable witnesses had to be assembled, and in their presence the man who was tired of freedom sold himself to a buyer in return for twenty pieces of cloth, and then went out and kept himself by bartering them. Usually they lasted them about a year. Then he went back and surrendered himself and his liberty to his master. It is not necessary to feel too tragic about this. The Spaniards, even the Spanish friars, who were not for slavery, felt that the Aztec slaves were well treated, and noted that they had often been freed by their masters on their deathbeds, and often lived out contented lives in households grateful for their good service. But that does not take away the horror of this suicide of status, in a community where status was everything; where the individual was of so little account that portraits are few and legends speak only of gods and emperors, where a man was simply the envelope of a social function. Yet one does not need to ask for reasons why Aztecs chose to become slaves. Some of them are obvious enough and can be imagined as showing their potency, were they given a chance, in our own society. There were all the people who had followed in youth occupations which had to be abandoned in maturity: players in the ballgame, which was the great sport of Mesoamerica as well as a religious ceremony, dancers, jugglers, and prostitutes. There were also the women without men, the spinsters, the widows, the female orphans. Well, if one stood outside a hotel in the grimmer parts of London or New York and shouted through a megaphone that people who came down and signed a short form promising to obey orders would get free food and clothing and lodging and a place in a household for the rest of their lives, most of the clients would pour out on the pavement, just to see.

There was, however, a more general consideration compelling people into slavery. If a slave had no rights, he had no responsibilities. He had certain exemptions. One was perhaps of no great use to him: military service was not demanded of him, but the Aztecs enjoyed fighting. Cortés and his captains' accounts of the battles with Indians give an impression of a frenetic ballet with thousands of performers in magnificent costumes, advancing under swaying banners to the sound of super-jazz played at screaming pitch on drums and trumpets, in an ecstasy of contempt for death possibly enhanced by the use of hallucinatory drugs. Some Aztecs may not have shared this love of warfare and may even have been politically revolted by the aggressive policy of their country. The character of Montezuma, as Cortés and Bernal Díaz describe it, suggests that a fierce tradition had not been able to breed out all gentleness, and that in this rigid society the mind had made some free play for itself. And some individuals, even in the areas where caste requirements would seem to be most restrictive, attained independent philosophic attitudes. If the centuries had suddenly fused, Montezuma might have got along very well with Adlai Stevenson. But such independence was rare, and the exemption from military service cannot have attracted one man to slavery as against the hundreds, the thousands, the tens of thousands, who were drawn to it by the exemption it offered from all demands of taxes and personal service.

It is important to recognise that this was an equitable society. All classes must have been taxed heavily, if only because the Aztec Empire was a welfare state. It recognised and honestly discharged its obligations to support its citizens in sickness and when nature turned against them; and in this country nature is a manic-depressive. Even in these days of improved agriculture it is recorded that in one year half a million tons of maize are destroyed by drought, and the next half as much goes in floods. The priests and the civil servants and the traders and the craftsmen were heavily taxed but at least they had the chance of offsetting their heavy taxes by exceptional rewards in goods and repute should they show exceptional merit, which everybody believes they will be able to do some time. But the peasant had less hope of this than any other class. His life was narrow and bitter beyond the experience of the European or the United States small farmer, because he had nothing, absolutely nothing, to rely on except what his strength and skill could make out of the soil and the weather. But there is another force which works for farmers elsewhere and did not work for the Aztec peasant: a beautiful force, which I never recognised for what it is until I went to Mexico and realised what its absence had meant to its ancient civilisation.

That lack accounts for some drops of the black draught in the gold cup which is the museum, for the despairing decision that slapstick caricature is the apt comment on humanity, that champing hate is the dominant characteristic of divinity. For life is tolerable only if sometimes, just now and then, it need not be often, one has the chance of receiving some benefit which one has not earned and perhaps does not even deserve. The football pools and the numbers game and the state lotteries spread hope which perhaps has a philosophic background. Such a windfall can be taken as evidence that God or fate really loves one with one's faults and all or as evidence that the indifference of God and fate does not amount to hatred. In most parts of the world a peasant gets that assurance every now and then once he owns domestic animals. Their reproductive organs work for him, and better at some times than at others. A bull can throw a number of heifer calves, a goat or cow can be a heavy milker, a ewe can have twin lambs, a sow can have litters over the dozen mark that all survive, one strain of hen can be a prodigious layer: a sheer bonanza not to be ascribed to human effort, except when animal husbandry has reached a high level. But the Aztec peasant had no domestic animals. There were turkeys and dogs, both of which they ate, but not often. They were in short supply and went to the rich. There was not a herd of cattle nor a sheep nor a goat nor any sort of hog that could be seduced into the service of man, nor a cock or a hen.

This means quite a serious shortage of protein and fats in the Aztec diet, and it also meant that the peasant had no luck. Of course a good season could produce a variation in his crops, but nothing like as much of an increment as the birth of, say, ten or twelve heifer calves in a row. The poor wretch fared strictly according to his own skill and conscientiousness, as exercised in an exhausting and monotonous routine, so intricate and so exquisitely adapted to the business in hand that strangers from Europe and the United States who see it in practice today invariably denounce it as the inefficient product of ignorance. It has always been the Mesoamerican habit to choose a patch of forest land, cut down the timber with axes—which in Aztec times were made of stone, since they had no iron—and fire it and the scrub, then make holes in the burned earth with a dibble stick and drop seeds into them and, after two years of such burning and planting, abandon it for from four to twenty years according to local conditions, then start the whole thing over again in another part of the forest. This sounds sufficiently onerous, but examination of the technique as it survives today shows that it was also a horribly fiddling business. The Aztec peasant had to go round looking for the rich patch, the *milpa*, as carefully as women used to try on hats. The researches on this subject by Professor Hutchinson and Ursula Cowgill of Yale are intimidating. The right patch had to be high in vegetation, as that showed it had lain fallow long enough, the soil had to be as near black as could be, not too heavily loaded with clay or sand and free from rocks; it could not be too high, in case it was windswept when it was cleared, nor too low, in case it got waterlogged, though it had to be near a water supply and should have been not too far from a village.

What seems the most obvious handicap on the ancient Indian, that the cutting had to be done with a stone axe, was not so grave. In the last half of the nineteenth century there was a French woman novelist who wrote mildly erotic novels under the name Gennevraye, while her husband, the Vicomte Lepic, went about looking into the efficiency of primitive tools and cut down a number of small trees with a flint hatchet without much difficulty and at a fair speed. (Freud could have had some good sport with this family. Obviously the vicomte was asking himself, "How does she get away with it—with that primitive tool of a mind?") The Indians were particularly able technologists in the creation of cutting edges, as they taught Cortés and his men by their attacks with flint and obsidian swords, which inflicted terrible wounds on the men and managed to decapitate a horse. Far worse was the necessity for constant attention to detail. In clearing, one could not simply swing that axe: certain tree trunks had to be left at a certain level, to facilitate the regeneration of the forest when the patch was abandoned.

Weeding had to be done at certain seasons. Several kinds of seeds had to be put in the same hole, squash and beans as well as maize. Moreover, the Indian peasant had to plan two emergency crops in case the main crop failed, which had to be sown at different times of the year, in high ground when it was designed to mature in the wet season, and on low swampy land when it was designed to mature in the dry season.

The visitors from Europe and the United States who exclaim at the survivals of this technique and declare that science must have discovered a better way of growing maize are moved by religion and not scientific passion. They babble because they cannot bear to think that fate, which they secretly concede is God, a God who loves, can send people into the world with no other opportunity of getting a living except by this routine. (Here we see the double role of science in the modern world: to be the other culture and to be its own antithesis, disguised fundamentalist religion, which imagines technological discoveries which take the pain out of living as their predecessors imagined miracles.) Yet Professor Hutchinson and Ursula Cowgill write of the survivors who still practice this technique: "The present system is by far the most efficient use of the land possible with the means available, and there is no evidence that the modern indigenous population is making any misuse of it." True, this routine did not take more than perhaps a quarter of the year, but it had to be carried out according to schedule, and things had to be done when they had to be done, though there were many competing duties. The only fuel was wood, and the supply of that for even a small household means much picking up and hacking and carting; and there was the endless hungry hunt for protein and fats, for the birds in the reeds by the swamps and in the forests, and for the fish that had to be netted or poked up with a wood and stone trident. There had also to be fitted in the trips to the market for barter, on foot, always on foot, there were no mules, no horses.

But there were also the taxes. Bad to pay them in kind, worse to pay them in labour. Bad for a peasant to stand beside a heap of corn cobs and squashes and beans and explain to an official that this was really the share of his crop which he had been ordered to contribute to the state, that if the heap was small it was because of the frosts or the rainfall or a drought, and bad for an official who wanted promotion or to keep his position or even to serve his fellow men because he would have to sift the true excuses from the false. He would have to accumulate stores of these not only to release them in times of flood and famine, but every year, in the bald patch between the harvests, in June and July. It is charming that this distribution was made in the name of Old Old Prairie Wolf, the god of gaiety in love, of extravagant expenditure, of jewellery and unexpected pleasure, which must have taken some of the chill out of charity. But the official had to do worse than bully the peasant into handing over any comfortable surplus, he had constantly to assail the basis of the man's life by ordering him to leave home and go off to repair a fortification or a bridge or a water-conduit or a strategic road and that, if the emergency was imperative, at the season of the year when he should have been planting or clearing his own plot. This civilisation, which was so excessively sane that it was almost mad, would always know when the interest of the many outweighed the interest of the few. And the peasant had no consolations as he went on his way to serve the many, he could not say to himself, "Never mind that I have to leave now, the sow will be farrowing next week, my wife and children can eat some of the litter and barter the rest." The misery of the maceualli afflicts us, for he was one of our great benefactors: the plants cultivated by Indian skill in the Americas were unknown in Europe till the white invasions, and they were to double the food supply of the white races. But he was not rewarded, for this is not a moral universe; and further proof of that appears if we reflect that no political idea and no idealistic movement, no Gandhi or Saint Francis, could have bettered the lot of this man as much as the genital organs of a bull and a cow, a billy goat and a nanny, a boar and a sow, a ram and a ewe, working away quite selfishly for their own pleasure in the shadow of his reed hut. It was for lack of this animal sensuality, not because of any weakness of his own spirit, not because of any wickedness in the spirit of his social superiors, that he gave up his freedom and became a slave. This overpressured society had to have a safety valve. It had to allow a certain number of its citizens to opt out.

Anthropological Museum II

The halls of this museum on Grasshopper Hill are lit with craft, so that the light within them is a pervasive bloom on space, but the works of art which are exhibited have their own sort of darkness about them, because of the gravity of their forms. However rigid a class structure may be, the woe of one class seeps through the whole. Several cultures had produced these objects, and all had appeared in different parts of the isthmus at different times, and all had disappeared, for causes unknown save in the case of the last, the Aztec Empire, which met an atypical fate, since it alone fell to external attack. The others had been struck down from within by catastrophes which, whatever they were, must have savaged all classes alike. But this is a cruel land for those who do the work, and so these works of art stand in their private night. But moving among them in an ecstasy of respect were the living Mexicans, their complexions warmed, their hands and feet refined by their heritage of Indian blood, but the whole of them converted from pessimism to optimism by the European strain in them, so courageous, or so incapable of learning. They are as if they were in a church; one can pick out the tourists because they are behaving as if they were in a museum.

By aesthetic standards, the Mexicans should spend the longest time in the classical Mayan rooms, for the works there are the most beautiful of Indian achievements, but local patriotism triumphs, the crowd is always greatest in the Aztec section, particularly round the large model of Tenochtitlán as it was at the time of the conquest. No wonder, for the story is a marvel. The Aztec tribe settled down on the banks of Lake Texcoco about 1325 and found that all the dry land was already bespoken, so set about making their own by piling mud from the lake bottom on the top of wickerwork rafts. By the time Cortés found them, less than two hundred years later, they had built up in the lake a city of a million inhabitants, which was the capital of a highly organised society, which had turned itself into a welfare state, so far as its members were concerned, but was the centre of an empire exploited by the most brilliant military and diplomatic techniques. Their technological development was impeded by mineral deficiencies and the lack of a handy written language, and their agricultural talents could not be extended in the absence of livestock, but their governmental accomplishment was staggering. They had not achieved anything like the democracy which we find ourselves compelled to prefer, unless we are to change our cultural skins, but they had constructed something like an efficient Fascist dictatorship, tempered by an element which no modern people has ever combined with Fascism: a scrupulous observance of the rule of law.

They conjured into being this elaborate structure during a couple of centuries, and the magnitude of their achievement can be grasped if one looks at what England was doing during this period, which lies roughly between the coronations of Edward III and Henry VIII. The English did very little except thresh out problems of power by crude civil war and answer such formulations by crude suppression. True, William Caxton learned how to print in Cologne and Bruges and in 1476 set up his press in Westminster and was daring enough to print in plain English instead of Latin. But against that we must look back at the Aztecs, who had no literature other than hit-and-run history, half inventory and half legend (how could they branch out into anything else when "To be or not to be" would in their language have been the sign for two, the pictures of a bee and an oar and a knotted rope, followed by the sign for two again and the picture of a bee) and note that they were getting on with their state-building exactly as they would have done had they read Plato and Aristotle and Machiavelli and Hobbes. They were indeed a people of genius and could even be counted as virtuous too, for though the state was oppressive and greedy, they were at least diligent in their paternalism. The poor were fed when the hungry season came, as a result of this obstinate absorption of taxes.

Taxes . . . "Taxes," I found myself saying to the museum. "The very word is like a bell to toll me back from thee to my sole self." A letter from the Inland Revenue had reached me that morning in its base brownish envelope. It asked me a question which it said it had asked me twice before. It wanted to know how it was that a Mrs. Clarkinson, a temporary secretary I had employed some years before and could not at the moment remember, had received from me a cheque for a hundred pounds, which appeared in neither her returns or mine as part of her salary. The letter was a piece of grit in my eye. Once it had come back to me, I could not see the museum, nor the lovely, qualified, faintly acid ripeness of the Mexicanised autumn day. It was not fair that an enquiry about Mrs. Clarkinson should come between me and my experience of this delicious world, which was so foreign that it gave me the delight one might suppose would be given by a new colour, as beautiful as any known colour but quite, quite different. Up to the moment when the knell had sounded, I had been very well off in the courtyard of the Anthropological Museum, which enclosed within its shimmering walls of grey and rose and violet stone a November day as they come in Mexico City, the autumn mellowness thinned by the altitude, its sunshine like a sweet white wine but a very light one. In the long square lay a second sky, white clouds and blue firmament studded with yellowing lilypads and reeds. All round me were doors opening on a new heaven and a new hell and a new earth. I turned my back on them and went out past the long pool in the courtyard, under the wall inscribed with a verse from the poem of an Aztec king:

Flowers wither, but must my heart wither too?
Shall my name be someday just a sound?
Shall there be a world which does not marvel at my name?
Well, then, let's gather flowers.
Let's listen to the singing.
I do not know how my heart can go on beating,
Knowing that all's in vain.

Chapultepec II

And down one goes the wide marble steps into the park of Grasshopper Hill, and there are the dead Indian forces alive again and in control. They animate most of the fountains. Some are as we know them in Europe and the United States, light-minded and involved with marble girls, and others light-minded in an abstract way, whirling jets about so that they change like song or laughter, and more so here than elsewhere. I once heard Walt Disney explaining his cartoon technique to the last issue of a noble house that had fallen into genetic decline. "But of course," said the last issue, "there's a man inside." In many of the fountains, particularly a large one near the restaurant, there might be a man inside, having his fun. But there are other ones, unusually solemn. Up a hill rise a line of small square cisterns, each with several jets rising, but not very far, and bowing to one another, like half-grown acolytes, and on the crown of the hill is a low, solid mass of brick, built over-solidly like the Aztec temples, and like them inscribed with cumbrous patterns in the sombre Aztec colours, brown and sunless yellow, while jets, tall like full-grown priests, bow towards the building and break against the roof and drop down again over the front of its walls, with hieratic lack of haste. Versailles knew nothing about these impressive, slightly dull, hypnotic fountains or about those others, which elsewhere in the park fall with this same ritual slowness at regular intervals from a weighty wall, each from the huge menacing mouth of an Aztec god, an ugly god, who might be salivating in a greedy dream of the next human sacrifice. Nor could (or would) Le Notre have contrived the curious diversion that lies outside the pavilion on Grasshopper Hill where the river Lerma wells up from the ground through a tunnel and passes into the city conduits. In a wide basin, half in and half out of a shallow pool, lies the water god Tlaloc, made in high relief out of the finest mosaic, but hideous to look upon, his ill-formed head and body further deformed by ill will. His hands make a moral claim for him, for one holds a corncob, the staple food of Mexico, and the other is calloused by the toil he has done for the Mexican people. But the head is brutish, the great teeth ravenous, it can well be believed that, since the Aztecs worshipped this god, they felt it necessary to placate him with gifts of drowned children. There is another god among the flowering trees outside the museum, who is stone-shaped and permeated and made denser by threat.

These sombre fountains, these enraged gods, are not authentic relics of the civilisation which Cortés destroyed. Aztec remains were not valued, unless they were of gold and precious stones, until fairly recently. Statues of Montezuma, He-who-gets-angry-like-a-Lord, and his father, carved in relief on the cliff below the castle, were defaced as barbarous rubbish in the eighteenth century. This tragic architecture and these sinister beings we look on now are copied from ancient models by skilful artificers: the mosaic Tlaloc in the pool is the work of Diego Rivera. They have been deliberately set here by a highly sophisticated government, in order to confirm its people in a choice it knows they have already made; in its adherence to the Aztec culture, on a certain important plane of being.

This choice seems the odder when it is thrust upon one here, in Grasshopper Hill, particularly at the weekend or on holidays, when it is thronged with families walking together in amity delicious and quite unfamiliar to foreign eyes. In Mexico the bottom has not yet fallen out of parenthood. Here it is rare to see a child staring in hatred at its mother and father, seeking with Spock-fed vitality for a grievance, which, if it goes on taking its orange juice, it will be able to convert into a cause of life-long war; nor does one see parents pale with that look of guilt-ridden panic which is the meal ticket of modern psychiatry. These Mexican families may be capable of behaving like fiends, but not to each other. Their relationship they act out very prettily in conjunction with the balloon-sellers, who form a large part of the population of Mexico City: a proof of poverty, for it must take little to set up in the trade. Down every vista can be seen one of these gay paupers, gliding-cum-waddling-cum-jerking to keep erect over his head his stock of multicoloured bubbles, which doubles his height. A big Mexican, a Papa Mexican or a Mamma Mexican, or both, with any number of little Mexicans round them, often more than seems possible, for nine months is nine months, approaching the bobbing and hesitant giant, and the little brown arms shoot up and point to lemon and cinnabar and scarlet and periwinkle spheres, a brown hand passes money to another, the weightless pyramid above the balloon-seller's head rocks as he bows his thanks, and the family is off, light on their feet and seeming lighter still, because of the bright chosen spheres straining up above them towards the upper air, as it might be blown on by a breeze of good nature.

There is good nature too in the amusement park, where it might not be, for of course the amusement park is too small. The Mexican uterus makes nonsense of all public enterprises before they get off the drawing board. But there is no peevishness, no parents saying that they can stand it no longer and it is time to go home, no children dragging angrily at their parents' hands and screwing up their knuckles in their eyes. The families stand there waiting their turn, fathers and mothers smiling at their children as if they were deliciously ripe fruit that could be perpetually eaten while miraculously remaining still intact and appetising, the children warming under their parents' smiles like fruit under sunshine. Yet these people choose to have gods about them whose faces could not shine with love like their own, whose faces, indeed, are mere champing machines for mincing human sacrifices.

This choice is to some degree a game: one assumes a harsh culture for the very reason that life is so delicious that one can afford to pretend for a moment that it is not, just as one puts on an ugly mask at Carnival time. There is no question of actual belief in the Aztec gods: they are used simply as imaginative furniture. But that is odd enough. This society, if not Roman Catholic in a way that can please Rome, is dyed indelibly with Catholicism. It can be taken that many of the happy Mexicans who promenade among the heathen Aztec gods on Grasshopper Hill are believing Catholics, and among these nearly all the women and some men are practising Catholics, and there are anti-clericals on the scene, though these are not invariably, as they are in some European countries, atheists. A Mexican anti-clerical may spit on the pavement when he sees a priest (nuns he cannot see, for they are forbidden by law) or he may be a regular communicant, who nevertheless resists every encroachment on secular power by the Church. Mexicans will explain to you at immense length that their religious condition is immensely complicated and special to themselves, but in fact the faith seems to be as it is all over the world today: worn down to the warp in places, the colours nearly gone, the floor showing through at places, but elsewhere the fabric is as good as new, and that where one would least expect it. The case against religion is the responsibility of God for the sufferings of mankind, which makes it impossible to believe the good things said about Him in the Bible, and consequently to believe anything it says about Him. This consideration rather more than any other has emptied the churches in our world; that and the fact that the human attention has received the liturgy to saturation point, and there seems to many no point in hearing it over and over again.

Yet history has recently discredited this argument. Our age has produced huge quantities of intense suffering. A great part of the sufferers can be found in the colonies of exiles which have been planted all over the world. Their case is extreme. Many people can, of course, tear up the roots and go to live in a strange country without a pang, but the very fact that a man has been exiled shows that when the blow fell he was happy where he was and hoped to continue to be there. Now he is in a place he never chose as his home: he will almost certainly have lost some of his family and his friends, and perhaps all of them; he may have made a fortune in his new country, but he has nevertheless not got the tables and chairs and beds his grandfather left him; he cannot open the shutters of his bedroom in the morning and look out on the field where the old white horse used to graze. He perhaps endures the most frustrating experience of all. As he gets into his seventies and eighties he may long to go back to his own country, on any terms, making any submissions that are demanded, only that he may die in a particular house, which, however, may now no longer exist. It has been bombed or burned. His case against God is very strong. Nevertheless, it is exiles who borrow churches left derelict by the comfortable population of the country of their exile, fill them to the doors, and find no difficulty in worshipping God, whom they do not only fail to blame for their misfortune, but regard as if he were the most unfortunate exile of them all, whom they must do all they can to comfort, even to listening to words they have heard a thousand times before, if that is what He wants. Just this attitude to Christianity is found in Mexico among the Indians, and this may seem odd, since they are the only people in Mexico who have a clear claim to be indigenous. But they are exiles. They are exiles from the Aztec Empire which Cortés destroyed. So they stick the life-sized effigies of the suffering Christ into crimson cotton velvet gowns, as if he were their defeated kind, whom they had found naked and paralysed by the roadside and have to clothe. If one goes over to the side of the Indians, one has to take over their Aztec gods, that is fair enough. But also one has to take over the Christianity in which they and their gods took shelter when the disaster came. This is the Mexican paradox.

A diagram of the situation is drawn in bright colours at the Basilica of Our Lady of Guadalupe, the great national shrine, which is the centre of Indian devotion. It lies about three miles north of Mexico City. There is a vast paved square, vast enough to be a football field, and looking the vaster because the stone catches the light, which is enclosed by fine pillars and arches and wrought iron. Beyond lie two great couchant baroque buildings, one the basilica, the other the office of the Congregation for the Propagation of Faith, tilting away from one another drunkenly, far too heavy for the uncertain soil of the district; and behind them rises a small pointed rocky hill, not so much higher than their domes, which is laced with stone staircases leading up to a chapel. Here is the magnet which attracts for ten days each December a huge pilgrimage of Indians who come from all over Mexico to worship, camp on the streets, get drunk, perform solemn ritual dances, and make that affirmation which is made by any pilgrimage, whether at Rome or Jerusalem or Moscow, or by a swarm of bees: we are going to do something new, go to a new place, enter a new year, be new persons, and we do it best packed close together, we find that that way we best generate our species' peculiar kind of force.

When we went to Guadalupe it was a Sunday like any other in November, but there was some sense of swarming. Through various gates people came in by twos and threes and briskly crossed the square, forming straight lines converging at the basilica door, like trails of insects bringing some contribution (presumably their souls) back to the nest, while other people came out of the door at an easier pace, their contribution made, and milled backwards and forwards across the square, cutting leisurely curves across the hurrying straight lines of the newcomers, so that the scene has a complicated rhythm. The people give an impression of being richly and archaically dressed, but it is hard to know why. Most of the women are wearing woollen sweaters and cloth skirts, and most of the men T-shirts and drill trousers, as they might in Brooklyn or Hammersmith, though here there are more glowing red sweaters and skirts and pullovers of a more swinging blue than would be seen further north; and though the Indian dress is so distinctive that at once one registers, "Here is an Indian woman wearing a traditional costume," the dress is so prim that it is hard to describe or remember. I followed an elderly woman who was as impressive as a Paolo Veronese court lady and photographed her, because I knew I was not seeing her properly. I find that she was wearing a dark headscarf, a small neat chestnut-coloured shawl, a black dress, and a black apron edged with white braid, with pockets picked out with a slightly wider braid of the same sort: simply that.

Animal vigour is what one sees on every side in Mexico and, as often, restraint. One might be looking on a flowering tree laden with leaf and blossom that is pruning itself. This effect is specifically Indian, and the pruning knife has not been wielded by the European invaders. The Indian is refined by nature, with his small bones and his quick, tactfully surreptitious movements. In the godly twilight within the basilica there stood a circle of little Indian girls, looking down at an inscription on the marble floor, their fine black hair hanging straight and clean down the shoulders of their fiercely laundered white dresses, their coffee-coloured, gazelle-neat legs wide apart, their narrow, plucking hands spread out to keep them balanced, bending so low to see the nearly vanished words that they would be sticking out their little behinds if they had any, but as yet they have only the smallest hint of such things. All these girls were beautiful, but not one of them was the obvious pretty girl. So subtle is the beauty of the race that it appears in its most novel and arresting form among the very old. All their superficial attraction has been pared away. Though they always keep their dignity, their aspect is often pitiful. They seem to be pronouncing feebly but with authority, "If this be the end of life, it is not worth it. We have not had enough. Not enough of anything." These ancients have an air of supernatural mystery, too, for it is the case with Indians that with age the skin fades like the hair, and the brown faces are overlaid with spectral whiteness, as if they were withdrawing gradually, not with the sudden shock and bump that is our crude custom, into another world. An old Indian murmuring prayers in a church is half-inside and half-outside an open door.

One would think that here life was rarefied to the cool thinness of mountain air, were it not that when one steps out of the basilica a blaring band marches through the main gate of the forecourt, ahead of a float banked up with mustard and puce immortals, on which a pile of orange and cream gladioli support a banner of a peculiar, tearing, rasping royal blue, on which Our Lady of Guadalupe is painted in the ferociously sweet colours used for lollies. To sneer at people with bad taste when they offer what they think beautiful to their gods is worse taste, but anyway we can take it that Mexican civilisation is not in danger of perishing through its refinement, and further security is given by the single dots which advance across the square bobbety-bobbety, and at a snail's pace, sometimes stopping altogether for moments. They are penitents who are kneeing their way over to the basilica, each carrying a candle, and some of the women a baby as well. It seems a gross idea of pleasing God, but a sideways look at these penitents' faces suggests not brutish superstition but rather oversensitivity. People know their own business best; and there is a certain propriety in the performance of extraordinary acts in this place which came into being for extraordinary reasons.

Juan de Zummáraga

The basilica was founded in December 1531, ten years after the conquest of the Aztecs by Cortés. An Indian named Juan Diego, a Christian convert, was walking by the village of Tepeyac, meaning Hilltop, which was hereabouts, probably on the rocky little hill where the chapel stands today, when the Mother of God appeared before him, radiant, and what was better still, distinctly brown. She told him to go to the Bishop of Mexico, Juan de Zummáraga, the same bishop who opened the school for the higher education of the Aztec nobles' sons, and tell him that she desired a shrine built to her on that spot. The bishop received the message sceptically, but the dark Madonna appeared to Juan Diego a second time and repeated her injunction, and when the bishop remained obdurate she made a third appearance and this time conjured into being, among the boulders where only scrub and cactus grew, a rose garden in full flower. She bade him gather the roses and wrap them up in his cloak and take them back to the bishop as a sign and a wonder. But when Diego laid his cloak at Zummáraga's feet he opened it on something better than roses. The inner side of the cloak bore a painting of the Mother of God, glorious and most certainly brown, in fact she might have been an Indian princess. The shrine was built, and later the basilica, and the painted Virgin has worked many miracles.

This is a beautiful story, far more beautiful than appears at first sight. Divine personages are doing no more than their duty when they become visible before the eyes of human beings and give them reassurance, which the poor things would not need were it not for the harsh peculiarities of the divine plan. But the full story of Our Lady of Guadalupe in Mexico gives a revelation more to the point. It was not for nothing that Zummáraga was a Basque; one of a small people who have survived intact in a corner of northeast Spain from the beginning of recorded time. They spoke—and speak—a unique language, not to be related to any other except by the slenderest ties, and they also form a blood group unique in Western Europe (Rh-negative 30.5 percent, which is about double that of any other tested Europeans). Their sailors were among the earliest whalers and fished for cod off Newfoundland before the Portuguese. Their peasants were reputed the finest shepherds in Europe, and as every farmer knows, a good shepherd has to be a man of better than ordinary brains and character, who can be trusted to use special skills in bad weather and for long hours far from his employer's eye. The Anaconda Corporation in Montana, which bought sheep with a sort of gourmandise over many years, used to import Basque shepherds. The Basques were also obstinate and able fighters though better at defence than attack. They did not want to go out and purchase glory, they wanted to be left alone to mind their own business, and so they were. The Arabs tiptoed past the Basque provinces when they swept through Spain and invaded France, and tiptoed back. When Christian Spain was reconstructed, the Basques became a self-governing republic within the monarchy, and this was not due to the tolerance of the larger unit. The Basques looked after themselves. They passed a law, for example, enacting that if an officer of the Spanish Crown presented a Basque with a note of demand not countersigned by a Basque local parliament, the Basque was entitled to resist him, and it would be no murder should he kill him.

Behind these safeguards the Basques built up a state which was liberal in all respects but one. They practised the grossest discrimination against lawyers. They used the creatures and regarded them as fulfilling a useful function, but felt, as society does about the prostitute, that the fulfilment was also a degradation. They would not allow lawyers to stand for election to the local parliaments, though the parliaments kept a roster of them for consultation, a sort of political red-light district. They were pious Catholics but were not attracted by the conception of the universal Church. Only the local priesthood was respected. When King Ferdinand came to take his oath at Biscay, he brought with him a Spanish bishop and was told to send him away; and no priest not Basque was allowed to enter a town where a local parliament was sitting. But even a Basque priest had to mind his manners. Some parliaments in the provinces had a rule that if a deputy were seen speaking to a priest before a session he lost his vote for the day.

Zummáraga was the son of a Basque peasant. He had been admitted to the Franciscan order and had made a name for himself as a scholar and a preacher and an ascetic. It was his inclination not to accept the Bishopric of New Spain when the emperor Charles V conferred it on him, for he was fifty-nine and cared only for letters and had no desire to become a man of action, as colonial clerics had to be. But he had to embark at once on the journey without waiting to be consecrated. He found himself put on a ship with the members of a body called the Audiencia, which had just been appointed to put Mexico in order by the small body named the Council of the Indies who acted for Charles in these matters. Zummáraga cannot have felt at ease. The Audiencia consisted of four members and a president. The president was Nuño de Guzmán, one of the great destroyers of history, comparable to Tamerlane and Hitler. He had been a provincial governor in the West Indies and there had demanded thousands of Indians as tribute, which meant that they were forced down below starvation level. He worked them till they dropped and died as carriers and sent them by shiploads to the mines. He burned villages and tied inoffensive chieftains to the tails of horses so that they were dragged along the rocks. He burned them alive. He was also a blasphemer; he would plead that he had tied the chieftain to the horse-tail because he had lapsed into paganism. There was raised by the burned village a cross, he was always ready with a text. And yet he could not plead the custom of the time as excuse. Cortés was much more merciful, feeding his appetites off the land but reasonably, ordering (and keeping the regulations himself) that the Indians were not to work for the Spanish more than three weeks in seven and were not to be taken far from their homes or employed in the mines, unless they had belonged to the slave class in their own civilisation; and women and children were exempted from all fatiguing service. He even ordained that Indian villages were not to be visited by Europeans without a government permit. Nuño de Guzmán was creative in his field, idiosyncratic in his cruelty, and instinct with a demonic energy. Besides this villain there were four lawyers, whom Zummáraga with his Basque prejudice against lawyers cannot have found ideal companions. True, two died on the voyage, which took thirteen weeks, but Basques knew that there were plenty more where those came from.

It would have been as well for Zummáraga if he had landed in Mexico with some official title as well as his ecclesiastical rank, but in the eyes of the temporal power he was only "Protector of the Indians," and though this was obviously an admirable thing to be, it unfortunately happened that, though the office had existed for ten years, its nature had by an administrative error never been defined. That is what fascinates in the study of Mexican beginnings; one can see in Spain the modern state getting cluttered up with functions. Washington and Whitehall were stirring in the womb of time, rich in inevitable error. Once Zummáraga landed in Mexico, he found his reluctance to accept the post had been the voice of reason. The oppression of the Indians was scandalous, although there were colonists who had no desire to oppress them. It was too sweet a racket for there not to be racketeers; and the president and the two surviving members of the Audiencia had hardly landed before they joined in the racket. The president turned out the chief of a delightful town and lived in his villa and diverted to the garden the water which the Indian villagers had used for the irrigation of their lands. They seized Indian girls from convent schools, they laid a tribute on the Indians working on the estate of Cortés, who had gone to Spain, and levied tribute of foodstuffs and timber, which had to be taken daily over a snow-covered pass, so that one hundred and thirteen carriers died. They got licenses to hold slaves, granted to their relatives, and servants and put them up to secret auction. Since Zummáraga protested, they spread libels about him and his Franciscan brothers, pointing out (and this is what the Basques never liked about lawyers) that Zummáraga had left Spain without being consecrated as a bishop; and when he put a preacher on Corpus Christi to defend the good name of the order, the Audiencia sent toughs and a constable to pitch the preacher out of the pulpit on the stone flags on the church floor. When Zummáraga told the president of the Audiencia that certain Indian settlements were being bled white by his exactions of goods and services and that as Protector of the Indians he must order him to moderate his demands, the president answered that if Zummáraga did not stop his meddling, he would punish him as the Bishop of Zamora had been punished.

This was a real threat. The Bishop of Zamora had been one of the leaders of a revolt in Spain which made a very necessary protest against

Emperor Charles's sacrifice of his own people's well-being to his international interests and the attendant wars. Emperor Charles would probably have admitted later, at least to his confessor if nobody else, that the revolt gave him a useful lesson in his duties, but it was too nearly successful for him to show mercy. One cannot be merciful, or even just, if one exercises more than a certain amount of power. It simply cannot be done. The Bishop of Zamora was arrested, subjected to a trial which lasted five years, ran mad with despair and tried to escape and murdered a guard and was garrotted. Since then Emperor Charles had given even more spectacular, if less drastic, proof that he was not to be overawed by ecclesiastical dignity. While he was genuinely extending himself to fulfil in Mexico the obligations imposed on the Spanish monarchy by a bull issued by Pope Alexander VI, he sent his troops in Rome to imprison Pope Clement VII, whom he quite rightly thought dangerous to the peace of Europe because he was weak and a trimmer. The history of mankind is a history of more or less controlled schizophrenia.

Knowing these things, Zummárraga sat down in Mexico City when the supreme political power was maniacal and wanted his blood and wrote a letter to Emperor Charles, setting down his accusations against the Audiencia and its president. There is no doubt that what he wrote was true. Many reliable witnesses, who knew nothing of Zummárraga, attributed the same atrocities to Nuño de Guzmán, before and after this time. Zummárraga dispatched the letter and presently learned that it had been intercepted by the Audiencia. He then set out for Vera Cruz, the seaport of Mexico, which lay at the end of three hundred miles of the only and poorly laid road in Mexico. He took with him a copy of his letter to the emperor. At Vera Cruz he found a sailor who was a Basque and from his own province. They built up a cake of wax round the letter, and the sailor took it aboard and floated it in a cask of oil, which must have been in the cook's galley and making its return journey, for there was no oil in Mexico. Thus there jiggled back across the Atlantic in the dark secret viscosity one of the most glorious sentences of all time: "One Spaniard I have heard of had such a diabolical spirit that he put a lord on a cross with three nails, like Christ, because he was not given all the gold he had demanded, and in this manner other Diocletian cruelties." In spite of what happened to the Bishop of Zamora, in spite of the violation of the papal dignity, Zummárraga dared to write this loaded sentence. He dared remind Charles V that to be an emperor was not to be exempt from sin: that a Roman emperor named Diocletian had crucified Christ again by his persecution of the Christians.

The ship having sailed, Zummáraga went back along the dangerous road to Mexico City, and waited among his enemies for the answer. It would take twenty-six weeks for the bare journey-time of the letter and the reply to it. This brought him no punishment, and no reward either. Zummáraga had asked that his legal title of the Protector of the Indians should be given some substance by being assigned definite duties and powers, and this was not done. When the crown found one of its servants performing an outstanding act, it never forgot its technical trick, then or any time after, of accepting what profit his gifts could bring it and at the same time cutting down his pride so that he was unlikely to venture on rebellion. Yet Zummáraga's letter had such an effect that Professor Byrd Simpson calls it "possibly the most important ever written from the Indies." It did not do its work single-handedly but, as so often happens in human affairs, developed its explosive force when it was combined with its opposite. It arrived in Spain at the time when Cortés had returned there—Cortés, the inexhaustible lover of women, gold and silver, jewels, fruits, flowers, silks, palaces, and wide prospects, full of original sin at its most attractive, so attractive that even the Indians he had conquered were seduced into sincere homage, which forgave his greed. (And indeed he was no greedier than their own emperors had been.) It must have been disconcerting for the emperor and the Council of the Indies when these two men, Cortés and Zummáraga, the natural man and the man who had renounced his nature, suddenly spoke together with the same voice, and said they could not stomach the disorder of Mexico which was a hell peopled by Indians who were delivered to the flames by inhumane colonists, corrupt officials, and bad laws. It was a convincing combination: it set a spark to what Rousseau was to call the general will, which is not the opinion of the majority, but the part of a society's beliefs which has dynamic power. The Council of the Indies dismissed the First Audiencia and took care over appointing a second; its president was a highly intelligent bishop and four first-class lawyers, one of whom later became famous as a bishop whose name lingers today in his diocese.

The Council of the Indies also availed itself of a device which had been borrowed from the ancient Eastern empires by Emperor Charles because his interests were so far-flung: Viceroyalty. The first Viceroy of Mexico was Antonio de Mendoza, member of a fabulous family, which had given Spain generals, heroes, cardinals, diplomatists, scholars, poets, novelists, and satirists, with several of these categories sometimes fused in one body. True, they had to wrangle with him for five years before they could meet his exorbitant ideas of a salary, but once he got what he wanted he gave fifteen years of selfless service in carrying out new laws which read as honestly and hopefully as any comparable code. They contained a notable confession, harking back to and owning up to the disgraceful character of Spain's first invasion of the New World: "The Indians left alive in the islands of Puerto Rico, Cuba, and Española are relieved of all tributes and services, so that they may multiply and be taught in the Holy Catholic Faith." They prescribed virtue for themselves in clear-cut terms: "No free Indian is to be brought to the pearl-fisheries against his will; if the loss of life in pearl-diving cannot be avoided, pearl-fishing is to be abandoned." These promises were often broken, sometimes because greed and cruelty do not die, and sometimes because circumstance will temper its wind to liberalism; but often those promises were kept. For the next three hundred years the state of Mexico was to be not so bad, compared to what was going on in the rest of the world.

Isabella and Ferdinand of Spain

In 1494 Pope Alexander VI issued a bull conferring on the monarchies of Castile and Portugal temporal dominion over the territories in the New World just discovered by Columbus, on condition that the natives were converted to Christianity. This was not the best of introductions to the Christian faith. Alexander Borgia was one of the popes whose election can be reasonably supposed to have surprised Christ. He was one of the greatest scoundrels who ever succeeded in dying in bed, and that a bed which had served too many other purposes. Today we despise the mitred bishops and the crowned kings who paid obeisance to Alexander VI for maintaining that it did not matter that he was a lecher and a murderer with incest on his conscience, he was nevertheless the elected pope. But they were right. It was the office that mattered. The bull he issued regarding the New World meant that every good Catholic felt under the obligation to protect every Amerindian as a part of the body of Christ. Very likely such a Catholic paid no attention; but he had at least had fair warning that it was an obligation, and in fact he was very often helped by this reminder to discharge it. Certainly, Isabella of Castile, wife of Ferdinand of Aragon, took it seriously enough. We tend not to love this couple. They committed the hideous crime of the expulsion of the Jews, at an inexcusable age. They were neither young and inexperienced enough to believe in cruelty as a permissible solution, nor old and frightened enough to run to cruelty as a refuge. They were entering their forties, a time when men and women should have committed enough sins to be afraid of further guilt and developed the intelligence to dodge it. It is said by some that they had to get rid of the Jews because they had just driven the last Arabs out of Spain, and they needed to get rid of the Jews in order to get a homogeneous population of non-Oriental character, not likely to rat to Islam.

Sighing, one has to admit that that is how it may have seemed to Ferdinand and Isabella. But that is what is meant by the square in front of the Lady of Guadalupe. All over Mexico there are the images of the cruel gods who impose cruelty on us as our duty, as our fate; and people come out of the city and cross the stone square on their knees, asking forgiveness of a kind God, claiming that it is we who impose cruelty on the world, that there is another interpretation to the apparent facts. We can never find out what the rights and wrongs of the matter really are, and Keats suggests in one of his letters that true greatness consists in getting on with one's work without unduly fretting at this lack of a balance sheet. Negative Capability he called it. But as for poor Isabella, she was a Catholic, she was willing to back the hidden explanation, and go on her knees across the stony world. She accepted the obligation to win for God all the souls occupying bodies in the New World, and it was unfortunate that these bodies formed a labour force quite indispensable if the Spaniards were to extract from the New World all the gold and silver which was the only reason for them to take an interest in it.

That reason was legitimate. It is commonly believed that the Spanish pillaged the New World out of beastly greed, but we should remember that Spain was then in the same state of need as Europe after the Second World War. The Arab occupation had lasted seven centuries, and if at first it had brought great benefits (by turning out the Visigoths, who were not up to the job), it had later fragmented the country and starved its people because of the civil war waged between Arab sect and Arab sect. Now Ferdinand and Isabella had to govern Spain and they had nothing but an army, much of it guerrilla and tatty and anarchic; they had to improvise a police force, a civil service, and a constitution; they had to shatter feudalism by getting nobles to come up from their country estates and up to court, where they were sobered, bribed, civilised by being given responsible offices; and they had to put on magnificence as a show of power, to warn off any other European monarchs who had a fancy to absorb them; and they had also to reform the church which had fallen behind under the Visigoths. All this cost money. Without any hypocrisy Ferdinand and Isabella could say that they could not afford the conquest of the New World unless it was a sound investment, and that if it were that, then they were morally bound for their people's sake to conquer it.

Immediately Isabella, who was not simply the administrator of the

New World on paper, who was really governing the New World, was faced with difficulties. Only a certain kind of man could do the job of conquering, could become that tough animal named a Conquistador. He had to face the horror of exploring countries which still are terrible, even today, and must have been much more so to sixteenth-century men who had no relevant technological knowledge and were working at the end of immensely long lines of communication. The only kind of man who could do this expected that, when he endured this hell and won the territory, he would be allowed to loot it and enslave the natives, and he thought he had the Bible behind him, with its injunction that thou shalt not muzzle the ox when he treadeth out the corn. Isabella was bound to respect this demand of the natural man, for if he were not satisfied he might have come home, saying the game was not worth the candle, and the investment would be a dead loss. It is unlikely that they would have come to this decision, considering the delicious charm of the New World, with its flowers and its birds and its penetration by another and charmed kind of space; but Ferdinand and Isabella were not to know that. They knew about as much about the New World from travellers' tales as the people at Cape Kennedy knew from photographs about the moon.

But Ferdinand and Isabella may have been conscious of a danger which we have forgotten. It may have seemed to them possible that some of the conquistadores, not allowed to tread the corn unmuzzled, might have transferred their loyalty to the Turks, then a great maritime people, and now known to have taken an interest in maps of the New World. At this possibility the hearts of the Spanish king and queen must have grown faint. They knew how susceptible their people were to the charm of Islam. The defections of Spanish ecclesiastics, now the discipline of the church was being tuned up, had been embarrassing to Ferdinand and Isabella, as the defection of scientists has been to Washington and London in our own time. Four hundred friars tucked up their habits and crossed to North Africa and became good Moslems. If Ferdinand and Isabella had not thought quickly and cleverly and boldly, I should have been looking across the stone square not at the Basilica of Our Lady of Guadalupe, but at a mosque, and the women about me would have been veiled and have had not faces but black snouts, and the men would have been looking their worst in that most unbecoming form of male headgear, the fez; and the fashion might have been running up all over North America. It is no use saying that it might not matter much if this had been the case. The Turks had their chance of colonisation in the southeastern corner of Europe, the Balkans, where in spite of their charm and intelligence they made a mess that brought on us the turbulence of Europe and the two World Wars.

The conquistadores declared that they must have slaves and, without getting permission from the home government, took them. Isabella did her best to administer her sacred charge in the light of that text, "Render unto Caesar the things which are Caesar's, and unto God the things which are God's": an odd text, for it reads like the acme of good sense, and yet people never look their best when applying it. She was against slavery. It was a cardinal point of morality at the time, so many Christians had found themselves slaves in Moslem hands. But she was at the same time faced with the reluctance of the Indians to give their labour to the invaders as freemen. When they saw a conquistador, they ran away and stayed away. If they were hiding in the forest, how could she get the transatlantic gold and silver into the coffers of the treasury? And how was she to arrange for their souls to be saved? Isabella's attempts to get her moral hat sitting straight on her head are described in a fascinating volume called *The Encomienda in New Spain*, by a California historian, Leslie Byrd Simpson, a scholar crackling with vitality. He was born out of his right time. If Shakespeare had read his books, he would have got a dozen plays out of them.

In Professor Simpson's study of the Encomienda (which is the name given to the form of slavery as it was worked out by the Spanish) he shows how Isabella was compelled to go into the slave trade by her better nature. The only way to get the Amerindians to work (and to save their souls) was to enslave them, and the only way she could fulfil her obligation to protect them was to claim them as her vassals and establish a crown right to grant Spanish subjects legal titles to her possessions of slaves. But her moral hat kept on slipping over one eye, text or no text. When she granted a royal patent to a Spaniard called Guerra, who wished to exploit an area on the Pearl Coast, she gave him permission, God forgive her, "to take Indians, men and women for slaves which he is to do as nearly as possible with their consent, without harming them; and in the same manner he may take monsters and animals of any kind, and all the serpents and fishes he may desire; and all this is to belong to him as has been said, the fourth part being reserved for me." As nearly as possible with their consent . . . and in the same manner he may take monsters . . . the fourth part being reserved for me. . . . No, Isabella was not looking her best. But after 1504 she looked much better, for in that year she died. It is a wonder that she lived so long and was so able all her life, for she was pursued by grief. Her only son died at nineteen and her posthumous son died at birth, of her four daughters one died in childbirth and her child survived only a couple of years, another was the insulted first queen of Henry VIII of England, another was insane. It was all to her credit that she was so resolute in behaving better than Providence, and Ferdinand cannot have been much help to her.

Now, to his discharge of his double obligation, spiritual and patriotic, Ferdinand brought the gnawing private greed of a rat, and like a rat he carried plague. He exploited the West Indies with so little mercy that in twenty years the native races were nearing extinction. His subjects often showed themselves his superiors, protesting at the exactions which meant that tens of thousands of Indians were worked to death on the plantations and in the pearl fisheries and in the mines. Some Indians might have been thought lucky, since they were born in the Bahamas, which lacked minerals and were therefore termed by the Spaniards "the useless islands," but they had no luck at all. They were transported in ships which were mortuaries. They slept in their own filth and were starved and sickened and died and were cast overboard. Professor Simpson quotes the report of a Dominican missionary: "every time the Indians are brought from their lands so many die of hunger on their way that we think that by their trail in the sea another ship might find its way to port." The Indian gods were externalisations of the forces they recognised as determining their lives. It is quite natural that a nation permeated by Indian blood, and now often recalled to memory of its past, should not let those of their gods who are hideous be pushed out of the way.

This is among the great horrors of history. According to the Dominicans, out of sixty thousand Indians brought in ten years to Española, which is Haiti, only eight thousand survived that period. A man on the other side from the missionaries, a civil servant, reported that of one batch of fifteen thousand, only two thousand survived. Such administrators left a mountain of documents dealing with their own inability to satisfy Ferdinand's demands for loot. Desperately they tell the home government that they cannot cope with the Indians' obstinate addiction to death. (One Spaniard complained of their tiresome habit of committing suicide "for matters of no consequence.") It was this labour situation which led the Spanish to initiate the transatlantic slave trade in African Negroes; and it is a horrid example of human liability to error that this policy was advocated by Las Casas, the Dominican who risked his life and freedom again and again to defend the Indians, who was an extreme, even unbalanced humanitarian. He was moved, by the quite sound observation that Negroes were more robust than Indians, to the belief that they could survive colonisation better; as if it could have been taken well.

It is strange that I should have stood in that square, whole European and unmolested by the people round me, who were dark with the pigmentation of these martyrs. An Indian woman had halted beside me and was taking stock of me delicately and obliquely. I looked at her with some unease. But she was old, with this blanched, spectral form of age which is an attraction of her race, with that air of being halfway through an open door into another world, and she was perhaps wondering why, at my time of life, I was so stolidly planted in this world, like someone not making a move to leave at the end of a party, not claiming the coat of etherality necessary for going out into the thinner air. But she was not hostile. The Indians have never been given to hostility that does not serve a purpose. But otherwise they stayed on terms with people, if only to observe them: they liked zoos.

Also, being subtle-minded, they probably knew that the case of one human being against another is never simple. The Spaniards acquired great guilt in their relationships with them. Yet they often could not help it. Once they got to Mexico, they were pitch-forked into sin. They could not help starving them, for the Indian population had never had an adequate food supply. The conquistadores were ill-equipped to increase the food supply to feed themselves, for most had been professional soldiers before they came abroad, and though of these a large number might have been country-bred, the basis of Spanish agriculture was sheep-farming, and there was not a sheep to be found in the New

World. As for crops, they knew nothing about those native to Mexico; they had never seen maize before, as the Indians had never seen wheat, the Spaniards knew nothing about the management of tropical soil, which in many areas would not take the plough, only a cultivator stick. The Indians knew more about irrigation than even the Arabs had taught the Spanish, and the ambitious works the Spaniards undertook when they had destroyed the Indian towns were often geographical disasters.

Minerals and Mines

But not only did they rifle the Indians' food supply and deface the land, they inflicted on many of them a martyrdom which inflicted torture by being totally incomprehensible to the martyrs: service in the mines. The Indians must have thought it one of their most hideous gods who put gold and silver in their land and then let it be invaded by foreigners frenzied with esurience for these very things, and esurient for reasons which they themselves could never understand. For many centuries, the Indians had worked in the gold mines, which were all placer mines: that is, deposits of gold particles or nuggets in the sand or gravel of riverbeds and banks, which they washed clean in gourds. Silver they hammered out too when they had the luck to find nuggets of that, which was not often, so it may have been more valuable to them than gold. They worked with sweat, but with pride, for what they found was used for the perfectly comprehensible purpose of making jewellery for the chiefs and the priests and the rich merchants: a purpose which was more than comprehensible, it was approved on a high level. In the field of ornament, neither gold nor silver was supremely desirable, for jade and turquoise were valued more highly. But on the people who were happily teasing out these luxuries at the luxury-maker's pace, there suddenly descended a frenzied horde of strange, uncoloured men, coarse with an unusual fullness of life but pale like the aged, who insisted that to them these only moderately important metals were as necessary as air. When Cortés and his men first came to the frontiers of the Aztec state, Emperor He-who-gets-angry-like-a-Lord sent out messengers to see if he could bribe them to go away with presents of gold and silver and jade and turquoise. Cortés told them, "Let your emperor send us gold, for I and my companions suffer from a disease of the heart for which gold is the only cure."

It must have seemed to the Indians that he was speaking the literal truth. They cannot have conceived that what meant to them necklaces and earrings and lip-plugs meant to these horribly vigorous intruders that for the rest of their lives they could be stuffed with food and drink and honours, could buy any woman and a place near the king and a safe conduct to the misty world where the dead go, since masses can be paid for. The Indians must have stared glassy-eyed when Cortés and his men, since the gifts had not been enough, at a later date rode them down in a delirious desire for these pleasant but not important materials, willing to kill if it were not satisfied, on horses which also seemed to be suffering from this mysterious disease of the heart. For, if one had never seen a horse before and it were such a horse as a conquistador would ride—a quick cart-horse, with great shining globes for chest and buttocks, and a barrel for body, and a neck as thick as it was long, and raised veins twisting under the polished coat, and broad nostrils that snorted out gales, and ears twitching like imperative demands—then one would take it for granted that the horse was like its master, a mechanism set in motion by the same desires, and able to use the same cunning and unfamiliar methods to gratify them. When a horse neighed, the Indians who heard it must have thought it was telling them to hand over gold. There may or may not be flying saucers, but the Indians thought they were seeing something just as strange.

The conquistadores and the horses won the day for their peculiar appetite. Therefore thousands upon thousands of Mexican Indians were led away from their homes into strange places, where they could neither be fed nor housed properly and were beaten on to work, often in improvised gallery mines such as they had never seen before, by strangers who attached an importance to their labours, which must have remained for centuries incomprehensible. Indeed, some Indians would not understand it today. There are remote tribes which have never latched on to the currency system. More than their own well-being was destroyed by this senseless rape; even the existence of their people seemed doomed. Their staple food, then as now, was maize, which in this land required delicate and unremitting attention. The land had to be cleaned out at a certain time of year, the corn grain planted out at another, the corncob harvested at another, and not by blind habit, for the climate is capricious and the rainfall sometimes so catastrophic that the programme has to be rewritten; and in any case it was believed that the maize would not grow if certain religious ceremonies were not performed. Collapse threatened the beautiful structure of their husbandry, which had brought into being by illiterate but exquisite science not only maize but the bean, the pumpkin, the sweet potato, the pineapple, the tomato, the vanilla shrub, the pepper; and the irrigation systems and the mills lay in ruins. For the first hundred years of the Spanish occupation of Mexico, the Indian population drained away at the rate of about 9 percent a decade. That is how the *latifundia*, the huge estates characteristic of the country, came to exist. The Spanish settlers liked to cross the seas and find themselves lords of more land than they could hope to own at home; and then they found they were forced to extend their boundaries further and further for they had to take in a large area to draw on even a small reservoir of Indian labour. The Indian towns had become villages, the Indian villages were deserted.

Yet the Spaniards did much for Mexico. Indeed, their gifts are beyond counting. They brought in, and that quickly, wheat and barley and rye and oats, bananas and oranges and limes and apples and pears, sugar-cane, horses and mules and, best of all, hogs and sheep and goats and cattle. They also introduced the use of the wheel. Not the wheel—that the Indians had discovered for themselves, but they used it only on toy animals, to let the children drag them about, or as controls on distaffs. But the greatest service the Spaniards did was not to Mexico but to the Old World, and this, ironically enough, they did by the exploitation of the mines. There was a currency crisis in the West. From earliest recorded time, gold and silver coinage had been the accepted medium of exchange, and as Europeans travelled further and further away from their homelands, opening up channels of trade into Africa and Asia, the more calls there were on the precious metals. In one quarter the calls were not what should have been made if the theory was to be given a chance. Asiatics, particularly in India and China, traded their silks and jade and ivory and spices for gold and silver, and then hoarded the metals or turned them into ornaments, which was a convenient way of cultivating two fields of interest at the same time. An Asiatic wife could be flattered by being hung with gold and silver necklaces while she was acting as an inside-out form of safety deposit vault. This removal of precious metals from circulation caused an adverse balance of trade so long ago that Emperor Vespasian and Pliny complained about it, and it is still an inconvenience, though a slighter one, to the world's monetary system, like an airlock in a pipe. Apart from this permanent refusal of the human element to carry out the system as reason demanded, there was at least one damaging interruption to the world's financial progress. During the barbarian invasions, which can be counted as lasting from the end of the fourth to the end of the fifth century, the mining industry came to a standstill, sometimes totally, sometimes piecemeal. The Spanish mines went out of operation for about seven centuries and had to be reopened by the Arabs. The renewed production never caught up with the demand. Then the conquistadores went to the New World and suddenly presented their country with a huge surplus of the precious metals, which other countries shared in through trade and then added to by their own contributions, when they sent their own adventurers across the Atlantic. Historians estimate that within a century or so the world's stock of gold and silver was multiplied fourfold.

The immediate result was a true and glorious inflation. Suddenly the flow of purchasing power ran like a shining full-fed river. Of course it was faster and broader than the flow of goods and services, and up went prices: a quarter of wheat was selling in England for ten shillings in 1495 and for twenty-eight shillings a hundred years later, and rents had doubled. But wages and interests kept rising with prices, and that they would never catch them up, then or at any later date, was not suspected. So the occasion was cheerful, as no inflations we have known since, for they have been sad businesses, usually due to the economic disorder incidental to war, with its proliferation of highly paid armament industries and its famine of consumer goods, and the social schizophrenia caused by the recognition by some that the boom would not last and the persuasion of others that it would. But this conquistador-made inflation was a carnival. It was that lovely thing—lots of money, in an almost pure state. Man knew a relationship with coin as sweet as love-making would seem to innocents who did not know that it led to the birth of children and the setting up of households, that people who make love happily may not like each other for ever, that children may turn out badly. Never was currency to exhale such cheerfulness again, for though an even more bountiful present of gold was given to the world by Australia and Africa and California during the second half of the nineteenth century, the effect was spectacular only in a limited field. The world's stock of precious metal was by then so large that even that addition could not drastically affect the currency situation, and their importance had been taken down more than a few pegs by paper money and the credit system. But when Cortés and Pizarro came back to Spain, it was as if they had found a beneficent god named Gold hiding among the flowers of the New World, and he was willing to work his miracles across the Atlantic just as well.

The mechanism worked perfectly. The gold they delivered depreciated the value of the gold already in Europe, so the debtor found his shackles suddenly weighing light. He could pay what he owed by saving a smaller proportion of his rising wages, or he could pay the same proportion and discharge the debt more quickly; and the creditor, getting his loan back more quickly, could reinvest it at a higher rate of interest, and again it would come back to him sooner than before. Therefore the man who wanted to open up a new trade route, experiment with a new agricultural or mechanical idea, found it easy to find capitalists to finance him. People had more money to hire professional help. So the ship owner, the manufacturer, the farmer, the merchant, the skilled artisan, the lawyer, the doctor, each was given a personal endowment of material prosperity and limitless hope. The miracle was, of course, not universal. The gods never do a complete job. The people who did not profit were the old, who lived on the savings they kept in old stockings and suddenly found that what was there could buy less and less; the proportion of the town population who from ill luck or physical or mental defect could not join the force of efficient labourers whose wages were rising; the landless peasants who were bogged down in rural mud and not to be dug out for centuries; and, ironically enough, the people who had sent Cortés and Pizarro to do this very thing, bring back substance for more currency—the royalty of Spain, and, later, all royalty.

Kings and queens felt the rise in prices acutely, because they had to put on a show. They had inherited the Byzantine tradition of magnificence, which itself was derived from the unsurpassed court of Persia and was actually a valid technique of government. A splendid tournament or wedding was as good a demonstration of a state's resources as arms estimates are today. But with the inflation, royalty's hoarded wealth shrank in value, and though the revenue from lands and taxes rose, it did not rise enough, and the profits from coinage diminished painfully. But nobody listens to the complaints of the old or the unlucky or the defective or the obscure, and though people will listen to the complaints of kings, it is with a titter, so well has the useful myth of royal abundance been fabricated. The task of kings became more and more exasperating, for they had to increase the inflation by which they suffered, because they still needed the material for money, and then again had to increase their expenditure in waging wars and sending out armed expeditions to the new ore-rich countries. "All these discoveries," wrote the Italian doctor Jerome Cardan, in 1575, "are sure to give rise to great and calamitous events in order that a just distribution of them may be maintained. The conviction grows also that as a result of these discoveries learning will be neglected and but lightly esteemed, and certainties will be exchanged for uncertainties. These things may be true sometime or other, but how," he adds, as one of the triumphant new middle classes, "we shall rejoice as in a flower-filled meadow."

It was the Indian miners who sowed that meadow with its flowers. But did they get gratitude? No, they were crucified on a hideous irrationality of the human mind. The importance of metal to Western man is written into its name, which is derived from the Greek word *metallon*—that which is sought. But nowhere, till late in history, have those who have done the real seeking been pampered. It is our natural impulse to savage miners. Between two and three thousand years before Cortés invaded Mexico, the kings of Egypt were working extensive gold mines in the burning and waterless deserts in their Arabian and Ethiopian frontiers. Did that highly organised and priggish society send caravans out to reward the miners with ripe fruits and nourishing foods, did it build tents for their shelter, with attendants to fan them through the hot nights, were they given long leaves in Alexandria and pensions and honours? No, they worked on mean rations under the blows of alien overseers, who could not speak their language, so did not become their friends and were themselves brutalised by fear, for these outposts were insufficiently defended from robber bands and enemy raids. These miners were supposed to be convicted criminals and prisoners of war, but gold was important to the Egyptian economy, and there is a strong suspicion that, to get a full labour force, blameless people were often accused of crime. The Greeks were only a little more merciful in their search for metals, in that their branded, fettered, underfed, beaten miners probably were the convicted criminals and prisoners of war they were alleged to be. But that is all that can be said for ancient Greece as a mine owner. There were miners' revolts significant in their desperation; and though archaeologists know that the Greeks discovered the essential technique of mining quite early, they never took any steps to improve the working conditions in the mines.

The Romans were hardly more merciful. Their role was different. The Egyptians and the Greeks were prospectors, but the Romans' task was chiefly to exploit the mines already in operation within the territories they conquered. They brought to the business considerable technological efficiency, so they usually needed larger labour forces than they found and had to look about for recruits. Either they conscripted the local populations for the purpose, or they brought in slaves from another area, sometimes far distant. That meant exactly what it meant when the Spaniards shifted the tribesmen between the West Indian Islands. Men dead of dysentery were tipped overboard into the Mediterranean as the Indians were tipped into the Caribbean. And in the third century A.D. the African Bishop Cyprian was complaining that in the Roman mines the miners were branded, fettered, underfed, and beaten, as they had been in ancient Egypt. This is a slow-burn Hiroshima.

Society's ingratitude towards miners is the more remarkable because once barter had been superseded by a monetary system, the possession of the precious metals at times meant the difference between survival and extinction. The Athenians staved off defeat for thirteen years by a fleet paid for by the silver mines of Laurium. When Rome fought the Second Punic War, it had Carthage by the throat as soon as it captured the great mines of southern Spain, which the Carthaginians had seized long before from the Phoenicians. After that, Carthage's finances were in disorder, and its dour people, who lived by pride, had that pride eaten away. The peace treaty provided that they must pay Rome a swinging indemnity, and sometimes they had to make the payment in such poor silver the Roman treasury turned it back. It was only a matter of time before they were utterly destroyed. Metal meant prosperity, power, and self-respect, yet the donors of these were punished.

This punishment was not inevitable, and that had been proved long before Cortés went to Mexico. It might be supposed that, if one had to pass one's life as a miner, the present might be the period to choose; and today there are certainly groups of mine workers, such as the white South African gold-miners, who lead privileged and well-rewarded if exacting lives. Yet the lot of the miners was probably at its peak during the Middle Ages, in Central Europe. There were found a mob of princes, the Duke of Saxony, the Duke of Brunswick, the Duke of Thuringia, all jockeying for power, and therefore all eager to mint currency, and a highly intelligent population, who could get the stuff out of the ground as never before, and were politically alive enough to form a guild which safeguarded their interests, even to gaining them the power to market their services abroad. At the close of the Middle Ages, the German miner was working an eight-hour day, receiving a wage fixed by negotiation and sick pay and having his wife and children looked after after his death in a pension system. Most important, they were respected, just as much as if they had been weavers or masons. This happy state of affairs lasted until the Peasants' War of 1525. Mining was organised in the cities, and the war was a rising of the countrymen against the town-dwellers, who at that moment were in no state to resist them, owing to a financial crisis which was largely due to currency disorders: the inflationary wave started by Cortés on the other side of the world had not yet had time or the opportunity to reach them. The revolt failed, and left the princes and the capitalists stronger than before, so strong that they could crush the guilds, so the good days were over. But the point had been established. Men could be just and treat with proper gratitude their fellows who served them underground.

There was a historical reason for this change of front. The miner and the non-miner were able to confront each other in more favourable conditions than before. The miner was not a criminal or a prisoner of war, nor was alleged to be so; he was not brutalised by servitude as one of thousands in a burning climate, for in this territory the work could be portioned out among units of sixteen men and their prentice sons, and even when they travelled, they rarely left the temperate zone. There was a desire for the rational in the air, Luther was presently to invent Protestantism just round the corner. Therefore the non-miner was willing to accept the view that mining was likely to be more productive if the miner was a free and well-nourished and respected man rather than a starved and beaten slave. But why had he ever been reluctant to make that obvious admission, why had he wanted to make a nightmare out of the mine, which is nothing but a hole dug in the earth, a loathed sacrificial victim out of the miner, who is simply the man who digs the hole?

The answer lies in a sentence spoken by Hamlet. "Oh, God, I could be bounded in a nutshell and count myself a king of infinite space were it not that I have bad dreams." Man is small, in an environment which does nothing to adapt itself to him, but he could conquer it with his mind, were it not that he has bad dreams; and two of these relate to mines. A number of modern psychologists, headed by Freud and Jung, have claimed to learn from their patients' dreams that the unconscious conceives of the earth as a person, as a vast mother; and that from the same source it appears that the love of money is a form of anal eroticism, and money itself a symbol for excrement. Ordinarily our persuasion is that when psychologists make these statements they are pursuing their subjects beyond the bounds of what is for us realism, like the physicists whose calculations make statements about atomic structure, revealing it as different from the structure of the world we see and smell and hear and touch and taste. So we can form no picture of it. But we have to believe them, for their calculations prove themselves correct in many manifestations of atomic power. We take for granted that this strange structure will simply provide a framework for our lives, and that never can our five senses bring it into the range of our experiences. In the same way we assume that no actual events in our lives are likely to be caused by the insistence of our unconscious that the earth is really a huge mother and money excrement. They might account for the larger vague movements that determine the direction of our personal dramas: the choice of banking or stock-broking as a career, and a lifelong tendency towards constipated stinginess from time to time correcting itself by sudden generosity, or towards diarrhoeal extravagance seeking its correction in periods of thrift. But we do not expect people to run at bulldozers with the command that they should leave Mum alone, nor a waiter to be ready at the end of a meal to accept with equal grace a two-dollar bill or a small sack of manure. Yet sometimes these insane and indecorous confusions thrust themselves past the barriers our reason puts up against them and set about breaking up the pattern we try to impose on our lives. We cannot do our trick of making ourselves kings of infinite space within our nutshell, because we have bad dreams.

The martyrdom of the Indians in the mines was just such a collapse of the human enterprise, an abandonment of the human hope. Their oppressors were not simply blinded by greed for the metal in these mines. If that had been their sole imperative, they would have been careful to preserve the life and strength of the miners. As it is, the Spaniards were perverse in their destruction of the labour force which got them the gold they had to take back to Spain were their ambitions to be gratified. Their perversity should not astonish us, for it has been matched in our time by the persistence the Nazis showed in starving the inmates of the concentration camps, even when the tide of war had turned against them and they needed all the workers they could get. On both occasions, not reason was in control but a bad dream.

The bad dream about minerals which was bemusing the Spaniards had been written down long before, and was to be expressed long afterwards. The younger Pliny, writing about the time of Christ, had gone so far as to suggest that earthquakes were the result of the writhings of respectable Mother Earth under the rude penetrations of mining engineers. He was not one to say what was novel, and the Roman Empire had already established its reluctance, or (which was as significant) was said to have done, by a Senate Decree forbidding the mining of metals within the mother country, Italy. There are some rationalist explanations for this prohibition, but none rings true. It cannot really be that the Romans feared to exhaust the mines and keep them as intact assets, for in those days minerals were thought to be crops. It was believed that one had only to leave a mine fallow to find a nice self-sown growth of ore. Nor can it really be that the Romans feared overproduction for they were busily engaged elsewhere. It is begging the question to say that the Romans recognised that miners were the most deprived of slaves and therefore the most terrifying when there was a slaves' revolt; for that the Romans could have rectified by improving the conditions. It can hardly be doubted that the motive for such a decree (whether it existed in reality or in fantasy) would be the protection of the motherland from violation, particularly as two modern peoples have expressed the same quasi-sexual concern for the land that nourished them. The

American Mormons had good social reasons for seeking to exclude from their territory footloose prospectors and miners not possibly to be integrated in the Church of the Latter-Day Saints; the Afrikaners of South Africa had every reason to encourage anybody who was willing to develop the mineral resources of their country, which gave much less lavish returns to the agriculturist. But both Mormons and Afrikaners alike write and speak as if the farmer's relations with the land were decorous and lawful, such as a respectable husband might have with his wife, while they denounce the miner as if he were a lustful man engaging in a continuous rape.

What is still stranger is the sympathy evoked by this attitude in many people outside these communities, who are entirely dependent on metal. They speak of mine owners not as if they provided a service to the community, which has to be scrutinised because of special conditions which make it easy to abuse the actual operatives, but with total condemnation. Yet these same people could not go to work or on holiday were it not for metal vehicles; most of them could not earn a living except by handling metal, and this even applies to many artists, such as musicians, sculptors, architects, and writers (who must have their books copied and printed); they could not be fed if the crops were not augmented by the use of agricultural machinery; they could not have any surgical attention at all, and they would have to have much less medical attention than they would normally require, were it not for metal instruments. It may even be that their lives are sometimes touched with singular beauty by metal. One of the few beautiful events I remember emerging from the last war was the cooperation between the British and German coal miners in getting the Ruhr going again after it had been blitzed to a standstill. All hatred died, there was no more estrangement, while these men who had been enemies for years got on with their task of digging out of the earth what keeps people warm in winter and kills the darkness. All those miners were saying, "Let there be light."

The Spaniards who went out of Spain into the New World were subject to bad dreams. They had been forced back into the darkness that is blacker than a winter's night, because they were in such constant and climactic danger from man and monster and disease, and so far from home. When they opened the mines, which might have been the foundation of a wholesome economic partnership between the Old World and the New, they imagined they were doing a vile cloacal thing: and by a familiar mechanism, which we all use, they cleansed themselves of their guilt by projecting it on their defenceless collaborators, whom they had forced to contrive this pollution. It is to be noted that when Columbus first started gold-mining in Haiti, the gold was found in not at all inaccessible streams and taking it was not too unpleasant, so some Spaniards became miners; and these men Columbus forced first to confess and take communion. He was moved to impose this rule after he had learned that the Indians lived apart from their wives and fasted for twenty days before they went on their stint of gold-mining, as they believed that a man on a normal diet who had recently had sexual intercourse never found gold. This technique the Spaniards rejected with bluff commonsense, pointing out that their food was so poor they could be regarded as fasting, and their wives were in Spain, so willy-nilly they were on a par with the Indians, and they saw no reason for the confessions and the communions. But the incident has its value in indicating that the invaded and the invaders had here a point in common. The Indians too had nightmares about metal; they had even made the anal identification: gold and silver were known to them as "the excrement of the gods."

But in the days when they were unconquered, they kept their fantasies well under control. The Aztec capital was undaunted by the anal. Tenochtitlán lay sweet on clean waters. There were public latrines screened off with reed walls, and the solid excrement was taken in barges to manure the mainland, while the urine was used as a mordant in tanneries, and the garbage was dumped on the marshes round the lake to make them firm and cultivable. A sanitation corps of a thousand men saw to this disposal work and also swept and washed the streets and squares. But when the Indians' pride was broken by defeat, the Spaniards, thinking of excrement, drove them down the mines, and the Indians' faint sense of excrement became obsessional too. None of the invaders talks of the Indian as dirty, other than the priests in the temples, who practised a ritual abstinence from cleanliness; but when the Indians took picks in their hands and set to financing the new Europe, then filth was with them, as if a malign god had sent it down instead of manna.

Also, there descended on the situation a sort of nastiness with which we have become familiar in our time, whenever a totalitarian power takes its inevitable turn towards cruelty. It has then become the duty of all humanitarians to make public the sufferings of the victims; but it would be insincere to pretend that the publication did not give pleasure to sadists, who took up the subject for their own purposes. The descriptions of concentration camps were more numerous in the thirties than could be accounted for by the lovingkindness of our species, and some of them were impure in style. There were similar dubieties in the sixteenth century. The courageous but frenzied book by the Dominican champion of the Indians, Las Casas, *A Brief Relation of the Destruction of the Indies*, went through forty-two foreign editions in a hundred years, being translated into Italian, Latin, English, French, German, and Dutch. It is to be wondered whether Europe was really as humanitarian as all that, and suspicions are heightened by the graphic representations of the suffering of the Indians which were published in Europe during the sixteenth and seventeenth centuries. That excellent work, Rickard's *Man and Metals*, gives three such plates from Jerome Benzoni's *New History of the New World*, printed in Germany. A collection of pornographic prints and engravings gathered by a famous pharmaceutical chemist was sold at his death, some forty years ago, by a careless executor to a short-sighted woman who kept an antique shop in a small Sussex town. Among the female fencers and the flagellants and the dwarfs and giants the poor lady proffered to her customers with a vague smile were these Benzoni illustrations and some others on the same subject printed in Holland and in Venice. They were not out of place, being drawn with a cold, inquisitive glee.

Hernán Cortés

Mexico was deep in bad dreams; and that was why Cortés had a value for it. We know very well what sort of man he was, for there are many contemporary accounts of him, of which the most notable were written by his chaplain and secretary, Gómara, a self-conscious literate, and one of his captains, a Spanish Harry Hotspur, Bernal Díaz, who, such is the injustice of this earth, was by far the better writer of the two. These make easy reading today, and they and the supporting testimony were magnificently used a quarter of a century ago by a Spanish writer, Salvador de Madariaga, a civil engineer turned man of letters and diplomat, who was Spanish ambassador to Washington in the early thirties and worked for disarmament between the two World Wars with a magnificent voluntary renunciation of perfect historical understanding. In the most gentlemanly way he gave Providence its chance; a gentleman is always bound to give the hypothesis that his adversary is a gentleman too a chance. Cortés's contemporaries and Madariaga both convey his valuable quality: his freedom from bad dreams. It is delightful to think of him; though he was physically undistinguished, unremarkable in feature, and though better in body, being tall and well built, with broad shoulders, he had the bowed legs of the cavalryman. A faithful visualisation of the conquest must allow for the fact that many of the conquistadores were bow-legged; they lived on horseback and the widespread disease of rickets made leg bones flimsy.

But Cortés possessed what seemed to his followers a great attraction, for it was rare: restraint, a man with no abstract passion for he practised it when it was necessary. It was not natural to him, he was contentious by nature, as he showed by his readiness to engage in lawsuits. But in the trials of every day, he abstained from blasphemy and bit back his violent temper, though his veins on his forehead were swelling, and at the peak of his anger he used to choke. In his youth he had squandered large sums on gorgeous clothing for himself and his wife, but latterly he dressed with a simple elegance. When other men of his rank wore massive and many gold chains and large brooches and badges, he wore one slender gold chain and a small pendant holding a picture of the Virgin Mary; for he was fervently religious. His hands were bare but for one fine diamond ring. He liked a large meal at midday, but the food had to be simple, and he drank little wine and could starve when he was on the field. Yet it was very important to him that when he dined he should be waited on by four butlers and a full complement of pages, and that there should be splendid gold and silver plate on the table. He liked, as he put it, "to eat by trumpets." For recreation he liked good-tempered gambling with dice, reading (for he was a lettered man and had written poetry in his youth) and learning new technical tricks about farming or the use of arms or sailing or mining, from the words and fingers of any man he could find to teach him.

He was an intellectual who had dodged his destiny. His father was a noble of the lesser sort in the sun-baked inland Spanish province of Estremadura, which to this day is three-fifths scrub, where only sheep and hogs thrive. Numerous Spaniards who made their mark in the New World went there to escape Estremaduran poverty. Hernán Cortés was a clever boy and at fourteen was sent to study law in the University of Salamanca and there spent two years "studying grammar," which meant studying Latin, to the point of being able to use it fluently as a conversational medium. This was then a highly practical education, for Latin was the international language, and in any case was the only subject which could conceivably teach the mind the exactitude we now hope to give it by scientific teaching. Though he was an excellent student and all his life could understand speeches made to him in Latin and respond in Latin, he left Salamanca at sixteen, perhaps because his parents could no longer afford to keep him there. He went home, was a nuisance there for a year, spent some time having the mild malaria then endemic in such parts and for another year took to the road and had unrecorded adventures. Then, at nineteen, he sailed to the Indies, to join the staff of the new governor general. When he landed and looked about him, he said, when he was told he would be given land if he would bind himself to stay for five years, "Neither in this Island nor in any other of this New World do I wish or mean to stay for so long." It was the kind of remark that sometimes leads to a marriage. He settled down as part-time civil servant, part-time "gentleman farmer," part-time lover, part-time wrangler with his fellow colonists, who were a quarrelsome lot. By twenty-six he had been sent to the newly explored island of Cuba, to act as secretary to its governor, a noted soldier named Diego Velázquez, and as king's treasurer as well. Here he showed unusual competence, particularly in the development of the gold mines and in the promotion of cattle breeding, but again got involved in local feuds so thoroughly that at one point he found himself in prison. During this imbroglio he performed the one deed of heroism ever recorded which belongs specifically to the civil service. To avoid deportation, he jumped out of a boat into the night and swam through shark-infested waters to dry land, a kerchief round his head protecting papers which he held as a notary of the municipal council and as an officer of the king's treasurer. That his purpose in preserving these documents was largely self-justificatory only links the deed to the civil service more closely.

So Cortés was a civil servant, civilian of the civilians, until, at the age of thirty-four, he turned overnight into one of the greatest of soldiers. He was sent by Velázquez to lead a third expedition into the unexplored territory of Central America, afterwards known as New Spain and after that as Mexico, when two others had failed, and it appears that, though he was from the first hotly interested in the commission, it was only as a means of advancement. He passionately wanted to be rich, as he passionately wanted to be saved by the Lord Jesus Christ. He called a city on the Mexican coast The Rich City of the True Cross. It corresponds with a certain union of desires, not often found so candidly united, in Cortés's mind. For the rest he was hedonist, enjoying what came. But he was overthrown in his sensuousness and taken up to greatness above the lot of ordinary men by this commission in a strange country, as a man might be felled by the wide wings of an eagle and then lifted up into the air. His achievement in Mexico cannot be belittled by any pretence that he had overwhelming technological advantages over the Indians. It is true that he and his men had horses, steel swords, guns and armour, and the Indians had none. But the Indians were not overawed by these novelties for long. They certainly mistook the horses for gods at first, but that ended when they decapitated the noble mare of Pedro de Morón in battle. As for weapons, they had arrows, javelins, stone-tipped lances, slings, and formidable wooden clubs with jagged obsidian insets which could inflict terrible wounds. It was by a swing from one of these that poor Morón's horse lost his head. For defence, they had useful shields made of close wickerwork covered with hide and suits like old-fashioned combinations made of quilted cotton toughened in brine, so resistant that the Spaniards adopted them as standard battlewear as soon as they could, since it was cooler and lighter than their own metal armour.

The Indians had, moreover, raised ambush to a fine art and had a brilliant intelligence service, which recalls the network of espionage the Ottoman Turks flung over their adversaries, and the resemblance sprang from a similarity in constitution. Turkish and Aztec officials travelled perpetually among the tributary nations, collecting taxes, confirming or modifying pacts and local regulations and naturally spied out military resources and subversive movements. This incessant circulation meant that the Aztecs knew every inch of the territory, to which Cortés had neither map nor even legend to guide him. He was victorious simply because of his courage and his command of arms, his handling of his own troops, his understanding of the nature of political warfare, and beyond everything by his freedom from bad dreams and his sublime objectivity. He had an intellectual quality which can be liked to normal vision, which does not mean average vision; it is indeed rare enough. It is enjoyed by people whose internal eye muscles rotate their two eye axes so competently, the gaze of each eye can be directed towards whatever object has aroused the curiosity of the mind, and the two eyes thus furnish a stereoscopic picture of the object which will supply coherent information about its colour, texture, size, and position. For this process to be successful there has to be harmony between the muscles and the nerves. Cortés was just such a lucky lens.

Doña Marina

The quality of his vision can be judged from an occasion when he looked at a certain woman. He had looked at many women before and was to look at many afterwards. All observers reported that he delighted in their company, and his chaplain says in a curious phrase that he "always gave himself to them." It would be wrong to call him a Don Juan, for that figure left discontent behind him. No lady ever seems to have waved him goodbye with the calm of repletion, and it may be guessed he was impotent. But Cortés was a polygamist who gave the sleekest satisfaction to all his loves except his first wife, who was doomed to misery because she was his wife, a situation thrust on him and her by her ambitious brothers. To marry Cortés was like being told to move into the National Gallery, first removing from its walls all pictures but one. It was, however, in an episode not wholly within the sexual sphere that his most significant encounter with a woman took place. On his first advance towards Aztec territory, he had to fight a battle with the Tabascans, a people which was independent but paid tribute to the Aztec Empire. After he had beaten them, the chiefs sent him placatory gifts, including some gold images representing men and animals, some cloaks, and twenty women, which Bernal Díaz describes with convincing simplicity as "the part of the present which we appreciated most highly." This *bonne bouche, bon sein*, or whatever one chooses to call it, stimulated Cortés to an action apparently naive. He made his chaplain, Father Olmedo, preach the twenty women a sermon on the Christian faith and then baptise them.

The priest cannot have liked the task. Not only was he an intelligent and dignified person, he was a member of the Order of Mercy, a prestigious Spanish brotherhood which organised the ransoming of Christian slaves from their Moslem owners. He cannot but have been shocked by the haste with which these brown women were cleansed of all the sins they had committed till that hour, as well as their share in original sin, and then were precipitated back into guilt the moment after by being distributed to Cortés's captains. Apart from feeling that a sacred rite had been profaned, Father Olmedo must have known the chagrin familiar to housewives who spend hours preparing an elaborate dish only to see their guests gobble it up in a few moments. It is ironic that had the twenty women understood his sermon, they might have shared his distress, for their own religion had familiarised them with the idea of ceremonial purification. But they had heard it only through an interpreter, a sailor accustomed to use his knowledge of the Indian language to enquire into such matters as the nearest maize field or well.

But Cortés was right in prescribing this ludicrous ceremony. He was first of all acting as a good subject of Emperor Charles, he was respecting the papal bull which granted Portugal and Castile the right to exploit the New World on condition that the aborigines were converted to Christianity. He was also very fond of women, and quite fond of Indians; he had always got on well with them in Haiti and Cuba, and on one occasion his Indian servants had rescued him when he was in danger of drowning in a rough sea. As he was a true believer, he would have liked these pretty brown Tabascans to have their share of salvation. Also, he knew his simple-minded conquistadores well enough to suspect that some might handle a woman less tenderly were she unchristened. Possibly at this point, he felt he had done his duty by the twenty and would know no more of them but the mate he had chosen for himself. But there was one girl, who had been given the baptismal name of Marina, so outstanding in her beauty that he had given her to Don Alonso Puertocarrero, a man whom he regarded highly, in much the same spirit that he had given this dear friend a handsome mare when they set sail for Cuba. The conquistadores soon noticed that she was treated with deference by the others, and called her Doña Marina, using a term that then denoted a woman of high rank, and thereby they proved the odd symmetry of their historical situation. They believed they were invading the land of a primitive people simpler in every way than their own, but they were actually in contact with a society just as sophisticated as their own and in some respects identical. For they were correct in their recognition of her social importance. She was in fact a princess belonging to another nation, who had been dumped as a little girl among the Tabascans, because her father had died and her mother had married his successor, and, as she had had children of this second royal marriage, she feared that her daughter's continued presence might raise disputes about the succession. So strong was the caste system that, though the girl was amongst the Tabascans only because she had been repudiated, they still paid her the respect due to her birth.

But she deserved respect on other grounds. She was intelligent and well educated, speaking several Indian languages, including Mayan, which meant that she could communicate with the Spanish sailor Jerónimo de Aguilar, who was Cortés's interpreter and knew only that tongue, and she could also talk with Aztecs and many of their subjugated peoples in Nahuatl, the Aztec language, which had spread like their power. She had also a marvellous double-being. She was on the side of sensual love, she became an exotic sexual symbol to the soldiers, a golden Venus rising from the land of gold; yet she was also their sexless comrade, who enjoyed the adventure of the expedition and rose to its dangers as they did themselves. Above all, she gave them her loyalty, and they knew it and could place their trust in her information and her advice.

Very soon these proved of decisive value. The twenty young women had been tipped out of sin and so enjoyably back into it about five days before Palm Sunday, and on Holy Thursday they arrived at the natural port called San Juan de Ulúa and were visited forthwith by Aztecs in canoes, come from afar to announce that their emperor was to send ambassadors to visit them. These arrived on Easter Day, laden with many presents of gold and textiles and feathers and food, and set up a temporary camp. They were the Aztec governors of a number of recently subjugated districts, and they were accompanied by a large secretariat and domestic staff and an intelligence corps, some of them artists who painted portraits of Cortés, his captains and soldiers, Doña Marina and Aguilar, the horses and, it is to be noted as evidence of their care, the greyhounds, and all their armaments. They stayed for something under three weeks, during which time two other delegations arrived from Tenochtitlán, laden with more and more presents. But they came to show dwindling generosity so far as food was concerned, and one morning the Spaniards awoke to find that their guests, or rather their hosts, had gone away in the night, taking no leave. The discussions so ended must have been subtle and elaborate, for they represented on the Aztec side a highly developed convention. A war for them could not begin until four conferences had been held between the empire and the object of its aggression, at intervals of twenty days (which was a month in the Indian calendar) held over three of their months. On these occasions, which were highly formalised, each side set out its attitude towards the casus belli, which was usually a refusal to trade or to pay tribute or interference with the Aztec traders.

The Spaniards' point of view was therefore not at all incomprehensible to the Aztecs: they were being told that they had better not dare to refuse the Spaniards and must prepare to become their vassals. They could understand these demands, but what they cannot have understood was the reason why they were being made. Their own claim to sovereignty over all surrounding Indian tribes was based on a bogus historical claim; they asserted, falsely but no doubt in good faith, that they were descended from an ancient people, long extinct, who had founded a great civilisation covering all the territory now occupied by these tribes. It would have seemed against all reason that Cortés should make such a claim, when he and his men were obviously strangers in those parts. The Aztecs may well have thought they were a band of maniacs, especially as they kept on asking for gold with this overstressed insistence. It is one of the great jokes of history that they would have made a saner impression had they asked for chocolate. On the other hand, the Aztecs would have a rough understanding of what Cortés meant when he talked about claiming the land by a title given him by the pope in the name of the religion, but they must have been hard put to it to distinguish him as a separate person from Emperor Charles, whom Cortés named as the monarch who was about to become their overlord; for their own emperor was chosen by an electoral college which included representatives of the priesthood, was committed to an endless round of religious observances, was a trained soldier and (like the president of the United States today) commander of the armed forces.

But what were they all doing in someone else's back garden? What they proposed to do next was all too clear. Cortés and Father Olmedo had explained at length the Christian faith and their intention to serve it by dethroning the local gods, and so well had they been understood that the news had gone back by runner to Emperor Montezuma, He-who-rages-like-a-Lord, and he had, by ordering this quietly terrifying departure, shown how a lord rages. That the essential argument was grasped so well as this is a proof that as good a job of interpreting was being done here as one would hope to find today at the U.N. The difficulties were appalling. The Spaniards spoke a beautifully terse and shapely and epigrammatic prose, like the best Latin writing. But the Indians used a repetitive style; perhaps for the purpose of leaving permanent impressions on their hearers, who, as there was no simple method of writing their language, could not hope to refresh their memories by consulting reports or taking notes. They broke their statements into short units, which they framed and reframed in nearly or quite tautological phrases; the effect recalls some German writers, notably Oswald Spengler. The duty of Doña Marina and Aguilar, which they had evidently fulfilled with competence, was to transpose these opposites into each other's terms.

Interpreting was to come into its own again on the day when Bernal Díaz and a comrade were on sentry duty outside the camp and were approached by five Indians of a sort they had not seen before, their lips painted with gold leaf and great blue circles dangling from their ears. Doña Marina and Aguilar were sent for and could not understand their language; but two of them, like Doña Marina, could speak Nahuatl, the Aztec tongue, and to her they explained that they were Totonacs, sent to tell Cortés that their nation was wearied of Aztec tyranny, which exacted from them back-breaking taxes and tribute. This gave Cortés, who had long been incubating a plan to attack the Aztecs with the aid of their discontented vassal states, the first inkling of where he could begin to carry it into effect. In July he went to the Totonac capital Cempoala, a prosperous place with a fat cacique. (This was the word the Spaniards insisted on using for local chiefs, though it is purely Haitian, thus showing the linguistic arrogance of the conqueror, exemplified in our own lifetimes by the German pronunciation adopted by Winston Churchill.) The fat cacique sent out twenty leading citizens to meet Cortés and his troops and give them bunches of scented flowers and make them speeches, and he himself welcomed them in his palace among a crowd of priests and nobles. This subjugated town, one of thirty in the Totonac lands, reminded the conquistadores of Seville, which was conceded by Europeans to be one of their finest cities, and the garments of its notables were magnificent enough to awe even those who had been to court at home.

The fat cacique lodged and fed his guests well and wept privately to Cortés over the ruin that the Aztecs were inflicting on them; and the next morning sent him and his army off to inspect a fortified town of his, twelve hours' journey or so away. It offered no resistance when they entered it next morning, and indeed the leading citizens received them with acclamation, and were joined by the fat cacique, who led them in a chorus of detailed and horrifying accusations against their oppressors. They were having a useful conference in the local palace and discussing means of freeing the territory, when suddenly a messenger entered and the agreeable hosts paled and disappeared. Cortés and his party found themselves quite alone. Through his interpreters, Cortés learned that five Aztec tax collectors had just arrived; and presently these passed through the room on their way to the apartments where they were to be lodged, with their heads in the air and not a look for the strangers. They were magnificent figures, splendidly cloaked, with long hair oiled and piled high on their heads, were attended by servants who fanned them and whisked away the flies, and they were indulging in a practice which the civil servants of today have not yet adopted. They carried roses, which they kept on sniffing, as if taxpayers gave off an offensive odour.

When the Totonacs wanly informed Doña Marina and Aguilar that these officials had been specially sent by the Aztec emperor to censure the tribe for having received and encouraged the Spaniards and to collect a heavy and terrible penalty, Cortés showed his peculiar genius. Keeping away from the tax collectors, he told the Totonacs to imprison them until he himself had informed Emperor Montezuma of the iniquities his officials had been inflicting on his vassals. The Totonacs showed reluctance, but Cortés insisted and managed to get them to insert the tax collectors into a curious machine, a strait-jacket-cum-pillory, made of a pole with straps attached for binding the neck, arms, and legs, of which he happened to have a sufficient number by him; and when one of them put up a fight Cortés directed that he should be subdued by a good beating. The Totonacs were so delighted by the spectacle that they wanted to go a stage further and kill the tax collectors. But this did not fit in with Cortés's plans, and he put the five men under a guard of his own soldiers.

At midnight, he had his men bring two of the prisoners to him in secret, and he asked them with an air of compassionate enquiry, as in the character of the Good Samaritan, who they were and how they had got into this unfortunate position. On hearing that they were Aztec officials and that they had understood that it was under his own orders that they had been arrested and manhandled, he expressed astonishment and horror. Solicitously he managed to get some food for them, and then, charging them with brotherly messages for their emperor, he had them smuggled out of the palace down to the seashore and into a boat with six Spanish sailors ready to sail them to a landing place outside Totonac territory. In the morning, Cortés affected great anger at the inexplicable disappearance of the pair, and when the Totonacs showed renewed eagerness to savour the pleasure of killing tax collectors, he assumed an appearance of ferocity, and, after loading them with chains, he sent them on board one of his ships, where they were kindly received and, as before, surreptitiously sent back to Tenochtitlán. It is to Cortés's credit that this was one occasion when he failed to call in Father Olmedo and engage in a joint exposition of the Christian mysteries.

The sound of laughter rarely travels from century to century; but we can still hear the guffaws of the conquistadores at Cempoala. Everybody was happy. Cortés and his men were delighted at having diddled the Totonacs; and the Totonacs were delighted at having acquired formidable allies in their struggle against the Aztecs, and they may also have been delighted at diddling Cortés and his men. For we know from the Totonac buildings and sculptures that they were a highly civilised people, and all the population in this area was caught in a network of intelligence services. It is very unlikely that they would have remained unaware of such massive horseplay as the nocturnal release of the two tax collectors and the packing off of the whole lot to Tenochtitlán. But their awareness of Cortés's impudence may have made them regard him as an ally really worth having; nobody thought less of Odysseus as a leader because he was cunning. Even the tax collectors must finally have enjoyed the experience. The tale they had to tell the authorities when they got home should have earned them promotion, and they too may have seen through Cortés. By this hilarious adventure he had gained military and political advantages: the Totonacs supported him, and in the heart of Montezuma interest in the white invader was mounting, and his intention to offer him a gentle welcome was confirmed. He had taken his first step towards the possession of Mexico.

The adventure could have been accomplished only through the efficiency of the interpreters. Farce has to be played at top speed; and Cortés could not have understood and planned and acted more rapidly had he been in a country where Spanish was the current language. This must have been the work of Doña Marina. Soon afterwards, the fat cacique presented Cortés with a present of seven young women, for himself and his captains, whom he accepted under the usual condition that they must submit to baptism. The most important of the batch was the cacique's niece, whom Cortés was obliged to take to himself; she was remarkably ugly, and Bernal Díaz records with admiration the chivalrous good humour with which his chief gave his hand to this undesirable prize. But another, who was christened Doña Francisca, was very beautiful and quite important, being the daughter of another cacique, and Cortés gave her to Puertocarrero. But Puertocarrero already possessed Doña Marina. About this time it became evident that some of Cortés's soldiers were impatient at the delay in going into action and at their small share of the presents the Indians gave their leader and were unsettled by the strangeness of the land (which even today is not only foreign, but strange). This discontent was being exploited by the agents of Velázquez, the governor of Cuba, who had sent Cortés to conquer Mexico because of his outstanding genius and for that same reason was jealous of him and could not bear to see him succeeding. Cortés rightly judged that this break in colonial unity made it imperative on him to send a direct report to the Spanish king, Emperor Charles V, to tell him what a great and rich territory was about to be presented to him, did he but give his soldiers time to do the job. This was not a mission for one man, given the uncertainties of subtropical travel and the political situation, so Cortés made two appointments, one quite disingenuous. Francisco de Montejo had been given, for no discernible reason, a disproportionately large share of an Aztec present of gold only a few days before he was told he was to be lucky enough to carry good news to court. Up till then he had been one of the most troublesome partisans of Velázquez. The other was Puertocarrero; and as soon as he had left, Cortés took Doña Marina as his mistress.

These events might give rise to a number of disagreeable interpretations. It might be that Cortés had performed a skilful operation in two parts: the first being the disposition he had made of Doña Francisca, the second being the appointment to the mission. It is never a good thing to steal a friend's mistress or lover, and here there might have been more than a sentimental offence. A woman was being passed from hand to hand, who, had she not been a prize of war, would have been honoured according to her chastity, and if the invaders did not triumph, might again be judged by this standard and be strangled and mutilated after death. It would have been true that her own menfolk had handed her over to the conquistadores, but, as history has shown again and again, men never remember that sort of thing. It might also be fairly suspected that after the events at Cempoala Cortés had formed a cold-blooded resolution to take every means he could to secure the loyalty of a talented interpreter, intelligence officer, and negotiator. It has often been said that this was his motive, and that he proved it by leaving Doña Marina four years later, when Mexico was his and she could do no more for him, and marrying her off to one of his captains, Juan Xaramillo. There is material here for the imagination of sufferings such as afflicted the victims of Byron's multiracial enthusiasms, like Lelia who ended at the bottom of the Bosphorus and Haidée who went mad and died.

But in fact everybody was happy. Of course Cortés's motives were self-seeking and moved by a desire to make sure of Doña Marina's loyalty, of course he was bound to think of his army's safety. But nobody could read Bernal Díaz and doubt that she must have been the most enchanting of bedfellows, and Cortés was not one to pass that up either. It is even to be presumed that his feelings for her were profound. The son she bore him was one of the two illegitimate sons whom he got legitimised by Pope Clement, and whom he invested with the great military order of Saint Iago. But that might have been automatic magnificence, a commandeering of the best for the family. But there is a phrase in a letter written when the boy was half-grown, which speaks of a special tenderness. Certainly Cortés married off Doña Marina when Mexico was his, but the date implies a possible reason. His unloved wife had been dragged out to him by one of the brothers who had forced her, for the sake of their ambition, to convert a cheerful love affair into an awkward marriage, and there had been an uneasy attempt at life together. After three months she died very suddenly, in the night, and the beads round her neck were broken. Perhaps she committed suicide; she had been made wretched by her family's importunities. Perhaps she simply died from a long-standing malady of the lungs, which had incapacitated her in Cuba and had been worsened by the altitude of Tenochtitlán. It gave her choking fits, which would explain the breaking of the beads. We may assume that Cortés did not kill her, given his habitual self-control, for the death happened on an occasion bound to cause scandal, they had had a flare-up of temper at the dinner table that night. He could have killed her silently and covertly. They were in a country where death was a major accomplishment; poisons grew in the fields and were perfectly understood. A Spanish doctor went out to Mexico and worked with the Indians in composing a medicinal herbal, and it proved they knew twelve hundred plants and used many of them for purposes they still serve in modern medicine. If Cortés's wife had evoked in him ill will instead of embarrassment, he could easily have contrived that she had a few days' sickness and troubled him no more.

But Cortés was now the legitimate ruler of Mexico; he was governor and capitan-general of New Spain, as it was then called. There were consequences which his eupepsia had not foreseen. The jealous hatred of him which had been kindled in the heart of Velázquez was now blazing through the whole Spanish colonial administration, the Spanish court, and even through the narrow brain and tepid heart of his sovereign, Emperor Charles V. This young man was already showing the qualities which were to be exercised through the centuries by the Habsburg dynasty and which we can appreciate most fully when we realise that he managed to be the ancestor of both Louis XVI and Marie Antoinette. How the dynasty became the guillotine's best friend can be grasped from the emperor's attitude to the extraordinary present and revelation Cortés had given him, which could be paralleled in our day if the moon proved to be studded with cities as beautiful as Venice and could send back by astronaut the means of ending all our poverty. Charles V's only reaction to finding Mexico in his hands was to suspect that Cortés had got too big for his boots. But the Habsburgs had no other reaction to any gallant behaviour, or indeed, to any behaviour.

They formed the same suspicion about the Slavs who saved their territory (and all Europe) from the Turks, about the Protestants, about the papacy, about the Jesuits, and finally about the whole of mankind, after which they lost spirit and staged the slow suicide of nineteenth-century Austria. Judgment Day will seem to the Habsburgs only a case of tight boots in a quarter which they had not previously suspected. Into the file which was soon stuffed with false accusations of Cortés's corruption, disloyalty, and incompetence, there was presently slipped the accusation that he had murdered his wife. As soon as Cortés had word of it he was under a pressing necessity to dissociate himself from Doña Marina, who was so well known to be his mistress that they called him by her name. They made of Marina Malina, since they could not pronounce the letter "r" any more than the Chinese, and they added "Itzin" to it, which was an honorific, and they called him Mr. Malintzin. It was time she was married off.

But the time and the place of her marriage prove it no abandonment. With touching simplicity Cortés tried to discount the mean decriers of his glory by piling up more evidence as to his title to be considered glorious. He set out on the great and profitless, but none the less great for that, expedition for Honduras, in the hope of making his emperor another gift equal to Mexico and compelling him to gratitude. He and his forces, which included three thousand Indian troops, went down through Mexico to the south, accompanied by Cuauhtémoc, the rightful but dethroned Aztec emperor, his cousin, the Prince of Tacuba, and several other chiefs, for fear they should rise were they left behind; a squad of priests, including some theologians to preach those sermons about the Christian mysteries; a physician and a surgeon; a large domestic staff, including a butler of the highest rank and a confectioner and persons in charge of a large service of gold and silver plate; a stage dancer (who was to die in the jungle), a puppet-player and juggler; and ten herdsmen for a large drove of swine. Two hundred miles or so south of Tenochtitlán, within sight of Orizaba, the extinct volcano called by the Indians Star Peak because the snow round its crater is so brilliant and so symmetrical, the expedition paused while two of its members got married: Doña Marina and Xaramillo. They had stopped there because this was the territory of her noble family who had abandoned her to the Tabascans. The event is chronicled by Bernal Díaz, who might well have regarded it with a jaundiced eye, as he was one of the conquistadores who had settled in the district to farm for the rest of their life, and now found themselves suddenly visited by Cortés and required *manu militari* to start off on a fifteen-hundred-mile trek which was expected to last at least two and a half years, for some political reason far from clear to them. Yet he makes it obvious that this was a thoroughly happy wedding, with nobody feeling deserted, and the bride more contented, or contented in a rather more inclusive way than is usual.

> Doña Marina had by her birth a universal influence and consequence through these countries; she was beautiful, her manners were candid, her wit was ready, and she had an abundance of being. She was an accomplished linguist and was of the greatest usefulness to Cortés, whom she accompanied everywhere. I was acquainted with her mother and her half-brother, who was by the time we met a grown man. The two governed their nation together, the lady's second husband being dead. They were both baptised, the mother by the name of Martha, the son by the name of Lazarus. When Cortés was passing through the district and had summoned all the chiefs to meet him, they were there. Doña Marina had always told me she was of that province, and the truth declared itself for she was very like her mother, and indeed, her mother instantly recognised her. Then both she and her son were terrified, thinking that they were sent for to be put to death, and they cried bitterly. But Doña Marina dried their tears, saying that she forgave them, and though they had sent her from their rightful place, no doubt they could not have done anything else at the time, and that all had worked out well. She thanked God, who had taken her away from the worship of idols to the true church, and had sent her a son by her lord and master Cortés, and given her a fine cavalier like Xaramillo for a husband, and she said she would rather be as she was than be the sovereign of all the tribes of Mexico. All this I heard with my own ears and swear it is true. Amen. At parting she gave them much gold, and sent them on their way.

Eden must have been like this before the Fall. Yet a more thoroughly fallen man than Cortés, and one determined to fall as often as possible, can hardly be imagined. He was the opposite of innocence. But he had no bad dreams about sex.

Nor had he any bad dreams about cruelty. He could be merciless. He hacked off the hands of the Indian spies who infiltrated his camp: there was a trick Europe had learned from Islam about compressing the stumps so that the man did not die. He was simply unable to earn a living or look after his own needs, for ever after. Also Cortés let Cuauhtémoc be put to the torture when Tenochtitlán had fallen, and he would not tell his captors the hiding place of the royal treasure; and later, on this same trek down to Honduras, Cuauhtémoc and the Prince of Tacuba were killed on his orders. But each time Cortés acted to save his own life. On the first occasion his conquistadores were half-mad with the horrors of their triumph and were near mutiny-point in their disappointment over the loot. The second time, if Cuauhtémoc and his cousin had chosen to revolt, he and every Spaniard, not only of the expedition but everywhere in Mexico, were doomed. It is to be remembered that there were three thousand Indians in the party, and only a few hundred Spaniards, who were feeling the shortage of food, more acute here than in any part of Mexico they had yet explored. Always when Cortés committed such deeds as these it was for the sake of self-preservation, never to derive disgusting pleasure from inflicting pain. Bernal Díaz tells us:

> Cortés caused a cross to be fixed in a large cottonwood tree close of the natives' temple, which joined to the building where he had made his quarters. He was at this time very irritable and depressed, he was vexed by the obstacles and accidents he had encountered in his expedition, and his conscience reproached him with the death of Cuauhtémoc. He was so harried by remorse that he could not lie in his bed at night, and got up in the dark to walk about, and once he strayed into the temple and went into a sort of shrine where some of the idols were worshipped. There he missed his way and fell down to a lower floor twelve feet below, cutting and bruising his head severely. This accident he tried to conceal, saying nothing about his suffering, and letting his injuries cure themselves as they could.

He rejected the sadistic nightmare (which could not be said of some of his countrymen) and also those dreams which are so subtle and so fantastic that they appear no more significant than the whirls of light we see behind our lids when we close our eyes, and this made him immune to Indian magic, which was very real.

Religion and Sorcery

The Aztec civilisation was permeated with a sense of the supernatural. This might seem surprising, for the Mesoamerican civilisation was strong on its scientific and technological and administrative sides. It excelled in architecture, in medicine, in astronomy, in agriculture, in many processes serving art and industry, and in the organisation of the military and civil services. They had a lucky start on the rational way, for two of the greater Indian peoples, the Aztecs and the Mayans (who were their superiors) had numeral systems which are quick and easy and even amusing to master today, and they had mounted from there to austerer slopes, reaching quite high levels on the astronomical field, to points where they could work out such matters as the length of the lunar month, which they alleged was 29.53020 days, as against our own estimate of 29.53059 days. Their superstitions helped them on their way in this particular approach to reality, for they were of opinion, as many men before and since, that the sun was the creator of the universe.

Nobody can call this belief illogical. Nothing exists unless it is made; natural objects, such as trees, are not made by man; this left primitive man convinced, like Joyce Kilmer, that it takes God to make a tree. The being who makes trees and mountains and rivers does not mix with men. He cannot be found on earth. Nobody ever meets him. Then where is he? In the sky, obviously. There is no other place. If we look for this being, we must search the sky by day, for plainly he must be interested in man, since he made our world, and hardly anything interesting happens by night except sexual intercourse. The nocturnal activities of the Mesoamericans must have been severely limited, for they got their lighting and heating only from resinous timber, which they used as torches or piled up in braziers. Royalty used a special sort of pine which gave off no smoke, and had mobile fire-screens (which appear not to have been known at that time in Europe) to ward off the excessive heat that comes when a wood fire burns up. But the lesser Indian must have coughed, felt alternately chilled and grilled, got tired of fetching logs, and gone to bed, and assumed that his maker would do the same. But there was nothing in the daylit sky except the sun. Therefore the sun must be the God who made the world. Nobody need be ashamed of following that line of reasoning. It is of the same order of thought that has led younger man to some of his most sophisticated discoveries.

From there the Indians went on with a peculiar dourness. Since life is no laughing matter, mankind assumes that God is solemn and this assumption became grim indeed in Mesoamerican hands. Though there are some agreeable experiences, they hesitated to ascribe this to their ferocious creator, and invented deities who could be allowed to be light-minded in their creativeness. There were the corn goddesses, whom they thanked for maize, springtime, twin births, and such felicity; and gods whom they thanked for flowers, youthful strength, and the joys of feasting. But these were counterbalanced by disagreeable experiences: for no fault a man got a cut in his foot and it swelled and matter exuded, another innocent man went blind. As everyone wants to believe the God responsible for this universe to be on a long haul amiable, he could not be charged with these enormities, so minor gods had to be invented to take the blame, and so they were, in numbers: but again we cannot bear to believe that the controllers of our destiny are cruel, so they were given compensatory virtues. Xipe Toltec, a most bloodthirsty god, the Flayed Lord, inflicted all eye disease, but was also the embodiment of the maize seed when it sends out its green shoot and, in order to become human, perishes itself.

Possibly, primitive man considers, the gods mean no harm, possibly they want us to do something which we are not doing, and they are so far off, up in the sky, that it is difficult to communicate. So he looked at the night sky, since there is nothing in the day sky but the sun, and there he sees the stars, which are either the minor deities or their means of communication, or a bit of both; but sidereal certainties come rarely. There has to be some deductive work done here on earth. Since we have displeased the gods by conduct which seems to us reasonable, we can perhaps please them by doing what is, according to our standards, unreasonable; and now we have achieved magic. Lévi-Strauss has said that "religion consists of a humanisation of natural laws, and magic is a naturalisation of human actions, as if they were an integral part of physical determinism." He is right about religion, as even the religious would concede. But he deals incompletely with magic, for that must consist of inhuman actions. All religious practice is directed towards an invisible and omnipotent spiritual intelligence, which, as often as not, refuses to acknowledge the attention by giving happiness to the good or to punish evil. Pure religion hammers on with the belief that this refusal is only temporary, and that in the end God will prove to be on the side of the angels. Magic gives up. It assumes that as God will not listen to sense, what he is waiting for is nonsense: that he lives in the state of being presented to us in the "shaggy-dog" type of story, where, if a guest at a dinner party empties a bowl of salad over his head it is taken as valid excuse that he thought it was spinach. A magical rite may be pleasing or unpleasing, beautiful or disgusting, a garland of flowers cast down in a strange place, or a newborn child's gut, but it must be front to back, upside down, meaningless. It must contain within itself the threat of producing no effect whatsoever in our universe, and the promise of producing an effect in the other universe, which was obviously the opposite of ours. Magic is, in fact, a shaggy-god story.

The Aztec Church covered a vast range of religion and all kinds of magical practices, excluding only the more criminal of forms, such as mass robbery by magicians, who would paralyse a family by charms (but probably by using some alkaloid like curare) and under their helpless eyes strip their house of all its contents. The church was one of the three main estates, which served and exploited and administered the empire, the others being the army and the civil service. In two hundred years, on the slender basis of bits and pieces of tradition left by past civilisations in that area, these nomads had created a complex society with institutions similar to those which European states have produced after a run of a thousand years or more. It helped its people through hard times like the modern British and French welfare states, and it dropped unworthy members of its lower castes, as Byzantium and the early Slav civilisations did; and in its broad outlines it suggests a microcosm of tsarist Russia, with its autocratic ruler, its military aristocracy, its bureaucracy, its irregular manifestations of democracy in local government, and its nationalist and aesthetically impressive state church, which oscillated between embarrassing servility and iron integrity.

But the Aztec ecclesiastical organisation has many other parallels nearer our own day. The heads of the state were the Chief of Men, an official dealing with such external matters as war and treaties, who often conducted religious services, and the Snake Woman, who was not a woman but was called after the fertility goddess and dealt with the internal affairs of the nation, including its religious life. But the real heads of the church were two high priests, the Plumed Serpents; of whom one, as it might be the Archbishop of Canterbury, served the God of War, Hummingbird of the South, and the Archbishop of York served the God of the Rain, Tlaloc, He-who-covers-the-ground. Under them were many bishops, attached not to dioceses but to particular gods, whose temples they supervised in all districts, while others took care of particular administrative responsibilities. The vicar-general bore a title which startles by its suggestion that the whole thing was a fake: "the honourable Mexican in charge of the gods." Another official kept the liturgy straight, another supervised the ecclesiastical colleges, and there was a treasurer with very heavy duties, for the wealth of the church was enormous, including the produce of many villages, and this had to be safely stored and dispensed for the maintenance of the priesthood, the poor, the aged, and the sick, including the hospital inmates, and as relief in times of famine and flood. The routine was in fact much as it is today in the Vatican or Lambeth Palace, and the Aztecs do not suffer by comparison. These priests were supposed to be men of intelligence and ascetic habit, killing the selves within them and living only for love of God and man, and the Catholic priests who took over the territory from them were of opinion that at least the higher clergy honoured their obligations.

No doubt there were bad priests, silly priests, priests who were no good for anything but blowing horns and beating drums. But assuredly the Aztec priesthood performed with distinction the task its culture had set it, in looking at the skies for what all cultures desire, an assurance that creation has a meaning favourable to man; but hopeless confusion was introduced by magic. In the latter half of September it was understood that the gods returned from a temporary absence and dwelt among the Aztecs for a time; a myth which dramatises the harvest. All through the nights the Plumed Serpents and two high ecclesiastics kept watch on the platform at the top of the temple pyramid in the heart of Tenochtitlán, kneeling round a bowl filled with fine-ground white maize, till the time when a footprint appeared in the flour. This was the sign that the first god had arrived, that the natural process on which man depends had not been suspended, that the foundation of life stood firm. The sign never failed to appear. Out went the proclamation of the four men that they had seen it, up went the cries of joy from the million people in the streets, the fires blazed, the dancing began.

Consider the complicated situation of those four men: the two Plumed Serpents jointly constituted an Aztec Astronomer Royal, and it is probable that both the other priests were conscientious scientists also. They were all exemplary in conduct, or the emperor would have dismissed them, and it can be assumed that in any given circumstances they would find it natural to tell the truth. Did they really see the footprint in the flour? Against the instinctive answer it has to be put that in preparation for this vigil they had long fasted and abstained from sleep, and most of us would be light-headed if we had sat for hours under the blazing Mexican stars with the altitude setting the blood drumming in our ears. It is also true that among the medicinal plants used by the Aztecs were the mushroom and the buds of the cactus peyotl, which produce hallucinations. It is also true that the most sceptical of men, if he found himself called to keep such a vigil, might think it served the public interest best not to withhold the guarantee of food for another year. But whether they told the truth, or whether they lied and thought they told the truth, or whether they lied and knew it, they were spread-eagled on a torturing occasion, for the god that left his footprint in the flour deserved no worship by our human standards. He was Tezcatlipoca, Smokey Mirror, whose name refers to the circles of black polished obsidian in which magicians saw clouds which dissolved into visions of the future. He was a conjuror, a fortune-teller, a trickster, he had brought the world into being by palming it out of the waters, he was Lucifer never challenged by a beneficent God, never defeated, never thrown out to the pit, but left to range free, under his other name Titluacan, He-who-is-at-the-shoulder, he who stands beside every human being and at the decisive moment whispers into his ear counsels of cruelty.

Here we see the crucial hardship of Aztec religion: too obstinate a determination to make the universe consistent. They lacked what Keats declared to be the necessary prerequisite of greatness, Negative Capability, the capacity for being in uncertainties, mysteries, doubts, without any irritable reaching after fact and reason. This quality the great religions of the world have possessed, as witness the vagueness of the Christian doctrine of the Atonement. Here in this magical rite, the Aztecs showed themselves altogether too busy. They had identified Flash-Harry cheating malice as a force in life and had called it Tezcatlipoca, and then bestowed a personality on that name; and then, appalled by what they had created, tried to confer on him pleasant attributes, as one might try to see the good side of an employer for whom, whether one likes it or not, one has to work. So the Aztecs contrived this situation of the footprint in the flour, as if to say, "Smokey Mirror has his good points, he brings us the harvest," as an employee, trying to soften his loathing of his boss, might say, "Well, he always sends us a turkey at Christmas." But all that did was to tarnish the innocent harvest with guilt by association; and indeed they so often smeared the earth with divine sinfulness that, in spite of their love of beauty, they were grimly puritan. It is relevant to remember certain photographs which have disturbed all of us who are middle-aged or more than that: photographs which showed tyrants, such as Hitler or Stalin, smiling and bending to receive bunches of flowers offered them by little children. These always caused a sense of despair. These men were permitted to rule by their communities because they were ruthless. Now these communities and these rulers were trying to get rid of the guilt of ruthlessness by showing that the rulers were not wholly bad, they loved flowers and children. But a bunch of roses and a child of five cannot wipe out mass murders; and the association is as unpleasing as the pornograph which shifts the field of sex from pleasure to pain.

But the Aztecs tried many devices to cope with the troubles arising from too precise a recognition of the prime forces of life: most notably a huge secondary calendar they erected on the substructure of the primary calendar they needed for agricultural purposes. They had the same year of three hundred and sixty-five days as we have, which they divided into eighteen months of twenty days, each under the protection of gods roughly appropriate to the season and certain others not related to time, eternal presences such as Fire. This left five days over, which were treated both as the *dies non juridici* of our legal systems and a Catholic Lent. It seems, though we do not know the details, that they adjusted these five days at certain periods as we use leap year, to smooth out the discrepancy arising from the fact that the real length of the solar year is three hundred and sixty-five and a quarter days. So far so good. But they had another year, which ran concurrently with the agricultural year, known as the Count of Fate, and seems to have existed purely for magical purposes; and this was split into two sequences of months which also ran concurrently. In one there were thirteen months of twenty days, each of which had its own name, and in the other were twenty months of thirteen days, each of which had its own number; and both name and number had quite distinct significances regarding bad luck and good luck, which affected people born on the relevant day and actions performed during it.

The importance of this triple calendar was that it was regarded as an absolute determinant of the fate of society and of every individual born within that society. It was assumed that the gods were really anxious to befriend mortals, but reasonably enough they only retained this good will if mortal behaviour was of a sort divinity could approve; and the standards were supposed to lie clear under mortal eyes provided they studied the calendar and its implications. That study was extremely complex. For the coexistence of the three sequences of different lengths meant that every day had three magical aspects and that these permutations were repeated only once during a cycle which ended when there had been fifty-two agricultural years and seventy-three magical years, having thus achieved 18,980 days. There was a fourth magical significance in the relation of the day to this fifty-two-year cycle. Not only the Aztecs but the whole Mesoamerican culture was in the grip of this rigid system.

Every part of life had to be put through this giant interpretation machine. If a man wanted to settle a day for his daughter's wedding, he had to consider the four magical significances of the day, and these would be considered in connection with the eight magical significances of the birthdays of the bride and the groom. Of course it was necessary to consult a temple-trained expert. The need for professional guidance became more imperative in the case of long-term plans. If one of the merchant class, a pochteca, was proposing a journey to another part of the isthmus which might take him months or years, he might be unable to calculate how the dates in the three series matched up. He might not know if the day he meant to arrive in important territory was Grass of

Penance 13 or Serpent 1: in the one case it was very perilous, in the other there was a challenging opportunity. The educated classes were of course able to avail themselves of the best advice, but this created fresh problems. The principles guiding the interpretation of the calendar were laid down in sacred books, inscribed in picture-writing on large pieces of vellum and bark which were joined and folded in long strips like a screen and kept in the temples, but as new generations brought in new material, other principles emerged and were adopted in the day-to-day practice of the priesthood. This must have left the laity, which is by definition at a disadvantage before the professional, even more dazed—as dazed as the growth of administrative law in the last half-century has left the British public. But the peasants, particularly in the remoter villages, must have suffered worse than that confusion. They must have passed their lives in fear and frustration and social resentment, dreading lest they brought on themselves ruin and damnation which they could have averted, had they been born in a different caste. The situation recalls the harassment of our own Western world by our complicated tax structures, exacerbated by cruder religious apprehensions than prevail among us today. The parallel would be close only if one imagined a taxpayer with a large income drawn from mixed holdings, some of them foreign, who believed that if he did not make an accurate return to the Inland Revenue he would be committing the Sin against the Holy Ghost.

But there are more parallels between our world and theirs than that. A large part of the Aztec population was withdrawn from productive labour to deal with the calendar and magical processes in the interests of the state (which stood or fell by its religion) and the public, just as a large part of our white-collar population is withdrawn from productive work to deal with our tax laws and the payment of taxes, in the interests of either the government or the taxpayers. The higher grades of the Aztec effort were accorded the highest respect, like the officials in the British and American Treasury Departments and the great tax lawyers, but the lower grades were treated with the impatient dislike felt by the public for the lesser ornaments of Inland Revenue and unsuccessful tax experts. The Aztec legends represent chiefs as laying about their priests who were beneath the level where the chief function was astronomical observation and who practised the routine of divination, should these venture to come up with a prophecy which was discouraging. In a Franciscan account of a miracle play composed and acted by Indians at Jalisco in 1587, it is noted that a scene showing Herod roughhousing his soothsayers was specially vigorous and assured, as if this was an idea they understood. Probably many such violent incidents occurred because of the lack of vocation by which a high proportion of professional magicians must have been handicapped, since boys born on certain days were considered under a divine obligation to join the profession, no matter how few occult gifts they had, or power to pretend they had them. If such were forced into competition with professional rivals of superior talent, the consequences might be serious. Montezuma's contemporaries believed that after Cortés had landed, the priests who watched the night skies from Smokey Mirror's pyramid in Tenochtitlán (and who would certainly have had surreptitious access to the reports of the Aztec intelligence force) came to the emperor and reported that at midnight they had seen a column of luminous smoke traversing the Valley of Mexico like a giant man that touched the sky. The next night Montezuma kept vigil with them and, one way or another, saw the great misty invader for himself and then sent for the court corps of magicians and necromancers and asked them what they had seen. Taken by surprise, they answered "Nothing at all" and were all strangled. Again there are parallel situations in our own society. The economic theorist, with ample leisure to collect information over a broad field, can foresee the trends of events, such as lead to a rise in unemployment. The executives responsible for the policy of an industrial corporation are more likely to err, since they have to cope with the problems directly relative to their product and its market; and they are likely to err badly and be put off the board of directors if they were appointed because of some hereditary or social advantage, comparable to being born on a lucky day.

It is a heavy charge against any social institution that it diverts able people from productive work, and Aztec magic was open to that charge. Montezuma was a man of fine natural endowments which had been finely developed. He was a good archer, a good swimmer, a good warrior, a good administrator, and, in spite of his summary way with magicians and necromancers, a lover of virtue and a father to his people, so far as their standards permitted him. Yet because of Smokey Mirror and all he stood for in the Aztec faith, Montezuma must have been cumbered at every turn by involvement with the evil, the disgusting, the trivial. How he must have been degraded, frustrated, bored by what he was obliged to patronise is shown by an experience that befell Cortés and his men when they were on their way to Tlaxcala. They had to go through a pinewood, and there they found that the track was crossed and recrossed by threads of cactus filaments with scraps of cactus fibre, scratched with odd markings. These were charms laid by the magicians of Tlaxcala to bar the way back to the men and the horses. But all the same Montezuma was a man of great nobility, who never gave rein to the rage and envy and desire for vengeance he must have felt against the invaders and never spoke a word that shamed himself, or, what was a great triumph, Cortés; and he would himself have claimed that it was his religion which exalted his spirit. There may be substance to that claim.

Smokey Mirror was not the only Aztec god. Supreme above the theogony were the god and goddess, who were perhaps one, Ometecuhtli, the Lord of Duality, and Omecíhuatl, the Lady of Duality. They lived on the heights of the universe, in the thirteenth heaven, "where the air is very cold, delicate, and ideal," and they were life and death, light and darkness, male and female, rest and motion, order and disorder, sound and silence, but it would have been coarse and presumptuous to build a temple to them, for though they were responsible for all earthly things, they were immaterial. They created the living and the dead, the day and the night, the man and the woman, the sleeper and the dancer, the growing maize and the sprawling bindweed, the song and the dumbmouth and the hushed wind, but these were brought into the world by the rhythm which pulsed through them or which they were. This Aztec conception recalls Louis de Broglie's ascription of wave nature to ponderable particles, which he presented to the world because he was infatuated with its intellectual beauty, which delighted his colleagues, so that they proceeded on the work which proved it true. The dual divinity brings to mind also the Pleiades, who are recognisably several yet seem one knot of light and must be stars but seem as little dense as moonbeams; and indeed the Aztecs, like many other peoples all over the world, were fascinated by this group, and they tried to build a bridge between them and their own life by using the position of the constellation as a marker for the beginning of each fifty-two-year cycle. It could well be that the contemplation of such eternal objects, or rather of such objects as seem to give time a significance, gave Montezuma the nobility we notice and that Cortés and the captains noticed. But there was also a general service performed by such a system, even by its magical aspect.

Any system which compels the study of a large group of phenomena by a large number of people has its achievement. Aztec religion was so pertinacious in studying the whole Aztec environment that it had to acquire much information and start many of those attempts to draw deductions from information which are known as abstract ideas. Even this was bound to be to some extent time wasted, for magic being what it is—an appeal to nonsense that it should find significance where sense has found none. It was inevitable that there should be much futile contemplation of those coincidences which abound in nature but are nature's mild delirium. A charming example of these is contained in a letter published in the journal *Nature* in 1940 and often quoted by Professor Michael Polanyi, which set out the gestation periods of various animals, including the English rabbit and pig, the Caracul sheep, the Black Forest goat and a Swiss variety of the same animal and an Abyssinian cow, and pointed out that these, measured in days, are all multiples of the number *pi* (3.142 . . .); yet there can be no possible connection between the pregnancies of our four-footed sisters and the ratio of a circumference of a circle to its diameter. Many Aztecs must have got trapped in such blind alleys of fact, considering now a migration of horned owls from a district where shortly afterwards the principal temple was struck by lightning, now an epidemic breaking out under skies which had recently been ornamented by an unusual number of solar halos. But the Aztecs' constant vigilance over their environment not only gave them a wealth of knowledge on such subjects as botany and agriculture, it gave breadth and subtlety to their understanding of human nature.

What they had to understand was human nature in a state of more acute apprehension than is our common lot. Montezuma was head of a state which believed itself doomed, not because of any quirk of morbidity, but in a sober reading of the form-book. The Spaniards' country had been swept across by several peoples, by the Phoenicians, the Greeks, the Celts, the Romans, the Visigoths, the Arabs, but this did not deliver the Spanish spirit over to pessimism, for all these invaders had either gone away or had been absorbed into the enduring Iberian population. The Spanish spirit had indeed just been lifted up by history to the heights of optimism, since they had sent the Arabs, so well qualified to stay, packing back to Africa. There was no fear in the heart of Cortés and his men that nations should die like individuals. But the Aztecs sent out many travellers over the isthmus and all returned with stories of great cities taken by the forests for their own; and legends told them the histories of these fallen cultures, getting the details wrong but the intimidating fact of final disaster right, and the lesson was pointed by the presence among their own population of a craftsman class whose crafts were an inheritance from a superior and vanished nation.

The Aztecs had no reason to suppose that they were any more likely to escape extinction than their predecessors, and they inscribed their anxiety on their calendar. They did not trouble to provide any but indirect clues for distinguishing any one of their fifty-two-year cycles from any other. It is as if we never bothered to number our centuries, and the date when Napoleon went to Elba was liable to be confused with the date of the outbreak of the First World War because both were simply 14. A state would hardly set a time system with such a defect unless it had had a short run and did not expect a long one. There is also an oddly repetitive chiliastic sense of disaster in the larger schemes of time within the system. Every fifty-two-year cycle ended in a moment of crisis when it was put to the people that the existence of the whole universe hung by a thread, and that thread might break. The Aztec people was dumb with fear lest the sun should set and never rise again. All over the country the fires were extinguished, sacred and domestic, and the slopes of all mountains in the Valley of Mexico were covered with crowds, who watched while the priests on the peak kept their eyes on the Pleiades as that knot of light mounted to the zenith. If it should halt and hang there, then the framework of the universe would dissolve, and a horde of monsters would charge from outer space and devour mankind. The Pleiades did not halt. After the performance of some repulsive ceremonies, the priests sparked a new flame from stone by means of a special holy instrument, and runners kindled their torches at the newborn spark and ran down to the valley to awaken heat and light again. This occasion represents the Aztecs at their worst. Nothing in our environment could lead a sensible man to suppose that the universe runs any special risk at the end of fifty-two years, and, what is more, a number of Aztecs were more than sensible enough to be aware that this is so.

But the general temporal landscape is more respectable. There was an abstract god above all gods, even the immaterial of them, and this was cosmic change, which conserved the old and made the universe anew, even casting out old gods and bringing in strange ones. Even so, among the Romans, Chronos was god above the gods. The sun itself was not eternal and was subject to change, and avatars of the sun gave their names to different and dissimilar ages. It is not known exactly whether there have been four or five suns, or how long they lasted, or by what name they were known, but each is nailed to a sense of catastrophe. The impression is of a past where man rose again and again to certain heights of civilisation and was hurled back by floods (which may well have happened in a country where instruments have recorded a rainfall in certain areas of ten feet a year) and earthquakes (also probable where volcanoes raise their head by the score) and high winds (also probable in the hurricane area). There are also allusions to military events, to conquest by a race of giants (who may have been very strong and tall men, like the African Masai, or, if there have been certain drastic geophysical changes, simply giants), and to the conversion of men into monkeys, which may be a chauvinist account of invaders of a lower culture. There may be very little invention or even distortion in these memories. To arrive at the Mesoamerican state of mind, read the Book of Revelation and consider what it would be like to have been already four times through the experiences there described, to have heard four times the loud voice crying to the birds in high heaven, "Come and be gathered together unto the great supper of God, that you may eat the flesh of kings, and the flesh of mighty men, and the flesh of all men, both free and bond," and to know no reason why that loud voice should not speak again.

Quetzalcoatl

So it was that Montezuma, after receiving the reports of his intelligence corps on Cortés, "could neither eat nor sleep, nor put his mind to anything, but was very wretched and sighed continually and took no pleasure in any pastime and kept on saying, 'What is to become of us?' His heart hurt him, and he prayed to the gods, 'Where do I go? How do I escape?'" He had known that doom was at hand as soon as he had heard that curious wooden towers had been seen balancing on the waves of the sea and that white men had climbed out of them and got into curiously shaped canoes and made their way through the surf to the land. The threatened doom might fulfil one of two prophecies. The first had foreseen a landing party of men with light skins who would dominate the country. The second was on a cosmic scale. It was believed that some day there would return from exile the great god Quetzalcoatl, the Plumed Serpent, who had left his people to go out to sea on a raft of serpents towards the east and would some day come back with his back to the east. This return was to the Aztecs as the promised coming of the Messiah. Quetzalcoatl was God and Man. He was the god of the Wind; he was the god who is one in two in one, the planet Venus which is the morning and the evening star; he was glorious by nature and by regal ornament, and he was the god of tender mercy and defeat. To be born on his day was to be unworldly and a wanderer and a failure. "Even though the man born on Quetzalcoatl's day became a great warrior, he would be esteemed poorly and would be admitted into no good company." But this was not doom. If Quetzalcoatl denied triumph with one hand he gave better than triumph with his other hand. He is alone among the gods and goddesses of the old Mexican faith in holding out such promises as were made to us in the Sermon on the Mount. Some of those gods and goddesses were joyful, like the Prince of Flowers and the Maize Princess, but only in Quetzalcoatl is there sweetness. Also, though his insistence on temporal royalty is firm and his trappings were gorgeous, his cult seems to confer a value on humility.

Quetzalcoatl's meaning as a god is obviously a superstructure built on what he was as a man, but though enough remains of the superstructure to leave an emotional impress on the present, the truth about his mortality has got sunk in the past. It would appear that at some time there was a ruler in the isthmus so greatly loved and respected that he was not only awarded divine honours by his own dynastic machine but was believed by his people to be a god, and that the god he himself worshipped, the Plumed Serpent. As later rulers adopted his name, there is a confused situation which only the archaeologist can examine with profit. The amateur had better confine his attention to the saga of Quetzalcoatl as it was taken down by Father Bernardino de Sahagún, that great man, who arrived in Mexico nine years after the conquest and patiently collected every scrap of Indian tradition he could find, sometimes under the discouragement of the Spanish authorities, till his death forty-one years later. What he gathered of Quetzalcoatl's saga is to be found, so far as the English reader is concerned, most easily in *The Gods of Mexico*, a learned and satisfying book, infatuated with its subject, by Mr. C. A. Burland, till lately an official of the Mesoamerican Department of the British Museum. From him we learn that Quetzalcoatl was the monarch of a civilisation remembered by the Aztecs as superior to their own in wealth and contentment as well as in artistic and technological achievement. This need not be dismissed as the familiar illusion of a past Golden Age. It is the opinion of archaeologists that if Cortés had landed a thousand years earlier he would have found splendours far brighter than those that dazzled him; the Mayans were then passing through their great classic age, the Teotihuacán civilisation was in flower, the Toltecs were in bud. The saga speaks of Quetzalcoatl's palaces, which were unfortunately called by the sort of names we now associate with Chinese restaurants, the Jade House, the Golden House, the Shell House, the Coral House, the Turquoise House, but then deserved their name; and from these were governed a people who wanted for nothing. By a curious detail it is stated that in those days even cotton was obliging, coming up from seed in colours ranging from crimson to "coyote." There was everything that later ages were to think of as rare treasure, but none of it cost very much. This earthly paradise was destroyed by Smokey Mirror, the Shadow, He-who-is-at-the-shoulder, the opposite of the Plumed Serpent, who was candour and light and virtue.

The evil power manifested itself in three magicians, each bearing a name under which Smokey Mirror was worshipped, who came to the palace of the Plumed Serpent when he was sick and worked their destructive magic on him through an intoxicating drink made from the cactus. The Aztecs had a great fear of drunkenness. This potion was a mellowing, cheating poison, and the saga then turns into an account of death seen from the solipsist point of view, which holds that all we know is that there is nothing but the self, and that the world is a construction of the self's sensory experiences, which if the self perishes must perish too. Quetzalcoatl is now shown us as leaving the delights of his kingdom, the delights are shown as ceasing to exist. His palaces were burned down, his treasures were buried under the earth, his famous groves of different varieties of flowering cocoa trees became scrub. The air had been full of beautiful birds, of quetzals and firebirds and roseate spoonbills and many songbirds, and they all flew away. Then Quetzalcoatl lost all the craftsmanship that had been his as the king of a craftsman people. It simply passed out of him and into the magicians, who thereafter knew all that he had known about gem-cutting and painting and sculpture and woodcarving and feather-weaving and the art of the goldsmith and the silversmith. But it was Quetzalcoatl himself who cast all his jewels into a spring. An old person has his death thrust on him, but when he realises it he resigns himself, he consents.

Travelling towards the sea, he climbed a pass between a volcano and a range of snow mountains, and here "all the pages of Quetzalcoatl, who were the sacred cripples and hunchbacks, who had accompanied him hitherto, died from the cold in the wind and the snowstorms which blew between the two mountains. Quetzalcoatl felt great sorrow. He wept bitterly and made up songs to their memory." That is a curiously acute vision of old age. The issues of life seem bleaker than before, it seems impossible that it has been possible to live so long. One's friends are crippled and deformed by their struggles with life's inclemency, but they appear as sacred, having endured this martyrdom, and their death is the only legitimate reason for tears. All the rest seems a fuss about nothing. When Quetzalcoatl had suffered that grief he changed. As he drew nearer the coast, he took up a cotton tree and cast it like a javelin through another tree, thus forming a cross. He stopped and built some mansions under the ground. When he came to the sea he walked on the water. He allowed it to be understood that he would return from where he was going on his raft of serpents. Perhaps he and his raft were burned as he sailed into the rising sun; the star which was his heart and in a sense himself vanished for nine days while he descended into the underworld, but shone again, prophecy and proof of his second coming. One can imagine, if one has a Manichaean cast of mind and could think of Christ not as the creator but as a force which aims at penetrating the gross matter of creation with his light, that here he attempted a manifestation and was defeated by the local grossness; or one can imagine that a rumour of Christianity spread to Mesoamerica across the Pacific from Asia, but this theory is hardly easier to accept, in view of the absence of proof of any but pre-Christian communication; or one can think that all over the world and in all ages men may dream the same dreams, the least, insignificant detail of which must, by that token, have a significance even when our reason cannot recognise it.

Montezuma

The dilemma of Montezuma was uniquely acute. If Cortés and his men were mortals, then it was his duty to send his armies against them, and this he could do with not too heavy a heart. Even if the seers were right, and the pale invaders were fated to conquer the isthmus and destroy his empire, the doom might take a long time to fall, according to the pattern of war the Aztecs knew. Each conflict began with prolonged negotiations setting out the issues between the two parties, went to a period of violent war lasting until one party or the other secured a positive advantage; and then the defeated party sought a temporary armistice which led to a peace conference as unhurried as the preliminary proceedings. They had no inkling of total war, though a succession of the moderate wars they knew might be a warning of the period of catastrophe such as brought a sun to its age. But the accent of even these moderate wars was on the violence of the fighting that was sandwiched between the two periods of negotiation. If Montezuma went out against Cortés and his men, he had to deal out death with his slings and javelins and obsidian swords with all the power of his warrior nation. But what if Cortés was Quetzalcoatl returned? We can grasp Montezuma's position only if we imagine the British and American governments of today faced with phenomena which might be either a hostile expeditionary force of spacemen or the second coming of Christ. Even at that, Montezuma was in a state of conflict we would never know. He was a gentle man. Many speeches were recorded for us as they fell from the lips of this head of a ferocious state, hopelessly committed to ferocity; and they all speak of a wistful longing for a meeker dispensation. He must have hungered for that quality of mildness which is mysteriously implicit in everything we read of Quetzalcoatl. Yet he had been bred in a civilisation which conceived godhead as a raging and raving state, and the Plumed Serpent was coming back to drive out Smokey Mirror, who had dispossessed him. Montezuma must have feared his Christ for himself and his people as we could not fear ours.

Montezuma at once made an effort to find out whether Cortés was man or god by applying a very sensible test. He sent him, in the hands of the first party he sent to visit the invaders at San Juan de Ulúa, certain presents which he should have recognised, were he Quetzalcoatl. Among these were the headdress worn by Smokey Mirror in his temple, which was made of feathers studded with gold stars, so voluminous that it fell about his shoulders as a cape; also the mask of Tlaloc, made of jewels and precious metals, and his standard; and a mitre of jaguar fur attached to another of these splendid feather-capes; and a number of magnificent jewels of ritual significance. These last were most important of all, for it was believed that they had belonged to Quetzalcoatl, and indeed they may have been possessed by one of the men who called himself by that name. Cortés's acceptance of these gifts was debonair, for he had no notion that he was suspected of anything but humanity, and he saw in them simply confirmation of his joyful recognition that he was delivering over to the Spanish Crown a pearl among colonies. But it was as if candour was a principle that operated in him independently of his senses and his intelligence. He did not understand the question, but he gave the answer. He said, "What I want is gold," and there is no shorter sentence by which a man could prove once and for all that he was not a god.

Yet the message did not pass quite clearly from one culture to another. The demand for gold sounded slightly idiotic to the Aztecs, since it was to them not supremely valuable, but then this fitted in with the magic view of divinity as liking to talk nonsense and listen to it. But among the embassy Montezuma had sent a slave, not even a prisoner of war, a bought slave, a lout, disguised as the governor of a province, and if Cortés had been Quetzalcoatl he would have seen through the deception. It seems that the chief of the embassy was at first fairly clear that he was dealing simply with men like himself, though differently coloured, but that situation shifted when he and his fellows noticed a gilt helmet worn by one of the Spanish soldiers: gilt and uncommon rusty, according to Bernal Díaz. They showed signs of awed interest and asked if they might borrow it and send it back to Montezuma, since it resembled a helmet which was worn by the god Blue-Hummingbird-to-the-South in his temple at Tenochtitlán, and which had come down to them from their ancestors of very long ago. (It is thought that this may have been another supposed possession of Quetzalcoatl.) Cortés kept a grave face as he acceded to the odd request and gave unwitting help to the hypothesis of his godhead by yielding to his trademark obsession and suggesting, with what seemed to his hearers divine dottiness, that the helmet might be filled with gold dust when it was returned to him. The helmet swung back the balance, and it perhaps never came down on the right side again. Salvador de Madariaga, the best judge of this story by reason of his deep knowledge and his poetic imagination, thinks that the Aztecs never quite knew whether Cortés and his men were gods or not, and that Montezuma never ceased trying to resolve his doubts and may have been doubtful when he died.

Many of his efforts to find certainty were frustrated by the unhappy consequences of a liaison between an able intelligence corps and an army of highly trained performing magicians. The emperor was appalled by the sight of the helmet and also by the paintings brought him back by the artists he had sent to paint Cortés and his men, their armour and their arms, their interpreters, their horses and their dogs and their ships, which did indeed seem beyond the frontiers of heavenly and human affairs as he knew them. To test the competence of his magicians he sent for a covey of wizards who lived on a lagoon at Chalco, Sweet Waters, which is near Tenochtitlán, reminded them of the prophecy of the conquest of Mexico by white men, and asked them how their studies had led them to picture these conquerors. Incautiously they replied that the invaders had heads growing out of their chests and had only one foot apiece, so huge that they could lie down and shelter from the sun and rain under their soles. Montezuma then gave another covey its chance, a firm quartered at another lagoon, Xochomilco, the Field of Flowers. These had better relations with the intelligence corps, and they alleged that their studies had shown the invaders as white of face and body, long in beard, and clad in many colours, arriving on things that looked like mounds floating on the seas and, once they had landed, much given to riding animals that looked like deer but much bigger. This was only one example of the disadvantageous consequences for the client arising out of the magicians' tapping of security lines. It was correctly reported by Aztec spies that the Spaniards took special precautions in guarding their camps at night, which struck them as strange, since Indians fought by day alone. The magicians then had a revelation that the Spaniards were the children of the sun and as such were invincible by day, but helpless by night. This led to a major defeat of an important Aztec allied force, which on these representations made a night attack. Nonetheless magic had accumulated enough information about human behaviour for the Aztecs to have some very ingenious tricks at their command; and some of the best arose out of their technique of juggling with identities.

Montezuma's substitution of a slave for the governor of the province had scored a double success. Quetzalcoatl would have detected the imposture, as Jesus Christ knew that the woman of Samaria had had five husbands, though she told him she had had none; and, thus proved mortal, Cortés was revealed as wholly at sea in the society he was attacking, unable to tell a gross caste difference and therefore vulnerable. But Montezuma had another trick up his sleeve. When the second embassy arrived from Tenochtitlán, it brought with it a cartwheel of gold, engraved with a solar calendar, a cartwheel of silver engraved with a lunar calendar, and a great lord who was Cortés's double. It was explained that when Cortés's portrait had arrived at court the courtiers were all astonished at its resemblance to one of their own number; so they had sent the double along for Cortés to see him for himself. Again two purposes were served. In every Aztec temple it was the custom to choose priests bearing some likeness to the god who was patron of this particular pyramid and to emphasise the likeness by similarity of headdress and cut of hair and pattern of paint on the face. If Quetzalcoatl were sent to a person who could be mistaken for him, he would recognise the priestly routine and approve; but if Cortés were plain Cortés, another end would be served. It appears that among the Aztecs, as among a number of Western people, a man who met his double felt terror and might even take it as a warning of imminent death. Presently Cortés's double left, and the Spaniards were told that he had fallen sick. It was shortly after this that the embassy vanished in the night.

The episode misfired gloriously. When first the double arrived, the captains gathered round him and guffawed at nature's freakishness and called him "The Other Cortés" and then got on with entertaining the guests by a sort of nonstop gymkhana, galloping their horses along the sands and firing their guns and shooting their crossbows and showing off their ships, and later they were distracted by increasing sulkiness about the shortage of food. There is no sign that Cortés or anybody else in the expeditionary force lost a moment's sleep over the doppelgänger. If Cortés had his uneasy nights, it was because he was under the strain of finding that a country he wished to annex for Spain by peaceful penetration meant to resist him, and that this country was so beautiful and strange that he did not want to make war on it and was also so horrible that, over an issue in which Spain played only a minor part, but which was vital to his own soul, he must break it and remake it. Also, no man wants to die before his time, and the supple Indian nature was twisting like a great snake in his hand. On his way to the capital and nerve centre of this country he would have to pick his way through these lying charmers who would offer him support which he did not dare refuse, but who would shift their allegiance as quickly as a snake can cast its skin. He understood perfectly that they had a right to betray him in their own interests, he was never fool enough to blame them for that, he knew he had no claim on their loyalty. Yet all the same he would have to punish them for resistance to this invalid claim, and that he hated, partly because of his eupeptic good nature, partly because of a professionalism which counted a killed Indian a failure, waste of one who should have lived to be a friendly and industrious colonial subject of the Spanish Crown. Neither Cortés nor Bernal Díaz writes of enemy losses with exhilaration. The game they were playing was scored not like cricket but like golf, the object was to get round the course in as few strokes as possible. When the Spaniards came to the city of Cholula, where there was a temple for every day of the year and a parent temple which stood up like a mountain over the plains, it was discovered by Doña Marina that the Cholulans were planning to fall on them in the night; and the Spaniards had to destroy the great temple and kill six thousand people before they were allowed to go on their way. It is with regret that they chronicled the incident. They were pleased with themselves because they had avoided ambushes on the road, and they should have walked round this trap too. Such ambitions and economies, military and colonialist, were their preoccupations. But fate managed to link their straight paths with the winding trails, half on earth and half off it and never direct, of Montezuma's preoccupations.

About it and about these went. When Cortés started for Tenochtitlán, he left a small garrison near Vera Cruz. Quauhpopoca, an Aztec official in charge of a district nearby, was commissioned by the Aztec central authority to kidnap a Spanish soldier in order that he might be sent to the capital to be examined by the emperor for signs of deity, whatever those were. Quauhpopoca sent a message to the Spanish garrison telling them he had wished to visit them for the purpose of tendering his allegiance to them and asking for an escort of four men to see him through the territory of an unfriendly tribe. When the four men reached him, they were seized; two escaped back to the garrison, one was wounded and one was killed. The killed and wounded men were bound to the backs of runners, but presently the wounded man died, and the runners found the grisly burdens insupportable, so cut off the heads and left the bodies by the roadside. When the heads were brought to Montezuma, he looked on them for a long time and grew pale, as well he might. One of the two had been a splendid young bull, with a great head and a strong black curling beard. The emperor decided that these were only men, but noted that they looked brave. With a characteristically sensitive and unimperial gesture, he ordered that the heads be taken away from the capital. He was for the minute free of his fear that Cortés was a god, but his heart was not in such doings. Then the scales trembled again when he heard of Cortés's visit to Cholula. Ironically, Cortés had been set on and nearly murdered by the dedicated worshippers of the god with whom he had been identified. The cult of Quetzalcoatl had its soul and being in that town. Now what was the emperor to think? The age was so committed to the belief that the worshipful was the disagreeable that Montezuma would find it natural for a god to celebrate his return by a massacre of the devotees. But would a god go so far as to overthrow his own great and glorious temple? The tests had to start all over again.

When the Spaniards marched down from the pass between the two volcanoes towards the Valley of Mexico, they found comfortable quarters in a caravanserai, one of the hostels for travelling merchants which were maintained all over the country, and when they had settled in they realised that the village round them was bubbling with a rumour that Montezuma was leaving his capital and coming along the road to greet them. And indeed an embassy did arrive before long, splendidly dressed, moving with ceremony, bearing presents which even by Aztec standards were munificent, and headed by an imposing figure who was treated by his suite with courtierly deference and who announced himself as the emperor, but who was not. It is said that this masquerade was designed to see whether Cortés, if he thought he had Montezuma in his hands, would lay hands on him and keep him as a prisoner, in which case all the Spaniards would have been slaughtered forthwith. But this is improbable. Montezuma knew enough about Cortés through his spies and ambassadors to be sure that Cortés would have taken no such rash step on an unknown terrain, surrounded by enemies whose military resources he had not yet assessed. More likely, this impersonation was another sprat to catch a god. Only a divine intelligence would see through the disguise, it was presumed. Actually Cortés, brought up in a household with some court connections, thought it incredible that a sovereign should be so careless of his dignity as to come so far from his capital to meet a foreigner.

Later the Aztecs told Sahagún a story, beautifully retold by Salvador de Madariaga, of the new folly to which Montezuma was inspired when the detected impostor returned. He sent out a posse of magicians to meet Cortés on the road and turn him back with their spells. While this party was still in sight of the capital, they met a peasant who was very drunk: possessed by Four Hundred Rabbits, as they would have put it, which was their Beatrix Potterish name for drunkenness, for possession by the wine deity or deities. The magicians instantly recognised him and fell on their knees, at which the god made rude remarks about Montezuma and told them to turn round and look behind them at Tenochtitlán; and, obeying, they saw the towers and temples of their city going up in fire. It can be guessed that not only the peasant but the whole lot of them were drunk. There were stringent laws against drunkenness, which by a unique act of kindness to the aged was only permitted to old men and women, and even encouraged in them; but for public drunkenness a plebeian got beaten and had his head shaven if it were his first offence and was publicly strangled if it were not, while a noble would be strangled in private for even his first offence. But as it is extremely easy to brew beer and spirits from the cactus plants which grow everywhere, it can be guessed that the risk was frequently taken; and indeed there can never have been any time when a magician was more in need of a drink. One can imagine a furtive resort to a reed hut off the highway where there was a shebeen installed, some steady drinking in the company of a peasant who was against the government, and the unsteady emergence of several muzzy magicians out into the fresh air, and a sudden view of Tenochtitlán, which might well have been wavering and fusing even to sober eyes, for the prospect lay beyond land and water; and all of us have seen the glassy disorder which affects a distant object when looked at through an atmosphere striped with variations in temperature. When they got home with this hiccuping story, it filled the refined, the intelligent, the imaginative, the experienced Montezuma with gloom of the same kind raised in him by the most serious intimations of Cortés's genius. It is the special misfortune of the magic-eater that he loses his palate.

There was another and honest embassy sent to Cortés, with a message which demonstrates the Mesoamerican technique of negotiation: Montezuma warned Cortés that he should leave the capital if he had any regard for prudence and should return to Vera Cruz and leave the country, and that an Aztec mission would follow him with a tribute, which they would deliver to him on the seacoast, a tribute of great magnificence and quantity. Some authorities say that the offer was of an annual tribute, to be collected at a port. When Cortés's refusal was brought back to Montezuma, he held the last of many councils, which was on a sophisticated plane, spending much of its time on a discussion of the status of ambassadors. Then it sent on a final embassy a nephew of Montezuma, a young man of twenty-five, Prince Cacamatzin, the king of Texcoco, ruler of an adjoining territory on the lakeside. He arrived at Cortés's quarters on a litter that looked as if he were borne on branches, but the wood was jewel-studded gold and silver, and the foliage was made of green plumes, and he was carried by eight lords, who deferentially helped the young king to descend and swept the path he had to tread, but were said by the Indian onlookers to be the rulers of important towns. The king of Texcoco gave Cortés a warning of cold and courteous ferocity that he had better be gone, and Cortés offered him patronising assurances that the Spaniards would do him no harm, and he left in silent fury. Cortés and his men had been informed by their Indian allies, who knew nothing if they did not know the truth about the Aztecs, who were their masters, that Montezuma meant to let them enter the city and there would put them to death.

Tenochtitlán

In a daze the Spaniards mounted their horses and rode out into the highway, which was crowded with sightseers, and presently they turned the flank of a little hill and for the first time looked on Tenochtitlán. Bernal Díaz has commemorated that moment: "When we beheld the many cities and towns settled on the water, and on the mainland, and saw the broad causeway running so straight and level across the lake to Tenochtitlán we could liken it only to the enchanted scenes we had read of in the romance *Amadís de Gaula*, because of the great towers and the pyramids and the mansions that were rising from the water. Many of us asked if we were sleeping or waking. Never yet did man see, or hear, or dream of anything equal to that spectacle we saw that day." It is to be observed that these men of action were thoroughly literate. There is little descriptive writing, and that not very vivid, in *Amadís de Gaula*, but Bernal Díaz had read the book with his imagination as well as his intelligence.

Not insensitive, not brutish, he and his party went on, dazed with fear, dazed with beauty, until they were met by a party from the court, who took them to a lakeside town, where they were lodged in palaces built of stone and cedar wood and hung with fine textiles and paintings and surrounded by gardens full of flowers and herbs and fruit trees, laid round canals of clear water. In the morning they awoke and set out, still in a daze of admiration and fear, and found themselves walking across the great causeway over the lake, which was broad as two spears, and lined with people, for all of its three miles' length. The waters of the lake were now a solid mass of canoes. They were conscious as they walked that they numbered four hundred and fifty and that there were multitudes of Indians about them, and indeed they must have been surrounded by more than a million. As they walked they observed that the causeway was broken at intervals by bridges which could be raised. They believed that the ruler of the city towards which they were going meant to kill them when they arrived, and they realised that the raising of a single one of these bridges would cut off their retreat. Bernal Díaz may be pardoned when he asks, "Now let who can tell it, where are there men in this world other than ourselves who would have dared this danger?"

To read of their meeting with the emperor, it is best to turn again to the admirable Salvador de Madariaga, who synthesises all the reliable authorities. The Spaniards were halted just outside the entrance to the city, where an assembly of splendidly dressed Aztecs, numbering about a thousand, passed in turn before Cortés and performed the gesture which was apparently the standard greeting to the ambassador of an important power: each touched the ground at his feet with his hand and kissed it. Then the party was led through the entrance into the city fastness—the only entrance—and walked along more of that causeway, over other of those bridges, into a wide avenue between shining mansions and there saw advancing towards them two columns of Aztec lords, even more splendidly dressed than those who had paid homage, but all barefoot, keeping close to the mansions' fronts, leaving the roadway empty. They stopped, while a hush fell on the people who were looking down from the roofs, and down the empty space was carried the imperial litter, more glorious than the king of Texcoco's litter as an emperor is more glorious than a king. Before Montezuma could descend it was necessary for the nobles to perform the ritual of sweeping the ground and covering it with cloths, and they had also to erect a canopy of green feathers hung with a fringe of dangling precious stones, and three heralds had to take up their stand with uplifted golden rods.

Meanwhile Cortés dismounted from his horse, and his men stood behind him in a trance. They had learned something of Aztec pomp from the royal embassies and the visit of the young king, but this was a greater glory. Díaz says with simplicity that the nobles they had seen before had changed into even better clothes; and indeed it is safe to think that when Montezuma stepped from the litter he was as magnificently attired as any human being since the beginning of time, for though the Indians had no silk their feather fabrics took its place. He alone was shod, wearing high thick-soled boots like the cothurns of the Greek tragic actors, but with the difference that the legs were encrusted with jewels and the soles were of gold. But this miracle of fantasy, this transmutation of a man and his clothes into a symbol of transcendent power, was seen only by Cortés and his men and the members of the royal house who stood under the canopy, for all others on the scene had their eyes fixed on the ground.

Then Cortés advanced towards the emperor and there was a curious fumbling, which the onlookers could not quite understand, before a handshake was achieved, and Cortés threw about the emperor's neck a necklace, part of the supplied paste jewellery he had brought from Cuba to give to the natives on the assumption they would be savages, which he had tried to better by stringing it on a gold chain and scenting it with musk. After that he opened his arms to the emperor in the embrace that was in Christendom the prescribed gesture between heads of state or their representatives but was frustrated by the two princes nearest the emperor, who caught him back in their arms to protect his sacred person from profane grasp. For they did not believe that Cortés was a god, they were sure that he was a man and as sure that he and all his company should be killed at once. Aztec society was so highly developed that it was not monolithic in its opinions, and those regarding religion ranged from absolute faith to scepticism. Probably nothing would have persuaded these minor kings and princes to abandon the faith of their fathers, both because their upbringing conditioned them to fear misfortune if they failed to propitiate the other world, and because their subjects might get out of hand were they not kept in order by sacerdotalism. But a joke is a joke, and they were not prepared to believe that a sweaty and travel-stained horseman (many of whose subordinates were known to have been killed in battle) was an immortal. When trouble brewed up later, they expressed their scepticism in words reported by the Spaniards, words reproaching Montezuma for the consequences of his bigoted faith and reliance on sorcery, which in spirit might have been uttered by contemporary liberals who found an elder relative committed to some reactionary political step by his fundamentalist faith. But Montezuma's power was still absolute, and as soon as all the nobles who had been standing with downcast eyes at the edge of the avenue had filed before Cortés and performed the act of greeting, he turned and led the way to the place where the strangers were to be lodged, walking with his hot-tempered young nephew, the king of Texcoco, while Cortés followed in the company of his brother

Cuitlahuac, a signal honour, for he was nearly as sacred a person as the emperor. At a sign a messenger came to the emperor and placed a packet in his hand. He bent over it for a moment and then turned back and threw over Cortés's head two necklaces of red shells, each hung with eight golden shrimps.

These were the insignia of Quetzalcoatl. The emperor had that morning received powerful confirmation of Cortés's deity. Cortés had been warned to turn back from Tenochtitlán for reasons of self-preservation that any mortal man would respect, and he had insisted on making the prohibited entry, on a day which by our reckoning was November the eighth, 1519, and according to one of the Aztec calendars the eighth day of the Month of the Wind, an ill-fated day, full of catastrophe and awkwardness, because it was under the sign of Quetzalcoatl, the Lord of Turbulence, of defeat, which somehow took precedence over triumph. A disconcerting aspect of this strange historical event is that the conclusion Montezuma drew from his superstitions was sounder than that of his rationalist relatives. It would have availed the Aztecs nothing to massacre Cortés and his men, for had he failed to return there were many other adventurers to persuade the Council of the Indies to sanction a larger expedition, which would certainly have been more cruel.

The palace set aside for the visitors was a former royal residence which had been for some time turned to use as a temple, a convent of priestesses, and the Royal Treasure House, and it was large enough to house not only the four hundred and fifty Spaniards but their two thousand native auxiliaries and their women cooks and camp-followers. Some rooms were so spacious that a hundred and fifty soldiers could sleep in one of them, each stretched out on the canopied sleeping-mat which was the Aztec form of bed; and there were gardens where they could wander, without feeling pent in. But this use of premises consecrated first to royalty and then to the gods must have been regarded as a profanation by all Aztecs not of the same mind as Montezuma, whose obsession showed itself again before the day was out. He left them before they were served with a dinner which Díaz, years afterwards, gratefully chronicled as "sumptuous." It probably deserved praise by any standards. The palace food was exquisitely cooked, kept hot at table on specially made earthenware vessels and eaten off the famous black and red pottery of Cholula.

But when they had finished, the emperor was back with them and sat down and talked to Cortés in the presence of his companions. Now they had time to look at him, and he charmed them. He was a man of forty, slender and well-proportioned, with black hair and beard very elegantly cut, fine eyes, and an expression of good nature and cheerfulness, which was balanced by his gravity. It is apparent that he possessed the seductive Indian quality of cancelled voluptuousness, of strong sensuousness pruned back by an inner delicacy. He told them that he was happy to entertain them, because he knew quite well that they were travellers from the east whose coming had been prophesied for centuries. He was tactfully asking, "Are you Quetzalcoatl, come back from the place where the raft of serpents took you?" With perfect truthfulness Cortés answered that he had indeed come from the east, and this plainly left Montezuma in an awkward position. He could not well ask him whether he was Quetzalcoatl or one of the mere men seen by the prophets, for fear of offending him if he were a god. He went on to make a hedging bet. He owned he had heard of the two lost expeditions of which Cortés had come in search and asked Cortés if all his soldiers were as brothers and were all the vassals of the same Emperor Charles. It may be suspected that not only was he interested in the two expeditions, but that his intelligence officers had reported the near-mutiny there had been in Cortés's camp when some of his men had shown themselves partisans of his enemy Velázquez. Like all emperors, he thoroughly understood the principle of *divide et impera*, and so did Cortés, who assured him of the perfect amity of all Spaniards, which was the greatest lie he told in all the conquest.

The next day Cortés and his captains went to the imperial palace, into which, so like was Tenochtitlán to Venice, a boat could row, though it was in the heart of the city. This was a splendid edifice, not long built. It had twenty doors, three courtyards, many large halls, one hundred rooms, and not small ones, for the most part about thirty feet square, one hundred baths, fed by a water supply which was controlled by a beautiful fountain in one of the courtyards. The carpentry was superb: cedar and cypress, palm and pine were carved into ornate ceilings and furniture and doors, all dovetailed, and the walls were of marble and porphyry and jasper and alabaster, and, where they were plain stone, they were hung with fine cottons, rabbit-hair cloth and featherwork. There was a great deal of decorative painting and wonderful carpets on the floors. Everything was exquisitely clean. The Spaniards held their breaths. Probably the only place in Spain where such luxury had been or ever was to be attained was the Caliphate of Córdoba in the tenth century, and there the scale was smaller; it is improbable that Córdoba had a population of more than half a million, while Tenochtitlán seems to have had its full million. Certainly not in the conquistadores' time had Spain had a ruler with such silken manners as Montezuma, who received the Spaniards in his private apartments, which normally only his family and his most important statesmen were permitted to enter, and who drew Cortés down to sit beside him on a dais, bidding the captains, with an air of being glad to have them there, find seats for themselves on the lower level of the room. The proceedings were watched by a party of Montezuma's relatives who, one imagines, had been addressing him on the beauties of scepticism and the necessity of keeping barbarians in their place, for Montezuma took a firmer stand. Cortés, not giving way for an instant to the convention that royal persons are allowed to choose the topics of conversation, at once launched upon the exposition of the Christian mysteries which he usually left to Father Olmedo. This is what he said, as it appeared to Bernal Díaz:

> He came to the emperor, he said, for the service of the Lord God whom the Christians adored, who was named Jesus Christ, and who suffered death for our sakes. He also explained to him, that we adored the cross as the emblem of the crucifixion for our salvation, whereby the human race was redeemed, and that our Lord on the third day rose, and is in heaven, and that it is He who created heaven and earth and sea, and is adored by us as Creator; but that those things which he held to be gods were not such but devils, which are very bad things, of evil countenances, and worse deeds; and that he might judge how wicked they were, and how little power they had, in as much as where ever we placed crosses, they dare not show their faces. He therefore requested, that he would attend to what he had told him, which was, that we were all brothers, the children of Adam and Eve, and that as such, our emperor lamenting the loss of souls in such numbers as those which were brought by his idols into everlasting flames, had sent us to apply an end to the worship of these false gods.

Here Cortés stopped, for Montezuma was showing signs of impatience, and said in Spanish to his captains that he felt he had gone far enough for a first interview and they could be considered as having done their duty, and they rose to leave. But Montezuma put up a detaining hand. He cannot have been accustomed to having an audience terminated by the persons he was receiving, and he had also to make it plain where he stood.

"Malintzin, Mr. Marina," he said, "these arguments of yours are already quite familiar to me. I understand that when you talked to my ambassadors on the sand dunes you put up a cross and kindly told him about your three gods, and your party seems to have missed no opportunity for spreading similar information during your journey across my country. We have made no attempt to argue with you, because we have worshipped our gods for a long time and know them to be good and just. So no doubt are yours. But please do not trouble to raise this matter again."

Pleasantly he continued, "As to your great king, I am in his debt. In other words, yes, I will pay tribute to him, I am ready to enter into negotiations with you for a settlement."

The prudence he owed to his subjects here asserted itself. "As I told you before, I heard of those two parties of your kind of people who landed on the same coast as yourselves. I should like to know, are you all under the same ruler?"

In other words: are you worth negotiating with, have you the authority? Once more Cortés assured him of the essential brotherhood of all Spaniards.

Then Montezuma's obsession seized him again. From the first he had wanted, he confided in them, to invite them to visit the cities of his empire and do them honour, and now the gods had granted him that desire, and here he had Cortés and his company all in his palace, which they must call their own and use as a place of refreshment and repose and never fear for their safety. If, he assured them, he had ever seemed reluctant to entertain them, it was not because of his own feelings, but because his subjects were frightened. And no wonder, for they had heard such terrifying stories about them. Why, he told them gaily, they had heard that the Spaniards carried thunder and lightning with them and discharged them when they wished, that their horses killed men, and it was even said that they were gods, and furious ones at that. But, he added, smiling at them as if they were long-known and much loved courtiers, he saw that they were men, simply men, though very valiant and wise ones. Doubtless there was a question-mark in his voice. The Spaniards beamed back at him, loyal as if they were his courtiers, and he turned laughing to Cortés.

"You know, people say such absurd things. Some of your Indian allies must have told you that I am a god and have nothing in my house but silver and gold and precious stones. But I'm sure you are too sensible to believe them. You've seen my palaces now and you can vouch for it, they're built of wood and stone, and look," he said, holding out his arms, "my body is made of flesh and blood. Like yours. I am a great king, and I have inherited the riches of my ancestors, but all the stories you have heard of my godhead and my bottomless fortune are lies."

He was asking two questions at once. Are you gods or men? And must you rob me?

But Cortés's Western ears could not hear the first question, and to the second he had the wrong answer, like all Europeans. Europe thought of itself in relation to the New World as a combination of missionary and entrepreneur, with a double duty to disperse the native populations' ignorance regarding Christianity and economics. The natives were certainly ignorant of Christianity, but it may be asked whether they did not know as much about economics as the next man. They had no monetary system, but they had evolved a rigid social structure, top-heavy with a large administrative class, where the civil service merged with the priesthood, and oppressive to the individual in its demands for taxes. This was all the economists of the admired Roman Empire had been able to produce, and it was not essentially different from what modern Europe has produced. The theory of the European invaders of the New World (insofar as they had a theory) was that they were conferring benefits on the native populations by inviting them to participate in international trade, and there they might have claimed to be genuine economic benefactors. But unfortunately they also felt compelled to confiscate both the accumulated wealth of the native populations and their natural resources, so far as these were mineral. This is not altogether the plain peculation that it appears, for they had an ingenuous belief that, as the native populations had no monetary system, these were wasted on them, and they were doing the only sensible thing if they took the minerals away and put them to useful purposes. It has to be remarked that these predators were actually conferring a huge benefit on another part of the world, on the Old World, by relieving its currency famine. This is not a moral universe.

It was no wonder that Cortés fell back on a compliment. "I do not expect to meet a more magnificent lord than you, not anywhere." He meant it, and he could not have spoken a truer word. He was to meet a lord not magnificent at all in his own emperor, that dreary Habsburg, who was to degrade his hereditary magnificence by his meanness; and indeed there have been few lords in all history as fine as Montezuma. Wherever he appears he leaves a sense of rich sweetness, like dark honey. Even the most ungrateful of routines he performed with a spontaneous yet not evanescent gravity, an ungrudging committal to pleasantness. At the end of this most unusual morning call he gave the Spaniards yet another present of gold and textiles, and they noted how handsomely he made the gift, seeming to delight in conferring a pleasure, showing no pang at all at the inroads on his wealth. They went back to their quarters talking of his gentle manners and his open hand and heart, and they decided to show him all the respect they could and never forget the courtesy of lifting their quilted casques in his presence. But the issue had been raised: between Montezuma and Cortés there had already flared up the one issue which was to sweep through this good feeling like a heath-fire and leave nothing but ashes, which was to break the heart of one of these great men and utterly destroy the other and his world.

The paradisal state of amity was to last four days. During this time the guests moved about their lodgings and grew more and more enchanted with the emperor and his works. His primary charm was a trait he shared with Cortés: both were specimens of an exuberant type, which they refined by their own innate artistic sense. Cortés was a conquistador who cut himself back and liked to eat to the sound of trumpets but eat little, was of an insatiable esurience but chose loyalty to the world of invisible things, which the senses cannot enjoy, who was greedy for vast estates but cared to cultivate them rather than exploit them. The emperor Montezuma was the head of a great and unpliable state which imposed a florid magnificence on him and renounced its advantages to the self. The pomp with which he was surrounded was extraordinary by European standards. All who were received by him in audience, even the greatest nobles, had to strip themselves of their fine clothing and go into his presence in a plain habit and barefoot, to show they were as nothing compared to him. They could not even come in a straight line to his door, but had to approach it deviously. Yet the emperor made it plain that this respect was paid not to him but to his office. He treated all the Spaniards, of whatever rank, with a courtesy which stated that within his office was a human being of like flesh to theirs and, that flesh being perishable, they all owed each other kindness.

They watched him as if he were not true. They were not homosexual, nor was the emperor, though the Aztecs were much given to homosexuality; yet they took much the same pleasure in him that they might have taken in an elegant woman who was also a good housewife. They liked the homely uses to which his fastidiousness turned the luxury, the cleanliness of his person and his garments. They admired the means he took to preserve his dignity, the screen which was set about him at the dinner table so that no one should see him eating, the precautions taken to prevent it being known when he visited his harem of two wives and many high-born concubines. They enjoyed the playfulness which made him, in spite of his moderate appetite, amuse himself by visiting his kitchens and watching the cooks at work and smile benevolently on the singers and dancers and tumblers who came to perform when dinner was over. They were impressed by the quietness of the palace, the hermetic quality of the gardens and the parks, where there were canals and shady groves and flowerbeds and theatres and picnic pavilions and an aviary and a zoo, which was also a temple, but never any bustle or display. Perhaps they would not have been sorry if they had been told that they were dead and this was paradise, and they could stay there for ever; and indeed it was much like a Moslem paradise, for they were even given lovely and well-mannered women.

But Cortés's inconvenient soul was stirring within him, and after four days he called together his three interpreters, Doña Marina and Aguilar and a page called Orteguilla, who had proved an apt student of the Nahuatl language, and sent them off to Montezuma with a request that he and his captains might be allowed to see the city. Montezuma immediately agreed, but his anxiety can be recognised in his decision that he himself should be their guide. Díaz records his own awareness that the emperor was apprehensive lest they should offer an insult to the Aztec gods in their temples; for that reason he would set aside his dignity and accompany them, to protect his gods, and also to protect them. The emperor's heart must have been heavy. The issue was to be openly stated, and emperors are used to prevent issues being stated that they wish to lie covert. But he had no chance. Cortés, who has come down through the centuries as the apotheosis of the amoral man, was faced with a moral decision, and he had decided it according to his standards of right and wrong, and that although he might pay for it with his life. Indeed, he had had other experiences on the way to Tenochtitlán than these which I have set down, which are all I knew before I went to Mexico, before I turned back to read the books. Why had I forgotten them? Because they represent a problem that my age ought to state and solve, that it refuses to state and has no prospect of solving.

Ever since Cortés and his troops had landed on the isthmus, they had found, wherever there was a town or a village of any size, large and well-constructed buildings of lime-washed stone, which were evidently temples, since there were altars and idols within. Their custodians were priests, not so different from the priests of Europe in their clothing, for they wore loose white robes like surplices or black hooded mantles like the Dominican habit; but they were conspicuously filthy, and their hair hung down to their waists or even their feet in twisted rats-tails clotted with blood, and blood dripped from lacerations in the lobes of their ears. There was blood on the walls and on the altars, but this did not come from the priests. There were always to be found on the premises some human bodies, their hearts cut out, and their legs and arms severed from their torsos. The sight revolted the Spaniards and more than the sight. There are those of us who have attended pagan sacrifices in parts of the world where only cocks and lambs and goats are offered up, and we know that the senses are sickened. Once, long ago, I drove up into the mountains on a pearly morning and got out of the car and looked through the clear air at a rock which shone red-brown. It was the altar of the sacrifice, and it was entirely covered with the blood of the beasts that had been slain on it during the night. As we got nearer, the stench of blood came and lived in our noses and throats like an infection. Later in the day, I was standing in a tavern in an upland village close by buying a bottle of wine, and suddenly the stench was with me again. Just behind me was the man who had stood on the rock and cut the throats of the victims, and the stench was in his clothes, massive as cloth itself. But there was more to offend than that. In the last moment of life the goats and lambs voided their bladders and bowels, and so would men. But there was a further horror beyond the blood and the sewage. The joints were taken from the temples to the public markets, were hung up there to air, in Bernal Díaz's words, "as beef is in the towns of Castile," and sold for food.

Race Relations II

So we believed what we heard from our friend Armando when we lunched with him in a restaurant on the Paseo de la Reforma. "We are very strange about the Indians," he said. "We babble about them perpetually, we put their gods up on our buildings as national symbols, but there is a colour bar. Oh, an Indian has full legal rights, and, except in backward and corrupt pockets of the country, he exercises them. But all the same, people don't have Indians to their houses, they don't let their children make friends with them, they don't ask them to their houses, unless they're very rich. No, I don't just mean that the white people and the mestizos have to be rich. I mean that *both* parties have to be rich, the white people and the mestizos on the one hand, and the Indians on the other. Yes, both have to be rich or very celebrated. If an Indian was very successful in politics or in industry or in the law or in science, then you would find him welcomed by the millionaires or by the elite of the universities. But by the bourgeoisie never. Never by any people who have any doubts about themselves, only by the exceptionally rich, aristocratic, and respected. It's not wholesome. For that's where the brotherhood should begin. That's the class we want to encourage, and which indeed we don't need to encourage, it's the Mexico of tomorrow."

Proust would have enjoyed the situation. It surely has not its exact parallel in Europe or in North America, the inability of the Indian to meet the grocer or the small-scale manufacturer of women's clothes, while he can enjoy the friendship of the duke and duchess and the winner of the Nobel Prize. It is true that some distinguished American Negroes would find it much easier to get to the White House, at least once, than to be entertained in their home towns by the run-of-the-mill white householder. Yet they can always rely on a certain amount of contact with the high-minded among the white population. That must indeed be part of the burden of being a distinguished Negro. How would any of us like to be restricted to the company of high-minded groups? That would be a kind of hell. But the point about the Indian is that once he makes his mark, unless he is a pure academic, he is rewarded by being precipitated into the sort of polo-pony society which was Scott Fitzgerald's ideal, and he never comes to know the Forsytes.

It is a bizarre situation, in view of the preoccupations of the Mexican mind. A great part of its energy goes into the business of making a living, which is difficult if one is a labourer and almost as difficult if one is a manufacturer, anxious to get foreign capital but hampered by legislation which discourages employers from employing foreign managers and foremen, who often are necessary if the foreign investor is to be satisfied with his returns and if local workmen are ever to be trained as managers and foremen. Most of the rest of Mexican cerebration goes into brooding on the Spanish-Indian situation and another historical crisis: the revolution. This is conceived as a contemporary event and one essential to the existence of the Mexican people, something like what Marx called a social revolution, but cozier. This does not mean that they are planning for the day when there will be barricades in the Paseo de la Reforma and a string of tumbrils bearing aristos to a scaffold erected on the plaza in front of the cathedral. Such goings-on the Mexicans regard not as a revolution but as part of a pre-revolutionary process, and they count themselves as having done all that in the nineteenth and twentieth centuries, and now they think of themselves as enjoying a permanent revolution. "Enjoying" is the operative word. It must be noted that the phrase "permanent revolution" does not mean to them what it means to the orthodox Communists, who think of it (roughly speaking) as the extension of the pre-revolutionary process from Russia outward to the whole world. What the Mexicans understand by it is the constant application of certain kinds of pressure on society. First, they see to it that Mexico expands without cease into a more and more ambitious welfare state, supported by the earnings of a mixed economy, in which private enterprise and public ownership exist side by side, careless of accountancy, never forgetful of social justice. This recalls Great Britain, but the Mexican contempt for the vulgar aim of balancing the budget stands to our contempt for it as Mexican cooking does to British: it is far hotter in the mouth; and indeed I cannot think how a state can get its figures properly prudent when it knows its population is going to multiply itself by six in a century.

The Mexican public has no illusions about its present situation. It knows it has not yet got social justice, it is conscious that its security benefits are limited to the city industrial worker. But Mexicans think they have found a way of putting pressure on the government so that it will get them social justice by steady installments, and they seem to be right. That is the queer thing. Here one finds warm, impulsive people thinking as if they were cold and took their time. As one goes about Mexico, one does not say, "here is the ideal democracy," but it seems possible that if the elite, the influence of which one feels on every inch of the ground, committed a downright betrayal of the ideal of social justice, its members would be likely to perish in their prime. But I saw no violence in Mexico. Yet I received the impression that a Mexican president who ceased to be the father of his people would instantly become its target. He and his government and his civil service have to keep going, keep going, keep going, in the direction of social justice, because the general will is like a gun in their ribs. The situation is controlled by the other form of pressure exercised by the Mexican people on their rulers. They recognise that privilege is something which springs up on the inside of a political machine as inevitably as fur forms in a kettle. One cannot prevent it forming, but one can have the kettle chemically cleaned at proper intervals. No president can be reelected after he has served his term of six years. Then out he goes and all his friends, with God, as the Spanish form of farewell put it. Let the new ones come in, but they must not stay a minute longer than the time that has been judged suitable for them to fill their bellies. One would almost call the Mexicans a cynical people, were it not for the hope that flashes on their faces like the reflection from sunlit water.

Cuauhtémoc

It is astonishing, this obsession with the Aztec past that governs modern Mexico. This French boulevard which runs through Mexico City, the Paseo de la Reforma, broadens out three times into wide circuses round huge enthusiastic monuments, which look as if about to do things stone cannot, such as burst into flower or explode or raise a cheer. All the two hundred and fifty feet of one monument celebrate the revolution, the winged and torch-bearing victory on another commemorates the heroes who died for national independence, but the one which exercises supreme authority is the monument to Cuauhtémoc, Swooping Eagle, the last Aztec emperor. He stands in hackling Aztec panoply, on a stone block rough hewn as Aztecs hewed it for their temples, and he is an indictment of the Spanish conquest. On the pedestal is represented the scene of his torture, which is the blackest mark on the name of Cortés.

I was told this story three times when I was in Mexico City, once by my hairdresser, and always with passion. The Spanish troops were discontented at the loot they got when they destroyed the Aztec capital, and the commanders had to scrape the barrel. Emperor Montezuma, He-who-gets-angry-like-a-Lord, the friend of Cortés, who nevertheless resisted him because he was an enemy of the Aztec people, was now dead. He had been a prisoner in the hands of the Spaniards when they took Tenochtitlán, and he happened to get accidentally killed. The Spaniards said he was sniped by an Aztec archer, either a traitor or a poor marksman, and they were possibly telling the truth. Montezuma's nephew and successor, Swooping Eagle, went on fighting against Cortés but was captured and was then questioned about the whereabouts of the treasure which the Spaniards had seen in Montezuma's palace when they had been staying there as his guests and friends, but which they could not then find. Swooping Eagle would tell them nothing. Cortés turned his back and, in the only moment of definite moral abdication detectable in his career, pretended to be unaware of what was going on when some of his captains put to the torture both Swooping Eagle and the king of an allied tribe. The lesser king groaned, and Swooping Eagle said coldly, "And what do you think I'm doing? Lying in a nice warm bath?" He would not speak, the torturers gave up. Later when Cortés made an expedition out of Aztec territory into Mayan land, down to Yucatán, he took Swooping Eagle with him because he dared not leave him behind, lest he became a rallying point for Aztec resistance. Somewhere on the thousand-mile-long trek there was a rumour of an Indian conspiracy to rescue him, and he was hanged by the Spaniards upside down on a kind of cotton tree known as the God tree. It is characteristic of the Mexican mind that it is not the scene of his hanging which is held up to perpetual execration on his monument: Aztec and Spaniard would agree that the leaders of men must sometimes kill to save their followers and the cause they serve. But they have agreed too that to torture a captured prince for the sake of greed is an infamy.

Were I to develop an urge to daub one of the monuments in Mexico City with bright red paint under the cover of night, this is the one I would compel myself to leave alone. I cannot run as fast as I once could. It is also according to Mexican fashion that the inhabitant of Mexico City who told me the story of Swooping Eagle with most passion was a pure-blooded Finn. I would fear all the people who caught me with my brush and bucket of paint near that monument, but I would not fear less than the Mexicans of long descent these other Mexicans who were, at the time that Swooping Eagle was put to the torture, in Lithuanian ghettos, or in northern Italy, or in Scotland. This whole population of Mexicans, down to the last Johnny-come-lately, has made a total self-identification with the Aztec Indians which amounts to a miraculous process like transubstantiation. This was initiated, of course, largely by the influence which sets the taxi driver shouting his history lesson to the foreign tourist: Diego Rivera and the other Mexican muralists, who so oddly used their brushes to exercise a power to change their society which elsewhere has been reserved for the written and spoken word. Even in the unlettered East this has been the rule: Gandhi and Nehru would have got nowhere without the platform and the printing press. But here it might be that Caxton had never been born, and nobody speaks of any public speeches except those uttered on some specific occasion of violence, usually in the past, say more than fifty years ago. It is these painters who have furnished the minds of these passionate people, who have built a city so modern that it gives a yesterday look to the recent quarters of London and New York and Paris, yet talk perpetually of a past remote by four hundred years.

Dr. Atl I

I might have understood this paradox better if only I had come here some years sooner, early enough to fulfil my purpose in coming to this country, or rather one of my purposes. For I came here not as a tourist but with a triple strand of intention. I wanted to see Popocatépetl and Iztaccíhuatl, Smoking Mountain and the White Woman, and any other Mexican volcanoes which were conveniently situated. I wanted to visit the Opera House, which had been the centre of entertainment in Mexico City in the late nineteenth century. I wanted to meet a person named Dr. Atl, who might be called the great first cause of the Mexican muralist movement, the irritant that sets up the pearl: all these desires were related to one another and, had they all been fulfilled, an area of teasing twilight, which has been troubling my curiosity for years, would at last have been irradiated. But only one among these desires was to be gratified, and that incompletely. I saw Popocatépetl, a delicate cone, of that peculiar shapeliness which affects the eye as a minor chord affects the ear, and Iztaccíhuatl, which is really like a gleaming girl stretched on a sacrificial pyre; and I saw Orizaba, the Star Peak, but that I could see only at such a distance that its splendid summit pretended to be the moon. It fooled me several times that way. I said to myself, "How beautiful the full moon looks, floating there in the faintly prismatic mist above the skyline," and then had the slight headache that comes when one looks to the north and thinks it is the south, and it struck me that we were at the beginning of the month, no time for a full moon, and that anyway the moon does not hang low in the west at noon. But there was a strike on the airlines, and I saw no other Mexican volcanoes. As for the Opera House, it had been pulled down long ago. And Dr. Atl had not waited to receive me. He had died in 1964, and not prematurely, for so far as can be ascertained he was born in 1875. This was a surprise to me, for the idiotic reason that my father had met him when he was a young man. He mentioned him in a letter and said nothing of interest about him: he was simply a young Mexican painter living in Paris. In my imagination he had remained so, encapsulated in their meeting, like a fly in amber.

This man I so much wanted to meet came of a rich Spanish-Mexican family and grew up with a passion for liberty and a burning desire to paint and that in the new nineteenth-century impressionist way. By a brutal irony of fate he was born the namesake of that mawkish sweet potato among painters, Murillo, and he early changed his name to Atl, which is a word in the Aztec language, Nahuatl. That it means water, sperm, urine, brain-stuff, cranium, head, and war suggests that conversation in Nahuatl must be a risky game; but, indeed, an idea can be seen passing in a stately way through these definitions, moving from an essential fluid (one without then one within man), extending to the idea of man's essential part, the intellect, and ending with what the Indians conceived to be man's essential occupation. When Dr. Atl was about twenty-one, he went to study law and philosophy in Rome, and he spent eight years in Europe. He was, however, not altogether as serious as one might deduce from the facts of his progress; he raised laughter as he went, laughter that, however, would not be wholly contemptuous unless those who laughed were contemptible. Working for some time in Paris teaching studios, he adopted the anarchist-syndicalist faith. Of the nature of his treasured faith, anarchism, most people will have to be reminded, for it is no longer modish. It rejected parliamentary socialism in favour of a society formed of self-governing unions of urban and rural workers who minded their own business and left a minimum of power to the state, which it hoped to confine almost entirely to the conduct of international relations.

This was the most fashionable of all socialist theories at the end of the nineteenth and the beginning of the twentieth century. To apply the current test, it would certainly have been asked to a Truman Capote party, while Marxism, though well established, was just a little too dowdy for that, and social democracy, of the sort which has won in Great Britain, would never have hoped to do more than read about the festivities in the newspapers. Anarchist doctrine had, indeed, certain compelling attractions. We must all concede, it would without question be the most convenient way of ordering life, if there were only a small number of human beings in the world, but the late-nineteenth-century anarchists held that the system could be adapted to the needs of a larger population by next Thursday at latest, through a combination of industrial action, including strikes, and a sustained assault on the operations of the state, including, if need be, physical attacks on its personnel. This doctrine runs contrary to the tactics and strategy of Marxism, though not to its aim. Communism believes that the state should disappear, but it holds that that happy event can only be brought about by first operating capitalism till it runs into the ground and then building on its ruins a socialist state and slowly organising the economic potentialities of the area till the existence of the state is no longer necessary: a long and painful process. Anarchism might be called Instant Revolution and offered the same advantages as instant coffee. But like that beverage, its manufacture raised technical problems.

Elie and Elisée Reclus

The great theorists of the anarchist movement, who tried to solve these technical problems, were two Frenchmen: the brothers Elisée and Elie Reclus. The inspiration of the movement came from the huge demented Russian bear, Bakunin, but he had not much to contribute to technique except bacchic exhortations to terrorism. And later Russia kindly exported another leader, but of a saintly type, in the person of Prince Kropotkin. But the Reclus brothers got on with the work in hand, and with the cooperation of a picked group worked out such possibilities of industrial action as the development of the strike. They refined that weapon by inventing two sorts, *la grève aux bras croisés*, the strike of the crossed arms, which was a simple downing of tools, and *la grève perlée*, the pearled, beaded, embroidered strike, which was the activist strike running to sabotage and attacks on scabs. The Reclus brothers were cultivated, charming, and virtuous men, sons of a Protestant pastor. Elisée was a distinguished geographer and a good man at a conference, but Elie was the better writer. Anybody who knows the brothers well will realise that Dr. Atl, after having made contact with them, came back from Europe to Mexico in 1904 not only a competent painter in the impressionist style, but an agitator determined to establish a militant trade union movement and also a connoisseur of volcanoes.

If he knew the Reclus brothers, this volcanic obsession followed. I am in a unique position to know. It happened that my grandfather, Major Charles George Fairfield, who served in the Third Scots Guards, though he was Irish, died in the year 1851, still in middle life. Infected gall bladders were not then understood by the medical profession. He left a widow much younger than himself, his second wife Arabella Fairfield, born Rowan, who looked like the figurehead of a ship and was a bigoted Protestant, ardently professing a faith hostile to ardour. It fell to her to find a tutor to prepare her four young sons for boarding school to which they had to go, like all children of their kind, for purely geographical reasons. A well-to-do family might find itself thirty or forty miles from any other children of the sort society then required to be educated, and if they lived in Ireland, they might be as far distant from any children of the same religion; and then, as now, homebred children had no opportunity of forming early ties with those they would have to work with when they were grown. Mankind likes to find a moral justification for everything it is forced to do by necessity. Hence, because the well-to-do had to send their sons away to boarding schools to avoid isolation, they alleged that this uncomfortable course helped boys to mature and develop exceptional powers of leadership and self-discipline, though obviously to shut up boys away from adults during adolescence must condemn them to immaturity.

Arabella Fairfield lived between County Kerry and London, where she had houses not at all grand but comfortable. Her London house was in Saint George's Square, which is down by the river near Chelsea, in a district named Pimlico, now desecrated and dreary. It happened that one New Year's Day, 1852, which was snowy and foggy, Elie and Elisée Reclus arrived in London, one twenty-four years old, the other twenty-seven. It was the dissenters' route: Karl Marx had arrived by it two years before. Elisée soon found work as a schoolteacher, and Elie became tutor to an aristocratic family and was soon dismissed, because the eldest son, still a little boy, had a courtesy title, and it was thought disrespectful that Elie would not use the boy's title but called him by his Christian name; also, he was accused of not shielding his charges from contacts with children of lower social station when they walked in the park. But Elie had followed the routine of the exiles by obtaining a ticket to the British Museum Reading Room, and there he had met an Irishman who was subsidised by my grandmother to write a thesis proving the Irish to be the Lost Ten Tribes of Israel, a work he had not completed when, many years later, he died of delirium tremens.

This Irishman was aware that my grandmother was looking for a tutor for her sons and sent Elie along to her on a foggy day, when the only way to get along the streets down by the river was to hang on to the railings. At last the right front door opened on a house full of light and small boys, who told Elie how anxious they had been about him, and how they would only have had to send their dog out and it would have found him, but unfortunately, the dog was in Ireland. There were servants, who took his damp greatcoat and his shoes away from him to dry and brought him the dead major's carpet slippers, and there was this handsome mother, who, muttering vague but sincere cries of sympathy, laced his tea with brandy and pressed on him buttery spiced currant buns. He was entranced by this family, which was entranced by him. "He was like an angel," my father recalled.

There began a relationship based on a wild misunderstanding. Arabella Fairfield assumed, in the light of her own obsessions, that since Elie and his brother had arrived in London as refugees, they must be Protestants, fleeing from the racks and thumbscrews in the cellars of the French branch of the Inquisition. In fact, Elie had lately earned local notoriety in his native town of Orthez, which was inland from Biarritz, by becoming an atheist just after his ordination as a Protestant pastor; and both he and his brother had long records of association with parties of the left at universities in France, Switzerland, and Germany. Their immediate reason for flight from their native country was a threat of arrest for armed demonstrations against Louis Napoleon when, a month before, he had overthrown the Republic and declared himself emperor. It is true that their demonstration was as mild as might be. They had got together at dinner with the youngbloods of Orthez, who cannot have been numerous, for it was a small town, and had resolved to make their protest the next morning by seizing the town hall. But the Reclus brothers were the only ones who kept the appointment. They had also been the only members of the company who followed a strange new practice known as teetotalism, a fact which they often recalled in later life. Indulgence in alcoholic liquor, they pointed out, might prevent such moral achievements as the capture of a town hall; it is a point certainly not often realised. They went home, but the authorities decided to arrest them, and it might have gone badly with them if the mayor had not sent warning to their mother, who snatched some money out of her desk and thrust it into her sons' hands and told them to keep going till they reached the English Channel. This episode was converted by my grandmother's kindly inattention into something as wildly off the mark as her persuasion that Elie and Elisée had been drawn by a common passion for Protestantism to the Irishman whom she was paying to prove that the Irish were the Lost Ten Tribes of Israel.

It is not imaginable how my grandmother failed to recognise that the tutor she was sustaining was an atheist and a revolutionary, and it is just as mysterious that the tutor did not identify the source of his sustenance as a Bible Christian and a high Tory. Yet there were elements that promoted confusion. The Irish famine had shocked my grandparents into austerity. In order that Arabella should give lavishly to the poor on her Kerry property and in Dublin and contribute to the relief fund, she reared her family on the plainest food and served only water at table, spent no money on pleasures even so simple as trips from London to Brighton, and dressed in the simplest widow's weeds. Elie Reclus rightly supposed that she made her sacrifices for love of the people, but did not know that her special fervour was due to the fact that she thought that the poor starving wretches were not only having a poor time in this world, they were bound to burn forever in the next, since they were Roman Catholics. When she railed against the pope, Elie thought it was because he was the head of Christendom, whereas she thought him a forerunner of anti-Christ. When she railed against Louis Napoleon, Elie thought that she and he were as one in detesting that poor character because he had been the president of the French Republic and had made himself emperor, whereas she believed, like most of her friends, that Louis Napoleon was a socialist, since he had got himself made president by promising the electors the elements of the welfare state. To many foreign observers this looked as if he were leading France backwards to a revolution, and this Arabella and her friends thought natural enough in a family as common, as unrelated to any of the best people, as the Bonapartes.

It was to Elie, and to him alone, that the truth of the situation came home. It was not long after he had been engaged as tutor, and the Fairfield household was still in London. He was absolved from all duties on Sundays and spent the day quietly with his fellow refugees, going with them to such green places as Hampstead Heath and Primrose Hill, happily talking about the coming revolution. Arabella Fairfield told him that on Sunday mornings she took the children to a meeting held by the body she had joined when she left the Episcopal Church called the Plymouth Brethren, and because some of the Plymouth Brothers and Sisters had come to the house and had spoken of their involvement in work among the East End poor, he took it for a sort of association resembling the Populist movement in Russia. But one day she mentioned a name that struck a chord in his memory, and he realised that the Plymouth Brethren was the English name for an evangelical sect known on the Continent as the Darbyites, after their founder, John Nelson Darby, a famous preacher. As Elie told my father long afterwards, he was deeply distressed by the discovery. It was as if, at the present moment, a young Communist, a draft-dodger and civil rights worker, found himself happily employed in a position of trust by a lady whom he had thought was of like mind but who was in fact an ardent Goldwaterite and thought him the same.

Elie realised that if he informed Arabella of his real principles she would burst into tears and ask him to leave, and he thought it his moral duty to remain with her. She was a good woman, and she was a helpless widow, specially helpless because she was a thorn in the side of her conventional relatives, who were members of the Established Church and loathed her Dissent, and she was too impulsive and too god-intoxicated to conciliate them. He thought the boys unusually intelligent and much upset by the loss of their father, and he believed that he was better qualified to educate them and steady their emotions than any substitute their mother was likely to find. Also, he suspected that my grandmother was not as well off as she was being led to believe she was and would soon find herself in financial straits. So he stayed on, for several years, taking an oath to himself (which he kept) that he would never instill any idea into Arabella's sons that she would not approve. From first to last he was utterly disregardful of his own interests. The financial disaster he foresaw occurred, and he insisted to Arabella that his salary be reduced. Later, Louis Napoleon declared an amnesty for all political offenders, and the brothers could have returned to France, but Elie stayed on still longer, till he had got all the boys on their way into the world, two into the army and two into the civil service. A later generation of the family suspected that Elie had been in love with Arabella, and it could be so. There are two types of women which eternally attract Frenchmen, one tall and pessimist and Racinean, and the other small and optimistic and Molierean, and Arabella was highly Racinean. It might have been a sign of transferred passion that, as soon as Elie entered the Fairfield household, he started a correspondence with a cousin of his and became engaged to her, and when, after five years, he at last returned home, he married her, but had certainly not hurried to her side. In any case, we may be sure he acted perfectly.

I have heard of few relationships that went as well as this one, which was founded initially on a profound misunderstanding. These people never tired of each other. All the four Fairfield brothers loved Elie Reclus so long as they lived, and they spoke to the younger generation about him as if they were showing off a family treasure, a beautiful piece of silver or a jewel; and how much Reclus loved them I learned not long ago, when I picked up in the dusk of a great library a bound volume of nineteenth-century pamphlets and found that one was an obituary of Elie, published just after his death in 1904 by the French Communist press, *L'Emancipatrice*. It was obviously written by someone much his junior, who had had to rely on the old man's reminiscences, and it must have been difficult to know what to choose from all his rich recollections. During his lifetime, politics had become an effective prescription against poverty, and the tongues of science had multiplied beyond counting, and the two brothers had known most of the men and women responsible for the change. The huge drama had been played out in terms of melodrama and comedy. They had been arrested and banished by their native France time and time again, bobbing in and out over the frontiers. Elie had taken a major part in founding the anarchist movement in Spain. They had been in the thick of the Commune, that abortive revolution which took over Paris in the name of the left wing when the Germans had defeated the French in the Franco-Prussian war of 1870. Elie had then been appointed keeper of the Bibliothèque Nationale, and there is a legend that, when the Commune had visibly failed, the committee in charge ordered him to set the Bibliothèque on fire. But that is a lie only interesting because it was told by Verlaine, who said in the course of an allegation that he himself had been ordered to set fire to Notre Dame. Certainly, Elie did indeed have his troubles as a librarian, but they were of a different nature. He had no difficulty in controlling the National Guard, whom he found most conscientious in their care of the nation's treasures, but he found real difficulty in checking a number of old scholars who felt this to be an ideal occasion for stealing books and manuscripts they had always coveted under the plea of taking them into safety. What makes the story endearing is that they pursued this purpose even under heavy bombardment.

But Reclus remembered the unhistoric also. In the French pamphlet, I read the name of one of my uncles:

> For several years in Dublin and London, Elie had to tutor four young people who certainly did him credit, and one of whom, Digby Fairfield, who died quite young in India, was far above the level of his generation in the nobility of his character and the brilliance of his intelligence.

It is as well that the old man had never heard how the other three brothers had also been engulfed by tragedy. But the engulfment had never destroyed in any of them their appreciation of that dedication to virtue, to kindness, to the alleviation of distress in friend or stranger and the abnegation of personal ends, which was characteristic of the Reclus brothers.

I tell at length this story which I heard as a child, because it is a perfect example of the process by which, my subsequent experience has taught me, culture and civilisation are carried on. Persons blinded by passionate prejudice collide with other persons blinded by passionate prejudice and the collisions engender a dynamic force which shapes our present and determines our future. If these persons were not so passionate that their prejudices blinded them, then they could not engender this dynamism. We develop by misunderstanding. It is possible to imagine better ways, but this is in fact the one that is most employed.

Naturally, my father was in part Elie Reclus all his life long. Of course, Elie failed in his intention of instilling into his pupils no idea contrary to their mother's faith. It is true that my father was a Tory, but of the extreme sort which exalts the individual and would give the state hardly any powers at all, which is very close to anarchism, as conservatism often is today. When William F. Buckley junior tells his students that the only thing the state should be allowed to do is to regulate currency, he is making a remark which most of the great anarchists of the past would have happily endorsed. Since my father was so largely Elie Reclus, so am I, and that is why I have a certain insight into the mind of Dr. Atl, who had certainly read the works of the Reclus brothers and claimed to have been closely acquainted with both of them, and probably with truth, for they were always surrounded by anarchist sympathisers from all parts of the world, including a number from Latin America.

This influence would certainly entail a measure of interest in the natural sciences, for Elisée was a professor of geography for most of his life; Elie had left the teaching profession to dabble in socialist banking, an enterprise much more successful than is now remembered. He worked with the brothers Jacob and Isaac Péreire, who, following the principles of the great socialist thinker Saint-Simon, had built the first railway lines in France and had now founded the Credit Mobilier, a joint stock company giving long-term credits for industrial and commercial projects, out of the funds collected by public security issues. This was for twenty years the most important single agency of its kind in France. When it was converted into a commercial bank for no other reason than the old age of the Péreires, Elie tried to imitate them by conducting such an enterprise of his own, failed, became the librarian in charge of an important private library, broke into the nascent science of anthropology, and ended up as a professor of comparative mythology in the same Belgian university, the Université Nouvelle in Brussels, where his brother was a professor of geography. But throughout his life, he continued, like his brother, to write popular books on scientific subjects. This was part of the left-wing pattern. A conspicuous example was Blanqui, the great apostle of the idea of conspiracy, who was twice arrested in 1870 for armed demonstrations, the first time because he went berserk at the funeral of a journalist called Victor Noir, who had been killed by a member of the Bonaparte family, and the second because he was caught stealing weapons from a military arsenal; at the same time he was writing a book on astronomy called *Eternity by Way of the Stars*. The idea behind this leftist tendency was that the existence of God had been disproved, but any sense of insecurity could be removed by investigations of the universe, which were bound to show it as a self-regulating and self-preserving machine, safe to carry passengers. Blanqui's proofs were not particularly convincing.

The natural phenomenon which fascinated the Reclus brothers most was the volcano. Lava being what it is, this seems an odd obsession for dedicated friends of humanity; a volcano is no pet. But doubtless a volcano was to them a symbol of the revolution and also of the aggressive impulse, which they were suppressing in themselves with an inhuman success in their personal relations but unsuccessfully in their political lives. The mildest of men, they could not bring themselves to denounce terrorism, even when it took the form of senseless bomb-throwing at crowds. Whatever the reason, the instruction Elie Reclus gave to my father and his brothers was heavily loaded with propaganda for volcanoes. It was pointed out to them that Great Britain and Ireland might be beautiful in their own way, but were shamefully deficient in volcanoes. If any hill aroused the boys' admiration, they were invited to reflect how much handsomer it would be were it surmounted by a fiery glow and a plume of smoke. The boys were encouraged to work hard so that they might get on their way and travel round the world, seeing volcanoes. This passion Elie successfully communicated to my father, and it never died down in him.

When he left the army, in his early thirties, he visited Mexico simply to look at Popocatépetl and Orizaba. Later, it pleased him very much that my mother had in her girlhood spent a winter at Naples when Vesuvius was unusually active, and that she would describe with ecstasy how at night the mountain used to look like a vast hand held wrist up between earth and sky, with the fingers and the lines picked out in flame as the streams of lava rolled down the gullies. This, his expression suggested, was how a woman of spirit should take her pleasures. On the other hand, my mother had been exasperated when, for the first time after her marriage, she had gone with him to Edinburgh in order that she might introduce him to her family, and he had disappeared from the hotel as soon as they had arrived there, having felt obliged to go at once and climb the mountain just outside the city, Arthur's Seat, because it is an extinct volcano. In his last years, he looked up at the glowing sunsets of the year 1902 and wondered whether they were really due to the dust of the Martinique eruption curling round the world, as if he hoped a tyrant had at last shown his splendid better nature. I must own that I have inherited this curious kind of piety. Any volcano seems to me something of the earthly yet sacred, like the pope.

In any landscape dominated by Vesuvius I feel as if I were in church. Etna shocks me because it is too dumpy for a divinity, but when I see the black fertility of the fields around it I realise that the divine is more than skin deep. But my satisfaction was complete when I saw Popocatépetl and Iztaccíhuatl in between the silver trunks of the eucalyptus trees.

Dr. Atl II

So I know where Dr. Atl got his passion for volcanoes, but I am not so sure where he got his other dominating passion, which was for the indoctrination of the illiterate Mexican proletarian with socialist ideas through propagandist mural paintings. This was in part a natural development of a long-standing trend in French art. As frescoes had in the past celebrated the pagan gods, the Christian mysteries, the cardinal virtues, and the monarchies, so in the nineteenth century very large paintings advertised left-wing causes. The exemplar of the socially conscious artist was, of course, Courbet, who has left a specific account of the propagandist intention which lies behind his *Stonemasons*. But even an artist who appears as neutral to us today as Puvis de Chavannes, whom we think of as the reconstructor of an antique world populated by wan nudes who had evidently been boiled for soup, even he began by painting pictures with such titles as *Mademoiselle de Souverin Drinking a Glass of Blood in Order to Save the Life of Her Father* and went on to vast decorative panels representing Peace and the Dignity of Labour. Mexican artists had been copying this kind of large didacticism on the domes and ceilings and walls of the public buildings erected by the various presidents who ruled over the country after it became a Republic in 1821, before which time most of its decorative energy had gone into churches.

But the idea of wall-painting to serve as propaganda to the illiterate is not so easy to trace. Possibly it was derived from John Ruskin, who of all English nineteenth-century writers cast the widest shadow on the future. It was Ruskin who made Gandhi a socialist, and what is more, made Gandhi the appealing kind of socialist he was. Ruskin was also a determinant factor in the development of Proust, who was to look at the churches of northern France with his idol's eye and himself translated into French his *Bible of Amiens*. It would seem as if a man who had influenced both Gandhi and Proust had cast his net as wide as one mental net can cover, but it is perhaps significant that in *The Bible of Amiens* Ruskin makes the point that the sculpture on the exterior of churches was meant to give religious education to the illiterate medieval peasant. It is quite possible that Dr. Atl came across this idea, or an echo of it, for as well as being a painter, an anarchist agitator, a volcanologist, and a student of botany and mining, he was a man of letters, writing prose and verse and being well read in several literatures; and it would be natural for him, as a painter, to take this concept of the pedagogic use of architectural decoration and switch it from sculpture to painting.

When Dr. Atl went back to Mexico in 1904, he meant to found his own Federation of Artists. Everybody still laughed at him, but he was so rich that he was able to carry out enterprises in spite of the laughing. And if there was nothing in Mexico City, no such constellation of genius as shone in Paris, he could still draw on a number of gifted artists. There was one supreme artist, Velasco, but he was of no service to Dr. Atl, for he was aging and a landscapist who could not be committed to anything but the earth of Mexico. There were, however, such juniors as Parra, who, astonishing as that may seem today, was the first to exploit the superb material offered by the Indians and their culture, and his follower, Harran, who treated that same material but bedevilled it with the influence of Gauguin and the Flash-Harry Spanish artist Zuloaga; and there was a far greater artist called Goitia, endowed with exact perceptions and a gentle yet arrogant certainty of design, who was just what Dr. Atl was looking for, since he was already a dedicated revolutionary. He came from the fantastically beautiful and ornate mountain mining town of Zacatecas, where the Franciscans, the Augustinians, and the Jesuits erected sumptuous churches among the colonists' palaces for three centuries; and he probably knew a great deal about poverty, for the lode had run out. Goitia's painting *The Old Man on the Dump Heap* is remarkable not only for the Goyaesque strength of emotion, which is kept from hysteria by the propriety of the design, but for its realistic portrayal of Indian poverty, which has its special character. A poor Indian seems to be tasting his poverty, trolling it over his taste buds, saying to himself bitterly, "Yes, it tastes as bitter as that." Then there seems to be a still bitterer after-taste. "I have nothing," he seems to be saying. "Can it really be true that I am going out of this world, having had nothing, absolutely nothing? If that is so, what is this world?" But the thinking is done quietly. Not a fraction of dignity is sacrificed.

In the great market of Mexico City, I saw an old woman sitting on the ground with the grace of a ballet-dancer taking a rest during rehearsal, while she haggled with a stall-holder over the rush mats she had stretched out about her. As the stout little man beat his arms up and down, doing the crawl through a sea of bargaining to the minimum price which was the winning-post, her eyes were looking over his shoulder, and while her voice cut into his, her whitish gaze was saying, "Can it really be true . . . ?" There is something of this secondary suffering in Goitia's great picture of Indians keeping their All Soul's Day, *Tata Jesucristo*, which is to be found in the Philadelphia Art Gallery. These studies of poverty make the great European specialist on that theme, Käthe Kollwitz, appear superficial. If her starvelings got enough food, they might simply put flesh on their bones, and even too much of it, and end like the people who had denied them food. Goitia suggests that want does not merely mean hunger and emaciation, it means the destruction of potentialities for good and evil. The old man who sits on the rubbish dump might have sat at the head of his table, looking fondly on happy wife and children, or he might have chosen for a seat a tyrant's throne. The indignity is not to be allowed to make that choice.

Goitia was not an unsophisticated artist. None of the revolutionary painters were that. Indeed, at the moment Dr. Atl returned to Mexico, Goitia sailed to continue his training in Italy and Spain. Meanwhile, Dr. Atl swooped down like an eagle on the centenary celebration of the revolt which led to the independence of Mexico and used it as a means of financing socially conscious artists by collecting them in a Centro Artístico and getting the government to give its members commissions arising out of the festival. This seemed a little inconsistent, for the president was still the dictator Díaz, who for over thirty years had been proving in a boisterous way that great soldiers make poor statesmen. But Dr. Atl was following an illustrious example. In 1871, Courbet formed a committee of artists, including Corot, who was over seventy, Daumier, who was over sixty, Manet, who was not yet forty, the sculptor Dalou, who was a particularly fiery spirit though his work was placidly academic, and a forgotten cartoonist called André Gill. This committee performed real services during the seven weeks of the Commune, assuming responsibility for the administration of the museums, but its usefulness was impaired by Courbet's sense of the dramatic. He rolled a red eye on the column in the Place Vendôme, because it commemorated Napoleon's victories, and ordered that it should be pulled down, and, unfortunately, the order was obeyed before the Commune had reached its allotted span. When the reconstituted government came back to work, it found that the column had been damaged in its days of prostration, and the cost of the necessary repairs and its re-erection was huge. As well as sending Courbet to prison for six months, it presented him with the bills, and on his release he was forced to flee to Switzerland, from which disadvantageous location he contested the claim, but in vain. When he died in 1877, the government seized all the pictures in his deserted studio and sold them by auction.

But his committee had achieved some permanent results. It had set up a Federation of Artists, which did not die with the Commune. It continued to exist, trying to grapple with the problem perpetually vexing to all art schools, no matter where they be; it tried to prevent the teaching from dragging its feet and loitering within the shadow of the last generation's triumphs; and it insisted on instruction in new technical processes. It also proposed, and the proposal was accepted by subsequent governments, a system by which artists would be employed to decorate public buildings with paintings and sculptures. This looks like a bid for self-preservation which might turn into graft, and so it often did. There are French towns and villages in which the inhabitants appear to be outnumbered by didactic statues produced by sculptors of the same political complexion as the local municipality. But the proposal was originally idealist. It was an attempt to free the artist from the caprice of the private patron and set him working for the nation; and it was also an anarchist effort to get artists into one of the unions which would form the governmental units of the anarchist state. Therefore the programme was jealously guarded and pursued by the next generation of left-wing artists, who included Seurat, Signac, Gauguin (who was the grandson of a pioneer socialist with the entrancing name of Flora Tristan), and, above all, Camille Pissarro, who, in spite of the quietness and measure of his art, was the fieriest revolutionary of them all. It must be noted that these men were not just vaguely against the establishment and ready to sass it, like the TV and nightclub and theatre people of today, who resemble them more than the painters of today in their obsession with politics. These Frenchmen were deeply read in political science, attended party congresses, and in some cases accepted full party discipline. It is one of the great ironies of history that, within a hundred years, the works of these men have become the money boxes in which millionaires lock up their savings.

In the complex which makes the modern Mexican, some genes are committed to the pictorial arts. Therefore, Dr. Atl's just duty (so far as artists were concerned, for he was simultaneously busying himself with trade union organisation), was to press the government to give commissions to artists, and this was the perfect moment for pressing such demands. Such commissions well might take the form of morally propagandist frescoes, for dozens of these had been painted back in the seventies, when the authorities followed a curious atheist-socialist-religious movement and commissioned many frescoes to popularise it. Mexicans were used to seeing Philosophy and Jurisprudence on the left and Science and Medicine slightly lower on the right. Mexico was about to celebrate the centenary of the revolution which gave the country its independence from Spain, and it was to be made the occasion of much junketting, for the native population had shown under the Aztecs and the Spanish alike a special aptitude for giving and enjoying huge public parties, and it was hoped also to make it something of a World's Fair, so permanent and temporary buildings might be erected. The idea of state patronage of the arts was already accepted and was applied with a singular lack of prejudice. For example, the governor of Vera Cruz was just about then awarding a travelling scholarship to a boy of twenty-one called Diego Rivera, although he was a demonstrative rebel. The government, smiling, showed every sympathy with Dr. Atl's campaign.

But there was a sour side to the situation. The impending festival was being blatantly converted from a celebration of Mexican independence to a glorification of the president in power, Porfirio Díaz, who was not a socialist. It is hard to say what he was, in political terms. Fundamentally, he was what the eighteenth century called a Roaring Boy, and he was inspired by the right idea: to draw Mexico out of the past into the present and develop its huge industrial potentialities and call in the foreign investor to negotiate the transition. But he furthered it by a technique all too familiar in the lower reaches of business enterprise. He was like the chairman of a corporation who manages to keep the shareholders happy by distributing to them money which looks like dividends but is in fact derived from capital assets. To foreigners he sold, or gave away, land amounting to one-fifth of the country, much of it belonging by legal title to Indian communities or individual Indians. He invited foreign corporations to come in and exploit mines and oil fields, set up department stores, run public utilities, make textiles, cut lumber, and engage in any other industrial process for which they could find the material, and he made the invitations the more seductive by guaranteeing that Mexican labour was underpaid, intimidated, and unorganised. This last was a great attraction to the backward-minded capitalists who were irked by the rise of the trade union movement in their native lands. No political party, conservative, liberal, socialist, anarchist, or communist, but would have refused President Díaz admission to its ranks. Yet the Federation of Artists, as founded in the Paris Commune, can never have found a statesman more wholehearted in his acceptance of their principles, nor more eager to carry them into effect.

Hence Dr. Atl faced a painful moral dilemma. Half of him was pure comedian; but half of him felt seriously about serious matters. He must have felt passionate hatred for Díaz, who was flogging, imprisoning, shooting helpless workingmen whose only offence was that they were founding the trade union movement which was the church of his own anarchist faith. But his prime business at that moment was with painters, so he went along with the Mexican government, who were indeed to prove how broad-minded they were by overlooking his known left-wing connections and offering him a truly munificent commission. It is useless to suspect Dr. Atl of greed or ambition, for at all times he gave away his wealth with both hands, and he was later to offer up his good name and every worldly prospect as a sacrifice to his principles. When he accepted that commission, he must have resolved to concentrate on effecting the nationalisation of art within a capitalist state, just as the founder of the Federation of Artists was then doing in France under the Third Republic.

But he must also have enjoyed accepting the commission, for his ideas were large. Most, if not all, of his frescoes have disappeared, either destroyed by his opponents or betrayed by his own use of perishable media, but they are said to have covered the widest walks and the highest domes with gigantic personifications of Night or Rain or suchlike natural phenomena, solemnised by the anarchist prepossession that these have a philosophical and political significance, and all in a state of nudity that itself made the same claims. This commission dealt with a Palace of Fine Arts which the government was erecting in honour of the centenary, a heavy, handsome, busty, more or less neoclassical building of the type that has served cultural purposes all over the world since the beginning of the nineteenth century. It stands on the edge of Alameda, Poplar Park, about which the patriotic taxi driver will cry out that it was a splendid market when the country belonged to the Aztecs and was converted by the Spaniards to a funeral pyre for the victims of the Inquisition. Within the plump matrix of the palace is a theatre, and Dr. Atl was invited to design a curtain for it.

That curtain is extant, and it is a richly meaningful whopper. It was made of mosaic glass by the New York firm of Tiffany, at a cost of forty-seven thousand dollars, and it weighs twenty-two tons. It takes the breath away by its odd displacement in artistic history. When Dr. Atl created it, he had just come back from a Paris dominated by Cézanne, Renoir, Bonnard, Vuillard, the Douanier Rousseau, Matisse, Modigliani, Vlaminck, Derain, Dufy, Marcel Duchamp, Braque, Ozenfant, Gris, Léger, Rouault, Bouchant, Lhote, even the young Picasso, who were all alive and still or already painting. Yet this work is a pure specimen of Art Nouveau, as glorious an exemplar as the restaurant in the Gare de Lyon or the ballroom in the Villa Hygeia in Palermo and much, much larger. The aim of that evanescent school was to render all forms, even if mineral or animal, with the flowing line seen in plant life, but, as it was urban in its origins, all represented objects showed the still and opaque colour and the lax forms of flowers not growing nor lately cut, but bought at the market or delivered by the florist on his rounds. Indeed, the huge monstrosity that covers the proscenium in the Palace of Arts recalls the lilies and gladioli and peonies and roses that glow behind the stream-washed plate glass windows of florists, their brightness not quite vibrant, and never a tense petal. But though this prodigy is pure Art Nouveau, it is impossible to imagine Swann taking Odette de Crecy to see it as a special treat, for so mysterious is the power of an artistic style to communicate without giving a single direct clue, it betrays its place of manufacture. Anyone would know that it came from the New York of Edith Wharton's early novels, that round the corner of its making was the old Waldorf Astoria, that, when the workers went home, nobly profiled young men drove through the crystalline unpolluted twilight in hansom cabs in the company of tall young ladies wearing ostrich feather boas. Since of all artistic styles Art Nouveau is the most closely associated with a specially pampered class of capitalists, it is odd to find it adopted by Dr. Water, Urine, Brain-stuff, Brain-pan, and War, at a moment when he wished to commemorate the chaste and violent character of his native country. But nobody can regret that it was.

When he was making his design, he must have been sorely troubled by the necessity to compromise with evil that he might do good. Hence he performed an expiatory rite which probably I alone understand today out of all the audiences which assemble in the Palace of Fine Arts to watch Señora Eva Hernández's enchanting Balet Folclórico. Dr. Atl's curtain represents the two patron volcanoes of Mexico City, Popocatépetl and Iztaccíhuatl, the Smoking Mountain and the White Woman. Before each performance these disclose their essence under the ever-changing conditions of time: a Platonic idea demonstrated by favour of an electrical device not often keeping such philosophical company, which exhibits their snowy summits first as flushed with the dawn, then radiant under noon, then as responsive to the moon under a purple night. The forms recall whipped cream, the colours suggest various kinds of jam. But here authority is still exercised by a double presentation of the symbol of salvation, as Elie and Elisée Reclus cherished it for all their joint one hundred and sixty-two years, as my father, soon to die, saw it written ethereally in the sky as he looked towards the sunset, that I acknowledge when I want to bend my knees reverently before Vesuvius. It is too bad that Dr. Atl did not live on into his nineties, instead of dying in 1964, so that we could have met. For I must be among the very few survivors who understand what moved him to set Popocatépetl and Iztaccíhuatl on that curtain. It was Saint Paul's belief that "God dwells in light which no man can approach unto." But an earlier faith, looking round for a Great First Cause, thought that God dwells in *fire* which no man can approach unto. It recognised that

Providence set earth and sky ablaze, often to the delight of men's eyes, but sometimes to end all delight and close all eyes; and it recognised that all the victims of this fire, by comparison with its huge, hot, indiscriminate guilt, are innocent and that this is the work of God, so either He does not exist or this fire also is worshipful. However it be, cry out the ghosts of Dr. Atl and Elie and Elisée Reclus from the twenty-seven tons of glass cubes in which they are forever enmeshed, the spectacle is superb, and what is needed is courage, and courage, and again courage.

Revolution

Here in Mexico I often feel as if I were among Slavs. There is an intelligent population, which uses words as if it were highly literate, even when it is illiterate, and is readier than the Westerner to switch from the concrete to the abstract, and is sincere, while not averse from attitudinising. Even the attitudes adopted are the same. Both love to pretend they boil in despair. In the lovely, almost too lovely, town of Cuernavaca there is an Aztec pyramid which is not looking its best, being involved with a railway station, and, when we visited it, a party of boys were lolling on its summit. They said loudly, in English, as we passed that they were smoking marihuana, and their spread laxity of limb suggested disillusionment, cynicism, everything that is negative. But their faces were bright with hope. The same combination can be seen in Mexico's beloved essayist, Octavio Paz, who argues that survival is so specially difficult for Mexicans that they might as well write it off, while his words sit on his pages as comfortably as if he were Montaigne. The same can be said of countless Slav authors, of all Slav refugees.

There is, of course, good reason why Mexico should have a Slav flavour, since it is Spanish. A thousand years ago the Slavs came into the eye of the Old World as an unlucky people always being pounded to pulp by their Germanic and Scandinavian and Asiatic neighbours, and their prisoners of war were regularly bought by the slave-traders of Byzantium and the Near East and marketed along the Mediterranean. The Arabs were then occupying Spain, which they were treating as an undeveloped country which had to be given know-how by the superior civilisation of Islam, and they needed labour. So they bought the Slavs in quantity, one khalif of Córdoba alone introducing forty thousand into his territory. They found their feet in that civilisation. Córdoba was then the equal of Constantinople and Baghdad, wealthier than any community today and liberal in the foundation of schools and colleges, hospitals, public baths, and morgues. "The pearl of the world," a Saxon saint called it, with no reason to praise Islam. The court was solemn: an ambassador sent by a great German king had to wait two years for an audience. Its splendours were protected by a corps of mamelukes, soldier slaves picked for their strength and intelligence and given special privileges so that the ruler could rely on a force detached from the people and loyal to their master alone. In the tenth century these numbered five thousand and were all Slavs. The population of Córdoba was alleged by the Arabs to number half a million, but modern archaeologists have measured the area of the old city and knocked the figure down to one hundred thousand. If 5 percent of Córdobese were Slav, and there was an army of other such importees working outside the city in the mines and on the fields and in the forests, it can be guessed how large the genetic chance is that a number of Spaniards in Spain and in Latin America will be prone to sit up all night and discuss ideas.

What happened to Dr. Atl and his friends will be more comprehensible if they are envisaged as not so unlike Russians and Poles and Yugoslavs. The Mexican situation began to go the Slav, left-wing way from 1910, when a young man was appointed governor of the cattle state of Chihuahua because, as one history book tells us, he "had seduced his niece and had been given office to steady him." The Chihuahuanese disapproved of this form of therapy and advanced on President Díaz with demands that he resign the presidency, which he had held, by means other than prayer or the normal operation of the electoral machine, for thirty-five years. Dr. Atl immediately left for Europe, not as a refugee but as a self-appointed representative of certain radical elements who were waiting to seize power as soon as Díaz left, which happened not long afterwards.

This did not work out so well as had been hoped, for he was succeeded by a weak liberal called Madero, in whom the country had no confidence. Quite unreasonably, this was largely because he had a falsetto voice, which aroused nonpolitical speculations which illogically had a political effect. It was also held against him that he was a teetotaller, a vegetarian, and a spiritualist and that he once wept publicly during a performance of Tchaikovsky's 1812 Ouverture. This utterly wiped out recognition of the saintliness which made him spend the profits of his cotton plantation on houses and schools and clinics for his workers, and the provision of meals for their children which were served in his own ranch. This gentle soul should have been welcomed by the young artists of the Mexican Federation, but it unfortunately happened that Díaz, just before his departure, had commissioned six artists (one of whom was Dr. Atl) to paint frescoes on the walls of a chapel which was being converted into a school in a slum district of Mexico City, and when Madero came to power he ordered the work stopped, though the scaffolds were already erected. The poor man could not be blamed. He could not pay for them, since Díaz had left the state coffers empty. It is possible also that the subject of the frescoes, "The Evolution of Humanity," made no powerful appeal to him, since he was possessed by fears that he was to be murdered, fears which were to be realised within two years.

President Madero's power was weakening, partly because of his private situation. His family were smelters of the sort which had benefited from Díaz's tenderness towards capital, so the family fortunes were declining, and only his brother Gustavo stood by him. He also, going over the top of saintliness into idiocy, took disciplinary action against corrupt subordinates and then recalled them to his service and expected them to be loyal and conscientious, simply because their country required them to be so. But it could not be said that Madero was his own worst enemy. That title belonged to the United States ambassador to Mexico, Henry Lane Wilson, a character insufficiently appreciated by contemporary Americans. A native of Indiana, he had become ambassador in Mexico because he had worked for McKinley in the 1896 presidential campaign, and a wave of the spoils system had washed him on the shores of the diplomatic service and retreated, leaving the diplomats to deal with this flotsam as they could. From the first, his quality aroused questions. He had a great desire to represent his country in Japan, but it was felt that the spoils system had better think again before it washed him on that critical area. He was therefore sent to Chile and then to Belgium, from which place he was removed just in time, in 1913. His presence there during the First World War might have put yet another crimp into that disaster. As it was, he went to Mexico and, finding a crisis such as the Mexicans had been handling for a century by ritual disorders, turned it into an international disaster simply by breaking every known diplomatic law and custom.

Madero was insecure in the saddle. The right hated him because it feared that he was going to expropriate the native and British and American capitalists; and the left hated him because they feared that he would not do anything of the kind. It was therefore important not to rock the boat. Henry Lane Wilson did his best to overturn it and very strangely, fourteen years afterwards, when most people had forgotten him, wrote a very long autobiography, *Diplomatic Episodes in Mexico, Belgium, and Chile*, in which he describes with a butler's calm in detail the enormities he committed. It is the first rule of diplomacy that no diplomat may interfere with the internal affairs of the country to which he is sent. But something had to be done to protect the Americans and their properties, who suddenly found themselves unwanted in Mexico. Henry Lane Wilson, however, did rather more than that, aiding the enemies of Madero by tactics which recall the preliminary softening up that Hitler used to prepare Poland and Czechoslovakia and Yugoslavia for annexation. He broke public confidence by spreading reports of general unrest in Mexico when nine-tenths of the territory was tranquil, he advised American residents to leave their homes without reason, he sent back dispatches to Washington which led the president to send a hundred thousand troops to the Mexican border, a step which automatically roused Mexican patriotism to fever-point, and, for good measure, alleged that Madero had become insane. When he had created chaos, he organised the deposition of the wretched man and his replacement by the most debased of his enemies, an able general who was also an alcoholic, a drug addict, a gambler, and an embezzler, by name Huerta. He then announced to Washington that "a wicked despotism has fallen."

He did not know beforehand what breaking the rules would do to him, and afterwards he was unconscious of the damage. Owing to his interference with the disposition of the government's defence forces in Mexico, President Madero and his vice-president found their position hopeless, and, to avoid further bloodshed, they agreed to resign on condition they and their adherents were given immunity. Washington instructed Henry Lane Wilson to see that Huerta honoured this condition when he accepted it, and Wilson did this to the extent of getting Huerta's promise that the men and their families would be sent out of the country, and these he passed on to Madero's wife. He describes what happened in a passage which brings to mind the official attitude of Pontius Pilate: "On the day following the events just recited Mrs. Madero came a second time to see me. She seemed still to be apprehensive about the fate of her husband and also about his comfort. During this interview she handed me, written on an ordinary piece of paper, an unaddressed note from the mother of Madero, which I understood to be intended for me, but which, nevertheless, I transmitted to Washington without alteration." It was a laconic appeal, bleak as a desert, for the life of her son. At that time Henry Lane Wilson could issue what orders he liked to Huerta. But he took no steps to secure that the prisoners should be handed over to him, nor to accompany them to the frontier. Three nights later Madero and his vice-president were, as Hitler used to say, "shot while attempting to escape." But Pontius Pilate is the closer analogue: "Profoundly as the violent death of Madero must be regretted by all right-thinking people, it should be remembered that he had resigned the office of President and at the time of his death was a simple Mexican citizen in no wise entitled through accepted international practice of the diplomatic intervention of any foreign government." That he stood where the text suggests he was standing is proved by his suppression of a fact. He omits to mention that, some days before Madero's wife came to him with the letter from Madero's mother, Madero's brother Gustavo had been murdered. He had been tricked into Huerta's hands by accepting an invitation to luncheon, had been tortured, mutilated, and finally shot; and both women knew it.

Dr. Atl III

It is hard to imagine what loyalty inspired Dr. Atl to continue his political activities in Paris after Madero's fall, but he had plenty of other irons in the fire. He haunted the Paris studios to see what was cooking, and the menu was satisfying, for it included cubism, surrealism, and the first response to African sculpture. The atmosphere was intoxicating, though perhaps Dr. Atl should have resisted the intoxication, since it was his mission to bring art to the common man, and it was then that art was taking a new direction which carried it outside of the common man's comprehension. But happily he spun round and round and blew his tin trumpet and was the life and soul of all the great festivities of the period, such as the demonstration which stormed the cemetery of Père Lachaise and tore away the tarpaulins which had for too long shrouded the tomb of Oscar Wilde constructed by the young Epstein. It was the plea of the authorities that they had been actuated only by a desire to protect its extreme fragility, but it was as rugged as a truck, and the real objection related to the male figures adorning it, whose genitals were large and scowling. The raid was inappropriately led by Aleister Crowley, a dingy practitioner of black magic, whose only connection with the arts was his perpetration of a large number of obscene watercolours, denatured by a prim and governessy technique. But he must have conducted this raid efficiently, as there were only about twenty demonstrators.

Dr. Atl also renewed his old political ties. Elie and Elisée Reclus had died, but he visited Switzerland, where there was a fine mixed bag of refugees. The mountains which now shelter the numbered accounts of nervous capitalists then harboured human repositories of dissent, to be drawn on when the historical situation called for its application. These dedicated beings would now be supported through foundations and universities and publishing houses and periodicals, by a society which has accepted the idea of the necessity for its modification and is toying with the idea of the necessity for its total destruction. But in those days the dissenters had to scratch a living out of what penitent capitalists (and there were more of these than would be supposed) contributed to the party funds or were sustained by family ties which surely have weakened since then. All over Europe fathers, brothers, mothers, sisters, were sending off remittances, which they often could ill afford, to adult relatives who had dropped out of their economic niche for the sake of ideas which their benefactors probably found shocking but which need not destroy their family's love; and this loyalty continued when the parties had not seen each other for years, even decades. Here and there a revolutionary kept his purchase on the economic machine. Martov was engaged for long periods during his stormy career in the manufacture of yoghurt, an operation which was not only profitable but had its symbolic value, for he was a Menshevik, and the bland substance he sold was not unlike his gentle kind of Communism. But for a great part the money that kept the exiles alive flowed over the frontiers from warm hearts that said in full banality, "What does it matter, so long as the dear one is happy?"

The dear ones were happy, perhaps happier than their kind has ever been since. They did not have to submit to the routine of employment. There were blueprints of the future to be worked on, and there were ample opportunities for them to practice their craft right at hand. The natives of Switzerland were making watches, milk chocolate, and cheese, all on a low organisational level. The German-speaking section of the population were therefore the objects of trade union propaganda by the German and Austrian refugees, while the French-speaking sections had long been affected by the influence of Bakunin and the Reclus brothers and responded to the anarcho-syndicalist refugees. There were also a number of refugees from the tsardom, centred round Geneva; it is said that there were more members of the Russian revolutionary parties within the Swiss republic than there were in Russia. They took no interest in the natives, whom they left to get on with the Gruyère, and spent their time working out the fine points of political doctrine and the strategy and tactics of the coming revolution. They had something of the prestige of a contemplative order in the Church, as compared to the orders which do good works—of Mary as compared to Martha. And indeed in Switzerland (and in any other place where they were exiled) they had another habit that recalls ecclesiastical organisation. As monks and nuns dropped their names to which they had been born and took holy pseudonyms, so did the refugees often adopt other names. It was in Paris that Gerardo Murillo became "Dr. Atl."

It was no doubt agreeable for Dr. Atl to pick up the threads of his former connections. Anarchism had its own culture, and part of that was a notable tradition of hospitality. Long afterwards, Emma Goldman and Alexander Berkman, old and discouraged, would greet any believer knocking at their door, even if he were a stranger, with a Homeric welcome. But Dr. Atl also tried his luck with the Russians and called on Lenin in Lausanne, and this was not a success. It could not have been. I know nothing of Dr. Atl's appearance except that he was bearded, but it can be deduced that he was exuberant, that if one poured him out one would never get him back into the container, that there was more than enough of him to go round. It is also evident, from his reported conversations and letters, that he was a case of premature Zen. He was also a large and happy giver; he loved to go into the kitchen and with his own hands cook his needy artists great cauldrons of spaghetti with rich, dark meat sauce. None of this was acceptable by Lenin, who found fervour in his disciples no recommendation at all and would not have appreciated the sauce. He was of the same mind as Henry More, the seventeenth-century Platonist, who wrote that "If Christianity be exterminated, it will be by enthusiasm." One of the most poignant letters Lenin ever wrote was to a colleague who was ill, begging him not to consult a doctor who was a Party member, since the faithful were such idiots. One sees between the lines of that letter a quiet elderly lady who has consented to take into her little house a friend's large dogs and finds them lolloping about her ordered rooms, licking her hands with their great wet tongues, rearing up and putting their paws on her chest and begging her for walkies. The same spirit is manifest in Lenin's last testament, in which he confessed, shuddering with fastidiousness and the determination to be fair, his unfavourable opinion of his colleagues.

That very large dog, Dr. Atl, must on his side have been equally dissatisfied. A similar visitor, the son of a Levantine millionaire who stole away from his father's villa at Nice and spent a year as a Party member in Geneva, described a few years later why it was that after an interview with Lenin, which he was told was a great privilege and a recognition of his potential as a revolutionary, he went home for ever. In a room which seemed voluntarily cheerless, as if it had been gone over by an interior undecorator, he was received by a colourless little man who talked trivialities which might fairly be interpreted as petty meannesses, as to who should be elected to certain committees and who should be kept off. Not till long after did he realise that Lenin was not making conversation, he was making history. Quietly he was nailing down the coffin-lids on all Russian left-wing parties except his own. We cannot blame Dr. Atl because he too failed to identify a procedure which, after all, was without historical precedent. But it was unfortunate that he turned his back on Lenin and fell under the spell of a socialist journalist named Benito Mussolini.

Benito Mussolini

Yet, here too, he was not altogether culpable. We know more about the primary character of Mussolini than is commonly known regarding unfledged eminence, which is apt to get into the shelter of a uniform or a system very young. But we have X-ray photographs of Mussolini's youth because, in the 1890s, there came out of Russia a young girl called Angelica Balabanov, who had persuaded her brother to exchange her share in her patrimony for an annuity, so that she could become a student at the Université Nouvelle in Brussels, which had been created to give professorial chairs to Elisée and Elie Reclus and provide higher education as much slanted to the left as it ordinarily was to the right. After she took a degree there and studied in Leipzig and Rome, she went to Switzerland to organise the Italian immigrants at Saint Gall, where many of them were textile workers and masons. She became a celebrated orator, going all over Switzerland and into Italy to speak at public and private meetings in French, German, Italian, and Russian, all of them acquired in her schooldays. Nothing is more strange than the decline in the power to master foreign languages from the high standard which was maintained so long as children were taught by uncertificated governesses.

Angelica was something of a female in the pejorative sense: a Little Me. But the moment she got up to speak, the disorder stopped, the whole hall was silent, wasn't that strange, she couldn't think why it was. But she was also, as a matter of hard fact, a great saint, who suffered want and danger and fatigue over many years in the service of the poor and the oppressed, and that is why she was able to give a description of Mussolini in her autobiography *My Life as a Rebel*, which is a classic picture of the left-wing panhandler. The two met in 1904, when he was an unkempt boy of twenty who had fled from his soundly anarchist home to Switzerland to avoid doing his military service in Italy and was wandering from job to job in a state of blasphemous and ambitious misery, sponging on the faithful. Angelica took him in hand and set about teaching him to stand on his own feet, and history shows that she succeeded all too well. But her gorge rose. To her a revolutionary was a priest of the people, and a base, greedy, lying revolutionary was as repulsive as a bad priest is to the devout. This gave her the spur of interest which is the secret of good portraiture; and the sensitive ear (which enabled her to pick up the inflections and rhythms of foreign languages) gave her a wicked understanding of dialogue as a revelation of character.

So there Mussolini is on her pages, demonstrating the essential qualities of the left-wing panhandler as against the right-wing panhandler, whom he greatly envies, for he himself has no school tie and wishes he had, as it would give him the run of a more opulent class of possible benefactors. As it is, he has an address book full of the names of people committed to compassion by their left-wing sympathies, and this means that they will give him their charity if they can, which satisfies his greed, and will suffer if they have to refuse him, which satisfies his sadism. Angelica's insight also recorded that though he was a revolutionary, this did him no credit. His father was an anarchist blacksmith in the most radical part of Italy, Romagna. "Not to be an anarchist in Romagna would have been to swim against the tide. For a worker to have been anything but a radical in that province might have required courage," writes Angelica. This was possibly among the earliest recognitions ever made of the problem presented by the left-winger who owes his faith not to conviction but to inheritance: who can be such a danger as Mussolini was, when he used his knowledge of the machinery of revolt to stage a counter-revolution lasting over twenty years, which cannot be defended since it furnished aid to Hitler.

But though Angelica realised Mussolini's immense potentialities for evil, she never threw him out. They were not alienated till the First World War divided them, and she even consented to be his co-editor on *Avanti* when she knew he was an infected growth. The obvious explanation for her continued patience does not hold, for the young Mussolini was sickly and a tedious hypochondriac. But his grip on her can be understood if one imagines a devout Roman Catholic attending mass and suddenly noticing that, as the priest stood facing the altar, he was not only saying mass but performing conjuring tricks, drawing out of his surplice those strings of coloured handkerchiefs, then those flying packs of cards, those rabbits. Nobody could help watching him to see what he would do next. That is why some people who loathed Lloyd George had to stay by him, just to see if the rabbits would be followed by the pigeons. Angelica was virtuous to the point of priggishness, but she could not kill her curiosity.

If Angelica was fascinated by Mussolini, it was no wonder that Dr. Atl, an impulsive man from far away, fell at his feet. It is said in Bernard S. Myers's *Mexican Painting in Our Time* that Dr. Atl and Mussolini together put out an anti-clerical paper in Switzerland, but by this time Mussolini was reestablished in Italy. He had, however, been a conspicuous anti-clericalist speaker in Switzerland in the years of his exile. Angelica relates with disgust that he had attended a meeting held by an Italian priest in the working-class district of Lausanne and had stood up afterwards and, with a borrowed watch in his hand, had proclaimed "I will give God just five minutes to strike me dead. If he does not punish me in that time, he does not exist." Angelica primly comments, "I immediately wrote him a letter pointing out how superficial and foolish was the approach. He did not answer my letter." That corny old remark must certainly have been uttered times without number ever since the invention of clocks (for one could hardly use it beside a sundial), but now her record of it rings on the air as a terrible plea with a meaning of which the speaker was unconscious: "Let it come soon. Or perhaps not. Perhaps I will have a lot of fun first. But anyway let me not be hanged. And not upside down, please, not upside down. Why can't fate be innocent?" The remark, as it sounded then, must have appealed to Dr. Atl, who was, like most Mexican reformers, compelled into anti-clericalism by his country's situation.

Wherever the Church is established in a disorganised country, it is forced to go beyond its spiritual duties and come to the aid of society by acting as a branch of the civil service; and thereby it dooms itself to being loathed by future generations. The state develops its own civil service, and the church is left with property and privileges which it acquired only by virtue of functions which it no longer discharges. This was the case of the Mexican church, which was left, long after it had ceased to play an important administrative role, with an abundance (shocking in a poverty-stricken country) of churches and monasteries and ecclesiastical palaces, which were sheltered under a legislative umbrella, for all property belonging to the Church and to individual clergymen was exempt from taxation. It is believed that when Mexico jerked itself free of Spain in 1821, half of the wealth of the country was in ecclesiastical hands. The clergy were ill-fitted to handle their property, for they were exceptionally undisciplined. Their tie with Rome was slight, for when the Spaniards drove the Arabs out of Spain, the papacy showed its gratitude by giving the Spanish monarchy the right to nominate within their territories its choice for all offices in the Church, and the right was extended to Mexico. Moreover, by its insistence on the celibacy of the clergy, the Catholic Church makes anti-clericals in all countries where there is a simple view of sex, where the male makes the same uncalled for and unfunctional fuss over the exercise of his sexual powers as the bull. Any member of the laity could point to a priest and suggest by derisive comment that he was on the other side of the street from this self-made eunuch.

Dr. Atl IV

No doubt Dr. Atl hardly noted that Mussolini's anti-clericalism was so much less intellectual and historical and sophisticated than his own, for he was probably very happy to be with a congenial soul in Italy, which was, like his own Mexico, a southern land and had its own volcanoes. These were still dear to his heart, and he sandwiched in among his other activities a further course in volcanology at the University of Naples. When Dr. Atl came back in 1913, all his native genius and his sound anarchist training failed to show him a clear line. Four leaders were trying to wrest power from Huerta. There was Carranza, an elderly landowner, who was primarily a proud man, a typical Mexican, enraged by Huerta, who was indeed the most squalid ruler Mexico had suffered before or since the conquest; and beyond that rage, Carranza could offer only a vague programme, vowing destruction to plutocracy, "pretorianism" (a splendid portmanteau word, applicable to anything that came up, which one thought ought to go down), and clericalism. There was Pancho Villa, a cattle-rustler and bandit and genuine populist, a blood-and-thunder Robin Hood. There was Zapata, a pure Indian, who cared nothing for the central government and simply wanted to reconstitute the vanished Indian social system; his armies ranged Mexico, seizing the land which had been alienated from the Indian villages and killing the usurpers and, when they had done that, dropped their arms and set about cultivating the fields without another thought for fighting, unless attempts were made to dispossess them. There was Obregón, the nearest to a modern man, a trained mechanic, who became a victorious general not by courage or cunning but by sheer efficiency, and when he had to write a constitution he produced something that would, on the whole, have been passed by the Labour Parties of most countries that had an effective Labour Party.

By rights, Dr. Atl should have cast his lot with Zapata, who was the nearest of the four to a true anarchist. Indeed, if he had reconstituted the Indian agrarian society (based on the communal ownership of land), while the Industrial Workers of the World organised the miners and industrial labourers, the world might have seen a most interesting attempt at the anarchist state. But not, it must be feared, for long. Great Britain and the United States, who at that time regarded Mexico with naked greed and nothing else, would certainly have strangled such a state at birth. Still, hopeless as the effort would have been, it might have been wagered that Dr. Atl would have had a hand in it. He certainly did not stand aloof. He organised "red battalions" of workers and a corps of soldier-artists, but it was in the interests of Carranza, the furthest to the right of the four revolutionary leaders, and when Villa downed Carranza, Dr. Atl and his artist-soldiers joined the army of the next most conservative leader, Obregón. But perhaps his loyalties were distracted because these armies had their headquarters on the slopes of that queen of volcanoes, Orizaba, whose crystal dome shines half across the isthmus of Mexico.

I had always thought of the Mexican muralist movement as a neatly developing organism, but it had the full untidiness of life. The socially conscious Goitia had returned to Mexico from Europe earlier than Dr. Atl and was not by his side; he was official painter to Villa's army and was never to rejoin the main movement of rebel artists. At that moment he was further left than they were and was to retreat before his death into apolitical religious mysticism. But others were to take his place, of prodigious quality. There was Orozco, born in 1883, a trained agricultural engineer, who had studied art at night classes and been indoctrinated by Dr. Atl with insurgent ideas and a taste for massive allegorical torsion and served beside him on the slopes of Orizaba. There was Siqueiros, much younger, born in 1896, and much more violent. By heredity he was a revolutionary, for his grandfather had fought in one of those Indian guerrilla bands which, so often in the nineteenth century, acted as conservative brakes on careening reactionary governments. What is characteristic of Mexico? The sound of brooms sweeping courtyards and pavements in the early morning; cotton-woolly tortillas stuffed with the clotted heaven of avocado-pear puree; gesticulating cactus; flowers so bright that they seem to be audible; people who walk silently; and this historical oddity of insurrections by a subject people on the side of stability and tradition.

Appendix

Three Book Reviews by Rebecca West

"Magnificent Mexican" (*Sunday Telegraph*, April 7, 1968)

The reproductions of Diego Rivera's mural paintings look quite frightful unless one keeps one's eyes in one's Left Wing, as so many people do these days. But a visit to Mexico creates a respect for him which is reinforced by this new biography, *The Fabulous Life of Diego Rivera.*

It is written by Bertram Wolfe, a gifted historian of our times, author of the study of Lenin, Trotsky and Stalin which Edmund Wilson declared the best study of that witch-knot of personalities.

Mr. Wolfe, who might well have disliked Rivera, being his gentle and reflective antithesis, dearly loved this 300 pounds of gesticulating brush-waving manifesto-writing flesh, who looked like Mao Tse-tung but was an amalgam of Pantagruel and Barnum and Baron Munchausen. He recognises what a spiritual triumph was achieved by this man, who could have wasted his time as agreeably as anyone ever born.

He was a superb joker-in-earnest, he held his own in Dadaist Paris by claiming to have discovered the secret of the fourth dimension and inventing for the purposes of demonstration "a curious machine, a sort of articulated plane of gelatin." He loved to weigh into all the doctrinal and disciplinary dog-fights arising out of his membership of the Communist party; all his life he was being thrown out of the party and shouldering his way back.

And this biography amply illustrates the paradox that when a number of women nod their heads and smile and sigh that some man was just a great child, an overgrown boy, it can always be deduced that he has been assiduous in the performance of specifically adult activities.

Mr. Wolfe conveys how remarkable it was that this scatty giant should have devoted himself for over 30 years to a task which, from a moral and historical point of view, is impressive. On the public buildings he inscribed a message which had to be delivered if the hearts of the people were to be lifted up.

More than a quarter of the inhabitants of Mexico are pure Indian, and of the rest the overwhelming majority have Indian blood in their veins. But their Indian ancestors were defeated by the Spaniards, and their civilisation trodden into the dust. That defeat has appeared to them and to their conquerors as a proof of inferiority and a heritable shame; and it is the illiterate who are specially apt to harbour this fear.

The Mexican Revolution of 1910 had liberated these people from the grosser forms of tyranny and given them a measure of control. They might have felt it was not for them to exercise it. But Rivera made an authentic record where all could see it of what the Indians had been—gifted artists, craftsmen, administrators, agriculturists, mathematicians—and he presented their defeat correctly as a matter of luck.

Thus he gave modern Mexicans—even the poorer ones who cannot read—power to face the White West with dignity; and it has enabled them to support the curious state of permanent compromise with which their country is experimenting.

It is true that sometimes Rivera fails to create space on the flatness of a wall, as the great muralists do, and one rarely recognises in his work that joy in paint itself as a medium which is the basis of most good painting. He also shows a certain disregard for brute fact. In his frescoes the ancient Aztec Indians look less like their sculptures of themselves (which resembled small Byzantinised Red Indians with features moulded by the sense of tragedy and satire) than Gauguin's Tahitians, surely a more cheerful and less cerebral people. It is odd, and sometimes disconcerting, that the contemporary Indians, who to the eye of the tourist are compact and bird-boned and light-footed, appear in Rivera's frescoes as stocky and obese.

There is difficulty in summoning the proper emotions before a representation of "The Distribution of Land after the Revolution" when the recipients are shown as well-covered little people with large behinds. Still, Rivera rendered his service. He helped his country, after centuries of subjection and disorder, to rediscover its identity.

This book throws light on some interesting aspects of the period. It is delightful to discover that the Rockefellers, who refused to allow Rivera to complete a fresco in Radio City because it included the head of Lenin, treated Frank Brangwyn with equal contempt because in another fresco in the building he had included the figure of Christ. In this anecdote is summed up all the silliness peculiar to the American 1930s.

But the value of Mr. Wolfe's book is enhanced if it be read in conjunction with *The Mexican Mural Renaissance* by Jean Charlot, a half-French and half-Mexican member of the group, who gives a most amusing account of how they knew nothing about the technique of fresco-painting when they started and had to worry it out for themselves. In the process Rivera emerged as a superb innovator, but also, when he felt like it, as a conscious and laughing charlatan.

The book gains still more if it be read in conjunction with another book: the third part of Isaac Deutscher's biography of Trotsky, "The Prophet Outcast."

At 43 Rivera married a girl of 19 named Frida Kahlo, half German-Jewish, half-Indian, very beautiful, already crippled by an automobile accident and doomed to die in her early middle-age through a creeping gangrene caused by her injuries. To read of her is to fall a little in love with her.

In spite of her protracted agony she made herself an admirable surrealist painter, collected pre-Columbian sculptures and became an authority on Mexican crafts, dressed herself with splendid fantasy and made herself a house that was simple and austere and yet a Chagall dream, and over-flowed with violent wit and kindness.

She and Rivera persuaded President Cárdenas to let Trotsky come to Mexico when no European country would receive him, and gave him a home. This was a splendid act of courage and charity. It worked out curiously.

As Mr. Wolfe tells us, Rivera drove Trotsky into a towering rage by talking nonsense about politics, and he and his wife packed their bags and left their goods on the sidewalk until they could find a new refuge. But of course there was a reconciliation, and Rivera put up with the injustice suffered by Cleopatra's messenger when he told Trotsky of the murder of his son in France and the poor old man laid about him.

But Frida's affection was less variable and they drew very close together, these three people who were all living under the expectation of death. It is odd to learn from Mr. Wolfe that just before Frida's death, long after Trotsky's assassination, he startled her by trying to borrow from her a pen Trotsky had given her, which she greatly prized. Rivera's reason was that he thought it would be historically interesting if he used it for signing his application for readmission to the Communist party.

This, and Rivera's arrangement of her funeral as a party demonstration, must be supreme examples of the isolation which can be achieved by the egotist. But egotists often perform special missions with greater success than those more easily distracted.

"Carmen at Gunpoint" (*Sunday Telegraph*, February 8, 1970)

Why did the Mexicans, children of two great peoples, produce for themselves the 10 years of bloodshed and chaos described by Ronald Atkin in his vivid and informative work, *Revolution: Mexico 1910–1920*?

Well, it was partly the superb climate, which is capable of producing such natural catastrophes as hurricanes which drop 10 thousand million tons of water "upon the place beneath," as Shakespeare said regarding another mood of Providence, but usually sends one perfect day after another in the dry season and in the wet season warms its rains and times them with convenient regularity.

When the leaders said to the masses, "Take up your guns in the course of liberty, and follow me into the hills," they were calling them to face hardship and death, but this cry, ideological as it might be in its origins, was affected by the weather. The proof of that is the rarity with which Esquimaux extend such invitations to each other. Selling the concept of guerrilla warfare from igloo to igloo, that would be a test of salesmanship.

The Mexicans made the revolution not so much because they were ferocious and in love with chaos, but because they had guns, as people must who live where homesteads are far apart and there are wild beasts, and there was this good weather they could ride out into, feeling they had a good day for it, whatever that it might be, a fiesta or a battle.

These are not prerequisites of every revolution. Those made on the French and Russian pattern, which depend on the application of complicated political theories, go all the better if the population has few guns and the climate is unfavourable.

Thus the unpolished-off leaders have plenty of time on wet and snowy days to sit down and check the stock and decide what to do next.

But as Mr. Atkin's book shows, the Mexican Revolution was of a different order. It was highly personal, but not for that reason of ephemeral interest. Each of the leaders was a political symbol. What the Mexican revolutionaries were trying to work out with these symbols was to establish something like what Rousseau called "the general will," which should control the ideal state.

What all the men with big hats and excessively ready rifles described by Mr. Atkin were attempting to do in the glorious weather, was to establish the general will of Mexico; to lay down the desires they felt by their people.

It is to be noted that none of the great principals were reactionaries. Madero was a displaced Fabian who should have been eating nut cutlets in the Hamptstead Garden Suburb and wanted to shove the camel through the needle's eye, force the lion with fair words to lie down with the lamb and make the possessed fuse with the dispossessed. Carranza was a land-owner who recognised the need for reform but put too much trust in the efficacy of administering the existing system honestly.

Pancho Villa and Zapata spoke for the dispossessed peasants; Obregón, a poor farmer (descendant of an Irish bodyguard to the last of the Spanish viceroys), by some strange chance spoke for the modern technological man, who needed more than mere abrogation of feudalism.

All, all were murdered. Not killed in battle, but murdered. One might be tempted to write off Mr. Atkin's book as a simple record of savagery, of melodrama that should have been acted on a stage and not lived; and this now appears to be borne out by the eye-witness account he quotes of a Villista soldier miming the action of a matador when under fire from a Government battery, twirling a tattered red cape at each shell as if he were playing a bull, while the military band obliged with appropriate music from Carmen. The only objection to this view of the Revolution is that it seems to have succeeded in its aim.

Mexico is still bone-poor, as any infertile land must be which doubles its population in 30 years. It also seems cynical about its politicians, cherishing the law which prevents any President standing for a second term with a warmth which leads to abrogation of the world-wide custom that street names are positive.

There are in at least two Mexican towns thoroughfares called the Street of No-re-election. What can this mean except "Do your best for us and we'll let you do the best for yourselves for seven years, but not a day longer." But why, in the view of this cynicism, do they let any President serve even seven years? Does the constant reference to the Revolution mean that they feel that the country then achieved a general will, which operates even through imperfect instruments? Rousseau's ghost would say so, and this highly metaphysical view might be right.

For the rest, Mr. Atkin's volume is full of timely information. It describes the terrible villainy of the American Ambassador appointed to Mexico by President Taft, Henry Lane Wilson, who plotted to overthrow the Government and did less than nothing to save the life of the gentle President Madero.

It tells the story of that resourceful Ulsterman, Sir Francis Stronge, the British Ambassador, who affected a passion for a parrot who perched on his shoulder at all times. When Sir Francis was approached by any representative of Britons holding mineral interests in Mexico, who wanted his intervention on their behalf, the parrot squawked and Sir Francis appeared absorbed in anxiety about its health.

He was thus able to behave with perfect correctness, until the Foreign Office unwisely listened to the Britons' complaints and recalled him, and replaced him by Sir Lionel Carden, who had no parrot and got into all sorts of trouble.

This is real history. One sees how things work, though not always quite clearly. It is interesting to see that Mr. Atkin, like many other students of Mexican history, has been puzzled by a sober historian's statement that a certain Governor of Chihuahua "had seduced his own niece and had been given office to steady him."

"Gilded Trap for Royalty" (*Sunday Telegraph*, November 28, 1971)

There is a lady who sometimes appears on television to demonstrate her power of taming fierce animals by breathing into their mouths. Joan Haslip has some such gift for compelling long-dead Hapsburgs to abandon their pretence of frozen nullity and give up their secrets, and this she manifests brilliantly in *Imperial Adventurer*, which is the story of the unhappy Archduke Maximilian and his wife, Princess Charlotte of Belgium.

Just over a century ago this couple were persuaded by that Professor of Social Science born out of his due time and place, Napoleon III, to become Emperor and Empress of Mexico, an ill-chosen territory, for the region was so anxious to govern itself that it very soon killed him and drove her mad. Maximilian was 35 when he was shot, Charlotte in her mid-twenties when she went mad.

This is one of the saddest, drowned-kitten, Princes-in-the-Tower stories in history, and Miss Haslip makes plain that it was sadder than we think. One harbours the delusion that Maximilian must have been a fool, perhaps because of his appearance. Tall and slender, he was the original tailor's dummy, and his whiskers seem, even in the eyes of this hair-infatuated generation, inordinate. They were bright gold, excessive in quantity, and the texture of the hair was curiously feminine. Indeed, those whiskers might have been raised from cuttings kindly supplied by Lady Godiva. The general effect resembles the caricature of dandies so common in *Punch* in Victorian days.

But Miss Haslip shows that he was serious-minded and gifted. The act of his brother, the Emperor Franz Joseph, in appointing him as Commander-in-Chief of the Austrian fleet when he was 22 has seemed to most of us beautiful only as a singularly pure example of nepotism. But apparently Maximilian filled the post admirably, thanks to a technological turn of mind which made him enjoy bringing the Austrian fleet clear of the age of wood and sail and giving it steam and iron on the advanced lines of Britain and Germany. He also had a remarkable aptitude for botany and zoology. One of the ironies disclosed by Miss Haslip is that Maximilian became more and more enchanted by the birds and the beast and the gardens and the jungle of Mexico, while the Mexicans became more and more determined to cast him out, into exile or to death.

With these talents, Maximilian might have been a very happy man, if he had never gone to Mexico; and one might add, if he had not married Charlotte. There can rarely have been a more disastrous bride than this girl, who was spectacularly beautiful, a marvellous dark glowing creature, who was unflinching in courage, desired nothing more than to love and to be loved and was willing to pay for this blessing by kindness to the world, and who had also a strange gift of eloquence.

Her words still burn the paper. An observer, judging her by abstract standards from a perch in eternity, might pronounce her one of the finest achievements of the human stock; but to those who encountered her in time she was sheer hell. Her priggishness was at first quite charming. In many pictures she looks like the 19th-century Salvation Army lass, forcing her way into an East End public-house to sell the *War Cry*. But her benevolence became a Moloch fire and worse.

She and her husband had adopted the son of a former Mexican president, to rear him as heir to the throne. They themselves were childless and the nomination of a Mexican heir seemed a good move to mollify the Mexicans, who objected to her and Maximilian as foreigners. The wretched mother of the boy, an independent young American, saw no reason why he should be taken from her. There is a monstrous quality about this adoption, as recounted by Miss Haslip in *Imperial Adventurer* and by Richard O'Connor, who has treated the Mexican tragedy much less wisely in *The Cactus Throne*.

The truth was that she had gone mad, and the chill of mania had set. But there we come on what must have been another factor in her instability.

Charlotte's letters to Maximilian are love-letters of the special sort that comes from a complete and satisfying and continually renewed relationship. His letters are not on the same plane, but they show a warmth of affection and intense respect impressive as coming from one who would any day have preferred the latest steam-frigate or a rare orchid to any Charlotte.

But there is evidence that there was no sexual bond between the two. The marriage was probably never consummated. Miss Haslip's representation of this tragedy is disciplined by regard for historic fact, but it has the exciting quality of imaginative literature, of a good novel.

Certainly this book will be skipped by weaker readers who want the novel in it and nothing else, being shy of the minutiae of 19th-century affairs. But such readers will be making a mistake, for the political and economic and international features of the period reveal how life has changed, and how it has not changed, in the past 100 years. For example: we can be fairly sure that no member of any royal family near at hand regards his or her position as due to any inborn aptitude for government. Rather would he or she hold that since people seemed to like having a visible head to the state in a king or queen, one had better go on helping the wheels go round, and that is that.

But this was not at all how Charlotte looked at it. Just as one assumes that Liszt could play any piano music, so she assumed that Maximilian could rule any country because he, being a Hapsburg, had a genius for government.

After Maximilian had retired from the fleet he would have been happy enough arranging his collections in his palace on the Adriatic named Miramar (Miss Haslip includes in her volume a photograph of the stucco battlements which reminds us that Miramar means "Seaview"). To Charlotte this seemed as wilful a renunciation as if Liszt had slammed down the piano-lid.

And those governors! They were not as we expect them to be. Both Maximilian and Napoleon III were convinced and proclaimed Socialists. With no mental readjustments, and perhaps a visit to the hairdresser's, both the emperors could have remained undetected had they joined the ranks of Labour backbenchers in any modern Parliament. The Mexican adventure was their ground-nut scheme.

From our ground-nut scheme the element of corruption was absent, but it was abundantly present in the Mexican adventure. Sharks had never been seen that size before, large and greedy, though Maximilian and Charlotte were untainted. But the whole enterprise sprang from the same complicated motives which make us today send aid to the under-developed countries, and we are not making a perfect job of that.

It is always difficult to exercise power; and it is the failure really to see this which makes Mr. O'Connor's *The Cactus Throne* such an unlikeable book. One suspects that to him monarchy is not simply a form taken by power in certain stages of civilisation. Monarchs are stupid and vicious people who grab the best that is going.

He nags at Maximilian and Charlotte as if they were naughty simply because they were royal. He also teases by unsupported detail. Can the Empress Eugénie's mother really have posed for Goya's *Maja Desnuda*? The picture was painted in 1798 and the young lady cannot be less than 16. This makes her task of bringing Eugénie into the world in a tent in a garden during an earthquake in the year 1826 even more remarkable than one had formerly considered it.

Notes

Text is identified by page number and the first few words of the passage being referred to in the note.

Introduction

xi Seva Trotsky: That West considered Seva, who lived at Coyoacán, a quintessential "survivor" is indicated by her choice of title for the oldest drafts, "Survivor at Coyoacán." Only the newest draft is entitled "Survivors in Mexico."

xii "Mexicans do not ever": Notebook diary, McFarlin Special Collections Library, University of Tulsa.

xii the life force: "I have . . . no faith, in the sense of a store of comforting beliefs. But I have faith in a process, in a particular process that is part of the general process of life." Rebecca West, in *I Believe*, ed. Clifton Fadiman (New York: Simon and Schuster, 1939), 322.

xii "the racial problem erodes": Rebecca West, "The Colour of Persecution in the Cape," *Sunday Times*, April 17, 1960.

xii "I regard Apartheid": Letter to Henry Andrews, March 21, 1960, Tulsa.

xiii "the secretary of the Treason Defence": Letter to Henry Andrews, January 25, 1960, Tulsa.

xiii "she came back and at some point": Private correspondence via e-mail by Kate Robinson Schubart to the editor, April 22, 2000.

xiv "It came to me that Mexico": Diary entry, notebook, Tulsa.

xiv "I just had to put": Letter to Emanie Arling, June 13, 1968, Beinecke Special Collections Library, Yale University.

xv "She began her book": Carl Rollyson, *Rebecca West: A Life* (New York: Scribner, 1996), 356.

xvi As I have shown elsewhere: In my "Genesis of a 'Might-Have-Been Masterpiece': Rebecca West's *Survivors in Mexico*," *Journal of Modern Literature* 24:2 (Winter 2000–2001): 251–69.

xviii "'tis not all the understanding": Michel de Montaigne, "Of the Inconstancy of Our Actions," in *The Essays of Michel Eyquem de Montaigne*, trans. Charles Cotton, ed. W. Carew Hazlitt, *Great Books of the Western World*, vol. 25 (Chicago: Encyclopedia Britannica, 1952), 162.

xviii She argues that even colonial invaders: Carl Rollyson called this attitude "liberal imperialism." Rollyson, *The Literary Legacy of Rebecca West* (San Francisco: International Scholars, 1998), 8.

xx Cortés was merely the lesser: This is a rather speculative train of thought, based more on West's resentment of Islam than on historical fact. Although Ottoman ships controlled the eastern trade routes in the fifteenth century and their navy dominated the Mediterranean until the Battle of Lepanto in 1571, the Turks showed little interest in capitalising on their maritime superiority to colonise the New World. Their primary theatres of conquest were North Africa, the Balkans, and Persia. Moreover, from the beginning of the sixteenth century, Turkish merchant ships to the East lost ground almost daily in competition with Portugal's rapidly improving naval technology. When the matter of global imperialism was brought before Pope Alexander VI, he settled it in the Treaty of Tordesillas (1494) to the exclusion of the Ottomans. The treaty decreed that Spain was free to colonise all territories west of an arbitrary line of longitude drawn down the middle of the Atlantic, while Portugal was welcome to colonise the hemisphere east of that line, under the condition that all the natives in the respective spheres were converted to Christianity. It was the English and the Dutch who challenged and eventually overthrew this imperial power structure, not the Ottomans.

xx "Although West excoriates": Rollyson, *Literary Legacy*, 224.

xxi "There is no such thing": Rebecca West, "There Is No Conversation," *The Harsh Voice* (Hamburg: Albatross, 1935), 60.

xxi "metaphysical rebellion": Albert Camus, *The Rebel: An Essay on Man in Revolt* (orig. *L'Homme révolté*, 1951), trans. Anthony Bower (New York: Vintage International, 1991).

xxi "God who blessed the merciful": Rebecca West, "The New God," 1–2, typescript, 1917, Tulsa.

xxii "That a father should invent": Rebecca West, *My Religion* (New York: D. Appleton, 1926), 24.

xxiii–xxiv "tongue like broken glass": Quoted in Carl Rollyson, "Rebecca West and the God that Failed," *Wilson Quarterly* 20 (Summer 1996): 81.

xxiv "not yet fully revealed": Rebecca West, *The Fountain Overflows* (London: Macmillan, 1957), 105.

xxv "truncated Mexican epic": Rollyson, *Rebecca West*, 356.

xxix relative chronology of composition: A detailed explanation of this procedure can be found in my *Rebecca West: Heroism, Rebellion, and the Female Epic* (Westport, Conn.: Greenwood, 2002).

Survivors in Mexico

MEXICO CITY I

3 Thirty years ago: Rebecca West travelled to Yugoslavia three times, in 1936, 1937, and 1938, and *Black Lamb and Grey Falcon* integrates these three journeys into one continuous travel narrative. During her travels, she visited Macedonia twice, in 1937 and 1938.

3 the Atatürk: Mustafa Kemal Atatürk (1881–1938), the founder of modern Turkey. As leader of the Turkish nationalists, he fought the Allies in World War I and then Greece and Armenia, which had benefited territorially from the collapse of the Ottoman empire. After establishing the Turkish republic in 1923, Atatürk pursued a policy of Westernisation, mandating Western dress styles and deemphasising the role of Islam. The honorific title Atatürk means "father of the Turks."

3 King Alexander: Alexander I (1888–1934), king of Yugoslavia. He was assassinated in Marseille by an exiled Croat. West describes his fate in the prologue of *Black Lamb and Grey Falcon.*

5 In 1521: Correction. West wrote "1520." The sacking of Tenochtitlán by the Spaniards lasted from July to August 1521.

5 Congregation for the Propagation of Faith: Correction. West wrote "Congregation for the Propaganda of the Faith."

6 GREAT STATESMAN JUÁREZ: Benito Juárez (1806–72), leader of the mid-nineteenth-century liberal revolution in Mexico, during which Catholic landholdings were parcelled out to landless peasants. He was elected president of Mexico in 1861 and organised the resistance to Maximilian's imperial rule (1864–67). He ordered Maximilian's execution in 1867 and was reinstated as Mexico's president from 1867 to 1872.

7 IN OUR NATIONAL PALACE: West's typescript originally read "IN CORTES PALACE," but she crossed out "CORTES" and replaced it with "OUR NATIONAL." Murals by Rivera are found in both the National Palace in Mexico City and the Cortés Palace in Cuernavaca.

DIEGO RIVERA AND FRIDA KAHLO

9 "pig's crackling": Crisp pork skin.

9 Rowlandson drawings: Thomas Rowlandson (1756–1827), English drawing artist and satirist. Rowlandson specialised in sexually explicit prints depicting their erotic subjects in a humorous light.

10 Soustelle: Jacques Soustelle (1912–90), eminent French ethnologist. The poem West quotes reads as follows in Soustelle's *The Daily Life of the Aztecs: On the Eve of the Spanish Conquest*, trans. Patrick O'Brian (New

York: Macmillan, 1962): "Does one take flowers along to the land of the dead? / They are only lent to us. / The truth is that we go; / We leave flowers and singing and the earth. / The truth is that we go" (242).

11 Teilhard de Chardin: Pierre Teilhard de Chardin (1881–1955), French Catholic theologian, paleontologist, anthropologist, and philosopher. Teilhard, whose main work, *Le Phénomène humain*, appeared in the year of his death, tried to bridge the gap between science and faith. Specifically, he aimed at harmonising the Christian creed with the materialistic principles of evolutionism, an approach that earned him the enmity of the Church and the scorn of the scientific community.

13 Bakst and Benois: Léon Bakst (1866–1924) was a Russian painter and stage designer. He won international fame for his orientalist stage designs, exulting in sumptuous colours and flowing forms. Bakst opened a private art school in Saint Petersburg and counted among his pupils Marc Chagall. Alexandre Benois (1870–1960) was a Russian stage designer, painter, and art historian. Benois is remembered for his groundbreaking stage sets and costumes for *Le Pavillon d'Armide* (1907), *Petrushka* (1911), and *Le Rossignol* (1914). He moved to Paris in 1926, where he died thirty-four years later.

13 The interior walls: Modification/excision. "The interior walls of the garden beyond were also painted this deep, singing, blue, slightly keyed down by distance and perhaps not so recently renewed; and in this blue world, the trunk of trees, their downstretched branches, upstretched creepers, in a profusion that gardeners would normally have cut away, not just because it was unhealthy but simply because it was too much, much too much."

13 "have her leg amputated": Frida Kahlo's leg was amputated below the knee in 1953, almost thirty years after the accident which had initially inflicted the injuries on her. Kahlo died on July 13, 1954.

14 The China Poblana who: Some historians would authenticate this story of the China Poblana. Linda A. Curcio-Nagy states: "Originally from India, [China Poblana] was brought to New Spain by Portuguese slave traders and eventually came to live in the city of Puebla. Until her death in 1688 she lived under the protection of the powerful Jesuits. She prayed for the entire Christian community and lived a life of reclusion and penance while experiencing visions. She prophesied regarding the souls of important political and religious figures." *The Oxford History of Mexico* (New York: Oxford University Press, 2000), 179.

Other sources cast doubt on the reliability of this account in relation to the dress: "Many legends have been attached to the China (pronounced 'Sheena') outfit, including the romantic story about the oriental princess sold as a slave in the city of Puebla, who then fell in love with a Creole, and created her wedding gown based on the local fashions but decorated with oriental motifs. The truth behind the costume is that every three months a ship carrying goods from the Philippines known as 'Nao de China' (Ship from China), anchored in Acapulco. The aristocratic ladies purchased a textile known as 'castor' to make skirts for their female servants, called 'Chinita' or 'china.' The word is completely disassociated from any Oriental background. As the length of this fabric was not enough to reach the floor, an addition of silk was sewn at the top of the skirt to complete the length. With time and dedication the women embroidered or applied sequins to highlight the oriental decoration of the fabric. The modern China Poblana's outfit is so saturated with sequins that the historic 'castor' fabric (which is only made in Toluca and Mexico City today) can only be seen if you turn the skirt inside out." www.propertyjournal.com.mx/jarabe.html, accessed June 7, 2002.

16 in the Zócalo: In a manuscript passage not rendered in this edition of *Survivors in Mexico*, West explained the origin of the word "zócalo" (Spanish for pedestal), which is the name given to the central square in every Mexican town. Since this explanation is not available here, I have exchanged West's ironic "Pedestal" with the common term "Zócalo."

16 "Above all," Fanny wrote: Quoted from Mme. Calderón de la Barca's *Life in Mexico* (New York: Dutton, 1931), 137.

18 I looked about me in astonishment: West's surprise is entirely justified—Coyoacán had changed dramatically since Trotsky's days. John Tarleton writes that "1930s-era Coyoacán was still a small town, 30 kilometers removed from Mexico City. Trotsky's house stood on a dirt road out on the edge of the Mexican countryside. The Rio Churubusco Canal flowed nearby. The adjacent land was used as horse and cattle pasture. Looking out beyond the high, fortress-like walls of Trotsky's house, one could see the legendary, snow-capped volcanoes Itzaccíhuatl (Sleeping Woman) and Popocatépetl (Kneeling Warrior)." http://cybertraveler.org/STORY12.html, accessed June 7, 2002.

18 Dolores del Rio: 1905–83, Mexican-born Hollywood star known for her "exotic" looks. She starred in more than forty movies, including silent films such as *The Loves of Carmen* (1927) and *Ramona* (1928), before making a successful transition to talkies like *Bird of Paradise* (1932). She eventually returned to her native Mexico and made several films there.

18 Isaac Deutscher: West obtained the raw data of Leon Trotsky's life and the circumstances of his assassination from Isaac Deutscher's authoritative three-volume biography *The Prophet Armed: Trotsky, 1879–1921* (1954), *The Prophet Unarmed: Trotsky, 1921–1929* (1959), and *The Prophet Outcast: Trotsky, 1929–1940* (1963).

Leon Trotsky

20 "I am a great man": Allusion to Shylock's speech in *The Merchant of Venice:* "I am a Jew. Hath not a Jew eyes? Hath not a Jew hands, organs, dimensions, senses, affections, passions? Fed with the same food, hurt with the same weapons, subject to the same diseases, healed by the same means, warmed and cooled by the same winter and summer as a Christian is? If you prick us, do we not bleed? If you tickle us, do we not laugh? If you poison us, do we not die? And if you wrong us, shall we not revenge? If we are like you in the rest, we will resemble you in that." William Shakespeare, *The Merchant of Venice,* 3.1.60–70.

20 It has been: Modification/excision. "It has been given to only a few that they should utter this plea with conviction. We give our compassion to Alexander the Great, to Charlemagne, to <blank>, it is really hard to compile a list, but certainly Trotsky was on it."

21 board the *Christianiafjord:* Trotsky boarded this Norwegian ship in New York on March 27, 1917, en route to Russia, only to be forced to debark again in Halifax, Canada, where he was detained by the British naval police for questioning on political grounds.

22 When Lenin was dead: Modification/excision. "When Lenin was dead, and Stalin showed his strength and ruin fell on Trotsky, he was turned out of his lodgings <?> Oppositionist who was still <?> of Home Affairs of the Russian Federal Republic, and who is remembered only because, in 1918, he transmitted to Ekaterinburg Lenin's order for the execution of the Tsar and his wife and children and attendants. A certain thing discloses itself. Trotsky was then falling into a state of apprehension about the safety of his family."

23 the cellar of Ekaterinburg: Ekaterinburg, also spelled Yekaterinburg (and called Sverdlovsk from 1924 to 1991), is the city on the eastern slopes of the Ural Mountains where Tsar Nicholas II and his family were murdered in 1918.

24 He had not: Excision. "He had not said it was unjust when the murders were done at Ekaterinburg, and he still said so."

24 When Frida Kahlo: Modification. "When Frida Kahlo opened <?> Trotsky was famined for kindness."

24 a Major Quisling: Vidkun Quisling (1887–1945), Norwegian politician and collaborator with Nazi Germany during World War II. After Norway's liberation, he was found guilty of treason and executed. His name became a synonym for "traitor."

25 *Enemy of the People:* The reference to Ibsen's play is fitting here, since *Enemy of the People* also centres on a lone protagonist, Dr. Stockmann, whose progressive radicalism and obstinate idealism are equally tinged by the heroic and the grotesque, thereby in some sense anticipating the fate of Leon Trotsky.

25 January 9, 1936: Modification. I have supplied the year, which was left blank.

26 In no other: Excision. "In no other place I have ever been are the peppers flashing green like emeralds, or the tomatoes red as coral but brighter; and I never saw anywhere else that fruit with a husk the colour of a young fawn, which splits open over veined flame-coloured pulp." A more detailed description of Mexican fruit and vegetables appears at a later point in the narrative, including the description of the "fruit with a husk the colour of a young fawn."

27 Beatrice and Sidney Webb: Fabian socialist reformers (1858–1943, 1859–1947). Their work on public education and their advocacy of "Poor Laws" led the way for the British welfare state. They were favourably impressed by the Soviet Union, which they toured in 1932, and wrote about it in *Soviet Communism: A New Civilisation* (1935).

27 President Cárdenas: Lázaro Cárdenas (1895–1970), popular president of Mexico (1934–40). Cárdenas was responsible for easing the anticlerical oppression begun under President Plutarco Elías Calles, for carrying out the largest land-reform programme in Mexican history, for organising the Mexican workers, and for nationalising foreign-owned industries.

28 Trygve Lie: 1896–1968, Norwegian statesman. He was Labour Party leader and minister of justice in Norway before being elected the first secretary general of the United Nations.

28 Kamenev, Zinoviev, Bukharin, Pyatakov: Trotsky's former political allies who were denounced, tried, and executed by Stalin during the Moscow purges of 1936.

29 Mr. Galbraith, the spy Vassall, Mr. Profumo, Christine Keeler, Stephen Ward: Thomas G. D. Galbraith was civil lord of the admiralty and a member of Parliament; William J. C. Vassall was a British spy for the Soviet Union during the 1950s; John Profumo was British minister of war; Stephen Ward was a pimp, a Communist, and an agent for the Soviet Union; and Christine Keeler was a call girl and Ward's aide. For a full treatment of the scandals surrounding these five people and the public's reaction, see West's *The New Meaning of Treason* (New York: Viking, 1964), 316–60.

29 It was Trotsky's: Excision. "Though it was Trotsky's lot to afford the world this form of gratification, and it really did not matter how his innocence was established by Otto Rühle, Liebknecht's old colleague, Weideler <?> Thomas, former Communist member of the Reichstadt, Carlo Gresce the anarchist syndicalist, Sisamon <?> La Follette, and the rest of the assembled radicals, gathered so incongruously in the romantic scene of The Blue House."

29 Otto Rühle: 1874–1943, Anti-Bolshevik leader of Germany's ultra-leftist

movement who rejected both Lenin's and Stalin's policies because he felt they were betraying the proletariat. Rühle emigrated to Mexico in 1935, served there as a political adviser, and helped with the defence of Trotsky.

29 Liebknecht: Karl Liebknecht (1871–1919), a militant left-wing activist and cofounder of the German Communist Party. After a failed proletarian revolt in Berlin, he was executed, with Rosa Luxemburg, by soldiers loyal to the Social Democratic government.

30 Trotsky had to: Modification/excision. "The Commission over Trotsky was alone with his wife, to bear another affliction not generally recognised."

30 Emma Goldman: 1869–1940, militant Russian anarchist and feminist. After immigrating to the United States in 1885, she continued her anarchist agitation in New York City, which led to her deportation to Russia in 1919. As an ardent anti-Communist, she had to flee Russia again in 1921 and was welcomed to England by Rebecca West, who introduced her to England's left-wing intelligentsia.

30 Mensheviks: Non-Leninist members of the Russian Social-Democratic Workers' Party, a minority wing that was permanently suppressed by the Bolsheviks in 1922. Contrary to the Bolsheviks, the Mensheviks opposed centralised state power.

30 She herself describes: Modification/excision. "She herself describes morning conversations with her husband, when he said that he was feeling very well, and that was perhaps he had taken a double dose of sleeping-powder the night before, he had noticed that that did him good; and she pointed out that it was not the sleeping-powder which did him good but the deep sleep which gave him complete rest."

31 Mexico in 1936: Correction. West wrote "1937."

31 Vehemently but without: Modification/excision. "Vehemently but without real vigour he formed the Fourth International which was to replace the Second (a Socialist) and the Third (a Communist) International and indeed is still strong in Mexico; in whose affairs Trotsky showed such lukewarm interest. It is still a force in the Miners and Metal Workers, which left the <?> Confederation of Mexico, and a certain federation of students and teachers."

31 the Fourth International: The First International was founded by Marx and Engels and was dissolved in New York in 1876. In 1889, a Second International was born, led by Lenin, Trotsky, and Luxemburg. The Third International, which came out of the Russian Revolution, was headed by Lenin and Trotsky. When the Third International adopted the Stalinist principles of opportunism, nationalism, and reformism, Trotsky founded the Fourth International in 1938 as the true instrument for achieving world socialism.

32 mothers often deplore. / He was an: Excision. "How little Trotsky understood what had happened in the world since the end of the Civil war can be shown by the way that he advised <?> in the Fourth International who ever found <?> lands occupied by the State to be 'most active in expropriating the landlords and capitalists, in sharing out the land among the peasants, in creating soviets, workers' councils etc. In doing so, they must preserve their independence, they must fight in elections for the complete independence of the soviets, and the factory committees vis-à-vis the bureaucracy; and they must conduct their revolutionary propaganda in a spirit of distrust of the Kremlin and its local agencies.' When we learn of what actually happened to the Poles, the Letts, the Estonians, the Latvians, this is a ghastly joke. He really had no means of learning about life after he went into exile. He did not latch on to it at any point."

32 Jules Romains: Also known as Louis Farigoule (1885–1972), French novelist, dramatist, and poet who became a member of the Académie Française in 1946. Romains wrote two internationally known works, *KnocK* (1924), a comedy, and an immense realistic novel sequence, *Les Hommes de bonne volonté* (1932–46), consisting of twenty-seven books.

33 the twentieth century. / He only once: Excision. "For the rest, he read (in 1939) Marcel Prevost, who had made a great success with *Les Jeunes Vierges* in 1894; Pierre Lorys whose <?> success was *Aprodite* in 1896; Victor Margueritte, of whose works he read one written in 1923; and a mediocre writer called Leon Frapier, of whom he read a quite sobering example called *La Maternelle*, written in 1904."

33 François Mauriac: 1885–1970, French novelist, essayist, poet, playwright, and journalist. A devout Roman Catholic, Mauriac probed the problems of good and evil in human nature. Among his most famous works is *Thérèse Desqueyroux* (1927), the tale of a young wife who, stifled by her loveless marriage with a coarse landowner, tries to poison her husband. Mauriac was elected to the Académie Française in 1939 and won the Nobel Prize for Literature in 1952.

33 Not for himself. / At four o'clock: Excision of a long digression on the misfortunes that befell Trotsky's relatives, notably his daughter Zina, who died destitute and nearly insane in Berlin in 1932, and his son, Lyova Trotsky, who died in 1938 after complications arising from an appendix operation.

33 The intruders machine-gunned: The first assassination attempt on Trotsky was organised by the Mexican painter David Alfaro Siqueiros, a Stalinist. Frida Kahlo was friendly with both Siqueiros and Trotsky's eventual murderer, Ramón Mercader del Rio, a fact West did not mention.

33 Then they heard: Modification/excision. "Then they heard a cry,

'Grandpa!' from Seva's bedroom, followed by silence, there was an explosion. The intruders had set the room on fire, and after firing another volley at the Trotskys' empty bed, they left. His elders did not go to his help. They cannot be blamed. They dared not. If they had shown they were alive they would have been killed and taken from him." To bridge the long excision that precedes this passage, I have interpolated the clause "Trotsky's orphaned grandson who had come to live with them the year before."

34 opening the door. / Harte's body was: Modification/excision. "The boy in the house must have been used now to sudden disappearances. When his grandfather wrote to him in 1938, explaining why he wanted him to leave France and come to Mexico he alluded to his father, Volkov, and said that it was not known where he was or even whether he was still alive, but that in his last letter, written four years before, he had asked urgently whether his little son was in danger of forgetting the Russian language. Volkov, Trotsky told the child, was an intelligent and educated man, but spoke only Russian; and it would be a terrible blow if they were unable to communicate with each other, *should they ever find each other*. The boy may have written of Robert Shelden Harte, whom he had known for six weeks before the midnight raid, as another of the lost. He must have heard when Harte's body was found buried under the kitchen-floor in a farm fifteen miles outside Mexico City, covered in a chemical that made it resemble a bronze statue, in an attitude which showed he had been shot when he was alive in there <?>."

34 Jacson Mornard: Pseudonym of Ramón Mercader, a Spanish Communist who was recruited by the GPU (the forerunner to the KGB). He served twenty years in Mexican jails for the murder of Trotsky. After his release in 1960, he went to Prague and later to Moscow, where he received the Order of Lenin.

34 Sylvia Agelof: Modification. I have added the name for the sake of clarity, since West later refers only to "Sylvia."

35 As it turned out: Modification. "As it turned out afterwards he never to have been primed with a satisfactory cover story, or if he had, he had forgotten it. He told a story of being the son of a Belgian Diplomat who the most superficial of enquiry could have been revealed as a mythical character."

35 three days later: Correction. West wrote "two days later."

36 Three days later: Correction. West wrote "Two days later."

37 house on the Calle Viena: Trotsky's house at no. 33 Calle Viena was converted into a museum and opened to the public in 1990. The museum is sponsored by the Institute for the Right of Asylum. The curator is none other than Seva Trotsky, also known as Esteban Volkov Bronstein, whom West had met in front of the house in November 1966.

37 I would have: Modification/excision: "I knew rather more about him than one commonly knows about a stranger whom one catches sight of standing at his garage door. . . . I would have liked to ask her grandson how much of that time he had lived with her, whether his presence there on that Sunday morning meant merely that he still owned the property and took advantage of the weekend to see it was in order, or if he had never freed himself from it and was still its prisoner."

38 a marble plaque: Harte's memorial plaque was placed not in the garden, as West thought, but next to the garage in front of the building. Its inscription reads "In Memory of Robert Sheldon Harte, 1915–1940. Murdered by Stalin."

39 I should tell lies: Perhaps West meant to write, "That I should tell lies in the presence of the dead!"

MEXICO CITY II

40 Paul Bourget and Maupassant and Marcel Prevost: Paul Bourget (1852–1935), Guy de Maupassant (1850–93), and Marcel Prevost (1862–1941) were French novelists of the naturalistic school who had spent a large portion of their lives in Paris. Many of their pessimistic and psychologically probing novels are concerned with moral decadence among members of the affluent bourgeois milieus of Paris.

40 The roadway is: Modification/excision. "The roadway is solid from sidewalk to sidewalk with a demonstration of what, were I a professor of Social Science, would be known as West's Law: once man has invented the internal combustion engine and succeeded in making automobiles at a price which makes it possible for enough of the community to purchase them for the manufacturer to earn a reasonable profit, then at all times when the purchasers of such vehicles feel the need to use automobiles which made them purchase them, then the automobiles will be unable to proceed at a speed as great as that attained by vehicles before the internal combustion engine was invented."

41 There is the: Modification. "There is the insubstantiality of its soil and a network of intractable lava; but also it is only fifty years since the Republic rose into peace from a century of unrest rarely rising quite clear of civil war or the risk of civil war."

42 How can one: Modification. "How one can groan as one dies without making public one's private death, like a poor lost French king?"

RACE RELATIONS I

43 marry them off to the Spanish nobility: During the conquest of Mexico, miscegenation was often strategically motivated. Cortés and his officers were given high-born local women as a show of loyalty from allied tribes; conversely, Spanish captains married Aztec women to form and solidify

political pacts with indigenous leaders. In most of these transactions, the women were passive objects of political negotiations or disputes. For the next two centuries, Spanish men predominantly married Indian women of pure indigenous descent, with their mixed-blood offspring normally relegated to a lower social status compared with either of the parents.

44 But innumerable dark women: Asunción Lavrin writes, "The process of *mestizaje* was carried out mostly between Spanish males and indigenous females. . . . Many fewer indigenous noble males married Spanish women, but this was by no means a rare event. Among the first was Diego Luis Moctezuma, grandson of the emperor, who married a Spanish woman and became the founder of the powerful family of the Counts of Moctezuma" ("Women in Colonial Mexico," *The Oxford History of Mexico* [New York: Oxford University Press, 2000], 250). By and large, the eligibility of both indigenous and white men and women to marry outside their race was determined by social class. High-ranking women could be courted by high-ranking Spaniards and elite Indian males would seek out well-born Spanish señoritas. In most cases the man would initiate the courtship, and the woman would have to accept whatever arrangement was made between her family and her suitor's relatives. Because of the frequency with which "consensual" extramarital relations were conducted between Spaniards and Indians, Mexico soon became populated by a growing number of illegitimate mestizos who were outcast, orphaned, or brought up by relatives. Nevertheless, by marrying among each other, these mixed-racial Mexicans gradually shifted the demographic dynamics until they were in the majority. The colonial elite at one point actively discouraged intermarrying by exhorting its members to preserve their *limpieza de sangre*, or purity of blood.

45 I was the youngest daughter: West's father, Charles Fairfield, was a brilliant though perennially insolvent journalist. He died in poverty and all alone when she was fourteen. For years before and after his death, West's mother struggled to make ends meet. In *Family Memories* (London: Virago, 1987), West recounts that "my mother's houses always had a certain charm, though the signs of poverty were blatant. . . . Our towels and bed linen were darned to patchwork, and the cleaning of our curtains and cushions was a crippling expense that had to be planned and saved for. We ate well but very simply, and our clothes were painfully shabby" (197–98).

47 the Forsyte Saga: A sequence of novels by John Galsworthy, published in collected form in 1922, chronicling the fate of an upwardly mobile bourgeois clan. The Forsytes share an abiding desire for property, accumulation, and wealth, something that is shown to be morally reprehen-

sible and in part responsible for the disappointments of love that punctuate the story.

47 old Jolyon and Aunt Juley: Modification. West wrote "Uncle Septimus and Aunt Julie," and in an earlier draft she wrote "Old Jolyon and Aunt Amy." Old Jolyon is a better choice for an example of an unimaginative, stolid man than Septimus Small (who is not referred to as "Uncle" in Galsworthy's novels). Septimus died shortly after marrying Aunt Juley (not "Julie") and remains off-stage in the novels.

48 in our village: Refers to Stokenchurch in the Chiltern Hills.

48 3,706 million human beings: Modification. West left the figure blank in the manuscript, intending to fill it in later. I have provided the number, the estimated world population in 1970.

48 57 million square miles: Modification. West left a blank in the manuscript for the figure, which I have provided.

48 likely to lessen pain and enjoyment: Modification. West wrote "liken to lessen pain and enjoyment." In view of her overall philosophy of hedonistic utilitarianism, it would seem almost certain that West meant to write "lessen pain and increase enjoyment."

50 It was a college: Modification. "It was a college founded for the higher education of the sons of the Aztec nobles after the conquest, by an enlightened Spanish bishop." The Colegio de Santa Cruz de Tlatelolco was founded in 1536 by Juan de Zummáraga and Antonio de Mendoza, Mexico's first viceroy.

CHAPULTEPEC I

52 He-who-gets-angry-like-a-Lord: Several variations of the literal meaning of "Montezuma" are in use. T. R. Fehrenbach explains that Montezuma means "literally, 'Sun Burning Through the Clouds'; symbolic Nahua for 'Angry Lord'" (*Fire and Blood: A History of Mexico* [New York: Da Capo, 1995], 82). According to Hugh Thomas, the name "meant 'He who angers himself'" (*Conquest: Montezuma, Cortés, and the Fall of Old Mexico* [New York: Simon & Schuster, 1993], 44).

52 Chagall: Marc Chagall (1887–1985), Jewish painter from Belarus who also worked in design, printmaking, and stained glass. His subjects, which are mostly taken from biblical or folkloric sources, are distinguished by a soft, dreamlike, fairy-tale quality.

ANTHROPOLOGICAL MUSEUM I

54 Charles Fort: 1874–1932, minor American writer, autodidact, and world traveller. Referred to as the Hermit of the Bronx, Fort is mainly remembered for writing *Lo!* (1931), a compilation of unexplained events gleaned

from innumerable newspapers and journals that he had combed tirelessly in search of paranormal phenomena.

55 If they could: Excision. "If they could lie on one's palm or had to be left in the open because no building was high enough to house them, they would still be right."

55 Cassius Clay: Later known as Muhammad Ali (1941–), legendary American boxer who lost only three of his fifty-nine heavyweight fights. In the 1960s, he won the heavyweight championship nine consecutive times and became internationally known for his aggressive charm, braggadocio, and indomitable self-confidence.

55 Rilke: Rainer Maria Rilke (1875–1926), German poet who wrote the *Duino Elegies* (1923) and *Sonnets to Orpheus* (1923). The intensive lyricism of Rilke's verses derives from his introspective emotionalism, combined with a metaphysical seriousness about existential themes such as time and eternity, death, and transcendence. A melancholy poet, Rilke believed that human beings were merely spectators on this earth, incapable of holding on to any absolutes.

56 Paradoxically, one of: Modification. West's notebook reads, "The paradox. One of"—that is, I have supplied the word "Paradoxically," in place of "The paradox."

AZTEC SOCIETY

60 They had not enough: Modification/excision. "The Aztecs had not enough food, they had not enough textiles. They practised an illiterate but exquisite agricultural science, which gave them and us not only maize, but the bean, the pumpkin, the sweet potato, the pineapple, the tomato, the vanilla shrub, the pepper. But they had not enough protein."

61 He did not: Modification/excision. "He did not take them from the class immediately below, the *pochteca*, which consisted of traders, not the small fry, not the retail tradesmen but the guilds who had a monopoly on foreign trade, and constantly sent out expeditions from the central valley of Mexico all over the Isthmus to the Pacific Ocean and the Gulf of Mexico."

62 risk, since we ourselves: Modification. I have added the word "since," for the sake of clarity.

63 Spanish friar Sahagún: Bernardino de Sahagún (1499?-1590), Franciscan friar who conducted proto-anthropological research in Mexico shortly after the Spanish conquest, translating and preserving for posterity a significant part of the Aztec cultural heritage. The speech West quotes here is from Sahagún's *Florentine Codex*, which was not published during his lifetime because of the Crown's censorship.

63 Cecil Rhodes: 1853–1902, English industrialist and empire builder in South Africa. After his aggressive territorial expansion resulted in the

country of Rhodesia being named for him, his plotting against political rivals in an attempt to expand his mining empire led to his forced resignation as prime minister of the Cape Colony. He bequeathed most of his enormous fortune to establishing the Rhodes scholarship.

65 Jacques Coeur: French merchant prince, circa 1395–1456. Coeur established French trade in the Levant, employed agents throughout the Orient, and owned factories and mines in France and abroad. Through his monopolies, he amassed a fortune, but he spent a large part of it to finance the military campaigns of King Charles VII. In 1451 he was arrested on the trumped-up charge of having poisoned Agnes Sorel. After an unfair trial, he was sentenced to imprisonment in 1453 and to the payment of a fine of several million francs. He managed to escape to Rome two years later.

66 "the class represented": Quoted from Soustelle, *Daily Life of the Aztecs*, 65.

66 Gottfried Keller: 1819–90, Swiss poet, novelist, and short-story writer. Keller specialised in vivid evocations of village life surrounding the inhabitants of his fictive Seldwyla (1856–74, trans. *People of Seldwyla*). He also wrote one of the great nineteenth-century bildungsromans, *Der Grüne Heinrich* (1854–55, trans. *Green Henry*), based on his own life as a painter manqué.

66 "Lass die Augen": West misquoted these two lines from Keller's poem "Abendlied," perhaps through recalling them from memory. The actual lines in the poem are: "Trinkt, o Augen, was die Wimper hält, / Von dem goldnen Überfluss der Welt!" The English translation of the lines is by West.

66 Dürer: Albrecht Dürer (1471–1528), German painter and printmaker best known for his penetrating half-length portraits.

67 "In all my life": Quoted from Soustelle, *Daily Life of the Aztecs*, 68.

71 Such a windfall: Excision. "Such a windfall can be taken as evidence that God or fate really loves one with one's faults and all or as may be required by many, evidence that the indifference of God and fate does not amount to hatred."

71 a sheer bonanza: Modification. "a sheer bonanza, not except when animal husbandry has reached a high level, to be ascribed to human effort."

72 in practice today: Modification. West wrote "in preactive today."

72 Professor Hutchinson and Ursula Cowgill: George Evelyn Hutchinson (1903–91) was a Yale professor, ecologist, and friend of Rebecca West's. He compiled a bibliography, *A Preliminary List of the Writings of Rebecca West, 1912–1951* (New Haven: Yale University Library, 1957). Cowgill was the author of *Soil Fertility and the Ancient Maya* (New Haven: Academy, 1961).

72 the name Gennevraye: Adèle Gennevraye, pen name of the vicomtesse de Lepic-Janvier de la Motte, author of *L'ombre* and other novels.

ANTHROPOLOGICAL MUSEUM II

75 They are as: Excision. "They are as if they were in a church; one can pick out the tourists because they are behaving as if they were in a museum, which is in the case, but all the same their attitude does not seem quite right."

76 William Caxton: 1422–91, first English printer, influential translator (French-English), and successful businessman. He printed about a hundred books, some of them adorned with wood-cut illustrations.

76 Machiavelli and Hobbes. / They were indeed: Excision. "Macchiavelli and Hobbes who had not been born yet. They were indeed."

76 "Taxes," I found myself . . . a new earth: Modification. "'Taxes.' I found myself saying to the museum, 'The very word is like a bell to toll me back from thee to my sole self.' Up to the moment when the knell had sounded I had been very well off in the courtyard, which enclosed within its shimmering walls of grey and rose and violet stone a November day as they come in Mexico City, the autumn mellowness thinned by altitude, its sunshine like a sweet white wine but a very light one. In the long square lay a second sky, white clouds and blue firmament studded with yellowing lili-pads and reeds. All round me were doors opening on a new heaven and a new hell and a new earth. But now the word 'Taxes' had done its wicked magic I was fettered to the recollection of a letter from the Inland Revenue which had reached me that morning in its base browning envelope. It asked me a question which it said it had asked me twice before. It wanted to know how it was that a Mrs Clarkinson, a temporary secretary I had employed some years before and could not at the moment remember, had received from me a cheque for a hundred pounds, which appeared in neither her returns or mine as part of her salary. The letter was a piece of grit in my eye. Once it had come back to me I could not see the museum nor the lovely, qualified, faintly acid ripeness of the Mexicanised autumn day. It was not fair that an enquiry about Mrs Clarkinson should come between me and my experience of this delicious world which was so foreign that it gave me the delight one might suppose would be given by a new colour, as beautiful as any known colour but quite, quite different."

76 "The very word": An ironic allusion to John Keats's "Ode to a Nightingale," which reads, "Forlorn! the very word is like a bell / To toll me back from thee to my sole self."

77 new heaven and a new hell and a new earth: Revelation 21:1. "And I saw a new heaven and a new earth: for the first heaven and the first earth were passed away; and there was no more sea."

77 I turned my: Modification. "One turns one's back on them and goes out past the long pool in the courtyard, under the wall inscribed with a verse from the poem of an Aztec king."

77 Flowers wither, but: The source of this translation is unknown. In Irene Nicholson's *Firefly in the Night* (London: Faber and Faber, 1959) the same poem is translated as follows: "Flowers, they wither: / everything goes to His Home. . . . / Shall I merely be gone, like the flowers that have perished? / Shall my glory be nothing one day? / Shall my fame be nothing on earth? / Even flowers, even songs! / Ah, what shall my heart do: / In vain we have come to abide for a while upon earth!" (185).

In *Daily Life of the Aztecs* Jacques Soustelle gives yet another translation of this poem: "Shall my heart go / As flowers that wither? / Some day shall my name be nothing? / My fame nothing, anywhere upon the earth? / At least let us have flowers! At least let us have some singing! / How shall my heart manage (to survive)? / We go about on the earth in vain" (241).

CHAPULTEPEC II

79 Spock-fed: Benjamin Spock (1903–98), American pediatrician, child psychologist, and pacifist. His *Common Sense Book of Baby and Child Care* (1946) influenced the child-rearing principles of generations of parents throughout the Western world. Spock advocated tolerance, common sense, and the absence of corporeal punishment as the cornerstones of a humane parent-child relationship.

82 Congregation for the Propagation of the Faith: Correction. West wrote "Congregation for the Propaganda of the Faith."

83 Paolo Veronese: 1528–88, Italian painter employed by the Venetian nobility to adorn their homes and palaces with gorgeous frescoes. He painted in the Venetian school of the time, which favoured the use of brilliant colours and lush decors, often depicting large, pageantlike aristocratic gatherings.

JUAN DE ZUMMÁRAGA

85 ten years after: Correction. West wrote "eleven years after."

86 Rh-negative 30.5 percent: Normally, one out of seven Europeans has Rh-negative blood. That one out of three Basques is Rh-negative may indicate that they are descendants of an "ur"-tribe of Europeans who had, moreover, not mixed much with other tribes.

86 King Ferdinand: Ferdinand V (1452–1516), king of Castile, Aragon, Sicily, and Naples. On July 30, 1476, Ferdinand V took an oath to confirm the privileges of the Biscayans, and they in turn accepted him as their overlord.

87 emperor Charles V: 1500–1558, king of Spain and Holy Roman Emperor from 1519 to 1556. He oversaw the colonisation of the Indies, warred with France and Turkey, and saw the rise of Protestantism, which threatened his vast territories with disintegration.

87 Nuño de Guzmán: 14??-1550, Spanish tyrant who began a rule of terror in Mexico in the late 1520s. Guzmán is sometimes linked to Joseph Goebbels for his skilled manipulation of public opinion (he started defamatory campaigns to discredit Cortés at the Spanish court) and to Heinrich Himmler for his unblinking brutality. He was eventually captured by Spanish authorities in 1536 and thrown in a Mexican prison. Two years later, he was brought back to Spain in chains and remained imprisoned there until his death in 1550.

88 Since Zummáraga protested: Excision. "Since Zummáraga protested they spread libels about him and his Franciscan brothers, pointing out (and this is what the Basques never liked about lawyers) that Zummáraga had left Spain without being consecrated as a Bishop, and they spread libellous stories about him and his friars, and when he put a preacher on Corpus Christi to defend the good name of the order, the Audiencia sent toughs and a constable to pitch the preacher out of the pulpit on the stone flags on the church floor."

88 The Bishop of Zamora: Modification. For the sake of clarity, I have added the words "of Zamora."

89 Pope Alexander VI: Rodrigo de Borja y Doms, or Rodrigo Borgia in Italian (1431–1503), pope from Spain noted for his corrupt lifestyle (he fathered four illegitimate children, including Cesare and Lucrezia Borgia), for his active political role (he led wars against the Turks and the French), and for his patronage of the arts (he commissioned Michelangelo to redesign Saint Peter's Basilica).

89 Pope Clement VII: Giulio de Medici (1478–1534), Italian pope. An illegitimate offspring of the famed Medici family in Florence and himself father of an illegitimate child, Alessandro de Medici, the first duke of Florence. Clement was an indecisive, vacillating pope.

89 At Vera Cruz: Excision. "At Vera Cruz he found a sailor who was a Basque and from his own province; one imagines that a younger priest, most probably also Basque, must have searched the taverns for such a sailor."

90 Professor Byrd Simpson: Lesley Byrd Simpson (1891–1984), professor of Spanish at the University of California at Berkeley, a master of Hispanic literature and specialist in Mexican history. West owned a copy of his book *The Encomienda in New Spain* (1929), which she heavily annotated.

91 Antonio de Mendoza: 1495–1552, first Viceroy of Mexico (1535–50). Mendoza's reputation as the "first and best" of the Spanish viceroys is based on his enlightened leadership, his educational initiatives (he cofounded two institutions of higher education for Aztec nobles and creoles in Mexico), and his economic acumen (he built up Mexico's infrastructure and encouraged agricultural innovations). He also promoted

the so-called New Laws intended to improve the legal status of indigenous peoples. After fifteen years of exceptional service in Mexico, Mendoza was installed as viceroy in Peru, where he died two years later.

91 gave fifteen years: Modification. I have provided the figure, which West left blank in the manuscript.

ISABELLA AND FERDINAND OF SPAIN

92 In 1494: Correction. West wrote "In 1493." She was evidently referring to the Treaty of Tordesillas of 1494.

92 monarchies of Castile and Portugal: Correction. West wrote "monarchy of Castile and Portugal," but these were two separate monarchies.

92 Isabella of Castile: Isabella I (1451–1504), queen of Castile. Her marriage to Ferdinand of Aragon united Castile and Aragon under their joint sovereignty, thereby laying the foundations of the modern day Spain. After a long campaign (1482–92), the Spanish monarchs succeeded in conquering Granada, the last Muslim stronghold in Spain. In 1492 Isabella supported the journey of Christopher Columbus to the New World.

93 and Keats suggests: West is referring to a passage in a letter by the poet John Keats, written to George and Thomas Keats in 1817: "Negative Capability, that is when man is capable of being in uncertainties, mysteries, doubts, without any irritable reaching after fact and reason."

94 thou shalt not muzzle the ox: 1 Corinthians 9:9.

95 "Render unto Caesar": Matthew 22:21.

96 queen of Henry VIII: Henry VIII was king of England from 1509 until his death in 1547. When his first queen, Catherine of Aragon, failed to bear him a male heir, Henry petitioned Pope Clement VII for an annulment of the marriage. Clement refused, whereupon the English king broke with Roman Catholicism, instituting the Anglican Church as England's state religion, with himself at its head. He subsequently divorced Catherine of Aragon, and married Anne Boleyn in 1533.

97 Las Casas, the Dominican: Bartolomé de Las Casas (1474–1566), Spanish colonialist, missionary, and philanthropist. He is called the Apostle of the Indies because he intervened on behalf of the indigenous Indian populations at the highest levels of the Spanish government. His *Brief Report on the Destruction of the Indians* (1552) documents and protests the savage oppression of the Caribbean and South and Central American Indians by their Spanish overlords.

MINERALS AND MINES

101 Emperor Vespasian and Pliny: Caesar Vespasianus Augustus (A.D. 9–79) was Roman emperor from A.D. 69 to 79. Vespasian added large new territories to the Roman Empire, notably in Germany and England, re-

formed the army, and raised taxes to balance the imperial budget. Pliny the Elder (A.D. 23–79) was a Roman scholar and the uncle of Pliny the Younger (A.D. 62?–113), who was famed for his elaborate correspondence, notably with the emperor Trajan.

102 from the end of the fourth to the end of the fifth century: Modification. I have supplied the dates, which West left blank. In A.D. 378, the Visigoths defeated the Roman emperor Valens at the battle of Hadrianapolis, initiating a series of "barbaric" incursions which eventually brought the Western part of the Roman Empire to its knees. The sack of Rome by the Goths occurred in 410, and in A.D. 476 the Germanic warlord Odoacer deposed the last emperor of the Western Empire. By the end of the fifth century, the great demographic displacements of the European *Völkerwanderung* had slowed down, followed by settlement and political consolidation. It is uncertain whether West was thinking about "barbarian incursions" in this restricted sense of the term or whether she had in mind a more broadly defined cultural disruption, lasting for centuries after the collapse of the Western part of the Roman Empire.

102 true and glorious inflation: This economic model of the consequences attending the Spanish importation of precious metals was authorised by Adam Smith in *The Wealth of Nations* (1776).

103 Pizarro: Francisco Pizarro (1475?-1541), Spanish conquistador who delivered the Inca empire to Spain. He betrayed the Inca emperor Atahuallpa by killing him despite the huge amount of gold that had been put up as his ransom.

104 Jerome Cardan: Girolamo Cardano (1501–76), Italian physician and mathematician. A true Renaissance man, he published mathematical treatises and wrote on topics in medicine, philosophy, astronomy, and theology. This man, who had pioneered probability theory, led an unpredictable life darkened by scandal, addictive gambling, and the execution of his son for murder.

105 African Bishop Cyprian: Saint Cyprian (A.D. 200?-58). Christian church father and bishop of Carthage. He was martyred under Valerian.

105 for thirteen years: Modification. I have supplied the words "thirteen years" where West left a blank between "for" and "by a fleet." She evidently refers to the Persian Wars. In 483 B.C., Themistocles persuaded the Athenian leadership to create a strong navy with revenue from the silver mines at Laurium. With the help of this navy, the Greeks inflicted a signal defeat on the Persians at Salamis in 480 B.C. Thirteen years later, Cimon eliminated the Persian threat altogether by destroying its navy in the battle of Eurymedon.

105 Second Punic War: This war, fought between Rome and Carthage,

lasted from 218 to 201 B.C. Hannibal's great martial feats and eventual defeat at Zama occurred during the Second Punic War.

106 Duke of Thuringia: Modification. I have added the word "Thuringia," where West left a blank. The Duke of Thuringia is a likely candidate, given that Thuringia, Saxony, and Brunswick were in close territorial proximity. Especially Saxony and Thuringia were wrangling over territorial hegemony during much of the Middle Ages. After the Duke of Saxony seized Thuringia in the tenth century, the Thuringian dukes of the Ludovingian dynasty took over the duchy of Saxony again in 1180.

107 "Oh, God, I": William Shakespeare, *Hamlet*, 2.2.260–62.

111 Rickard's *Man and Metals:* T. A. Rickard, *Man and Metals: A History of Mining in Relation to the Development of Civilization* (New York: McGraw-Hill, 1932).

111 Jerome Benzoni: Girolamo Benzoni (1519–?), Italian merchant adventurer who spent fifteen years in the Antilles and Central America. He published *La Historia del Mondo Nuovo* upon his return in 1565. Despite being an anti-Spanish polemic of poor workmanship, Benzoni's book was capitalised on by philanthropists and by politicians eager to challenge Spanish predominance in the Indies.

HERNÁN CORTÉS

112 Gómara: Francisco López de Gómara (1511–66), secretary and chaplain to Cortés. Gómara published his *Crónica de la conquista de Nueva España* in 1552.

112 Bernal Díaz: Bernal Díaz del Castillo (1492–1584), captain under Cortés and writer of the *Verdadera historia de la conquista de Nueva España* (True History of the Conquest of Mexico), published posthumously in 1632.

112 Salvador de Madariaga: 1886–1978, Spanish poet, historian, philosopher, and politician. A passionate defender of liberty and international cooperation, he founded the College of Europe in 1949.

114 Diego Velázquez: 1460–1532, Spanish conquistador and first governor of Cuba.

114 Pedro de Morón: Modification. I have supplied the name, which West left blank. The manuscript reads, "They certainly mistook the horses for gods at first, but that ended when they decapitated the noble <blank> in battle. As for weapons, they had arrows, javelins, stone-tipped lances, slings and formidable wooden clubs with jagged obsidian insets which could inflict terrible wounds. It was by a swing from one of these that poor <blank> lost his head." Bernal Díaz describes the death of Morón's horse as follows: "[The Tlascalans] began with a furious attack, and laid hands on a good mare well trained both for sport and battle. Her rider, Pedro de Moron, was a fine horseman; and as he charged with three

other horsemen into the enemy ranks—they had been instructed to charge together for mutual support—some of them seized his lance so that he could not use it, and others slashed at him with their broad-swords, wounding him severely. Then they slashed at his mare, cutting her head at the neck so that it only hung by the skin. The mare fell dead, and if his mounted comrades had not come to Moron's rescue, he would probably have been killed also. . . . After this they began to retire, taking the mare with them, and they cut her in pieces to show in all the towns of Tlascala." Bernal Díaz, *The Conquest of New Spain* (London: Penguin, 1963), 145.

DOÑA MARINA

116 *bonne bouche, bon sein:* French, "good mouth, good breast."

118 Jerónimo de Aguilar: Modification. I have added the name for clarity. Aguilar was a Spanish priest who had been shipwrecked on the Yucatán peninsula and taken captive by the Mayas, whereupon he acquired their language. He was picked up by Cortés on Cozumel and later played an important role as interpreter of native tongues. If an Aztec wanted to converse with Cortés, he would first address Doña Marina in Nahuatl; Doña Marina would then turn to Aguilar with a Mayan translation of his words, and Aguilar would translate this into Spanish.

118 she gave them her loyalty: Doña Marina, also known as Malinche, is viewed by Mexicans today as a blot on their history. The success of the Spanish conquest depended significantly on her service as a translator, which facilitated the forming of alliances between the invaders and disaffected native tribes and allowed Cortés to gather intelligence. The term "malinchismo" has therefore become a byword for the betrayal of native Mexican values, and Malinche stands as a symbol for selling out to the conquerors. It is astonishing that West, whose fascination with traitors was a lifelong concern, did not comment on this aspect of Doña Marina.

119 On these occasions: Excision. "On these occasions, which were highly formalised, each side set out its attitude towards the *casus belli*, which was usually a refusal to trade or to pay tribute, or interference with the Aztec traders, who were a separate caste uniting the functions of commercial travellers and intelligence officers."

120 Oswald Spengler: 1880–1936, German philosopher and writer of the deterministic history *The Decline and Fall of the West* (1918–22), which claimed that civilisations passed through cycles and that Western civilisation was embarked on an unstoppable downturn.

124 Haidée who went mad: A character in *Don Juan*, the unfinished epic picaresque written between 1819 and 1824 by the English romantic poet

George Gordon, Lord Byron. The poem describes the character's death and resurrection at great length.

125 Louis XVI and Marie Antoinette: The last king of France (1754–93) and his wife (1755–93). A French revolutionary tribunal condemned both to death by the guillotine.

125 studded with cities: Modification. I have supplied the word "studded." The word in the typescript is illegible.

126 Cuauhtémoc: 1495?–1522, the nephew of Montezuma II and last Aztec emperor, from 1520 to 1522.

126 butler of the highest rank: Modification. I have supplied the word "rank." The typescript does not contain a noun after the qualifier "highest."

127 Doña Marina had: There are countless editions and translations of Bernal Díaz del Castillo's *The True History of the Conquest of Mexico* in circulation. The one that comes closest to West's transcription here is Maurice Keatinge's translation, published originally in 1800 and reprinted in New York by Robert M. McBride in 1927. The corresponding passage can be found at pp. 79–80. The popular Penguin translation of the *True History* by J. M. Cohen contains an abridged version of this episode.

RELIGION AND SORCERY

129 It excelled in: Excision. "It excelled in architecture, in medicine, in astronomy, in agriculture, in many processes serving art and industry, and in the organisation of the military and civil services, which were so highly developed that in feeling Tenochtitlán was a precursor of Washington."

129 Joyce Kilmer: American poet, 1886–1918. His most famous poem, "Trees" (1914), contains the verses "Poems are made by fools like me, / But only God can make a tree."

130 Lévi-Strauss: Claude Lévi-Strauss (1908–), Belgian-French anthropologist and leading exponent of structuralism. By studying social organisation, myths, and languages in diverse cultures, he aimed to demonstrate that all intellectual and social functions of the human species are ultimately governed by universal mental structures.

132 The routine was: Excision. "The routine was in fact much as it is today in the Vatican or Lambeth Palace or the offices of the <blank> in <blank>, and the Aztecs do not suffer by comparison."

132 favourable to man; / but hopeless confusion: Excision. "Their people—and they were part of their people—were desperately apprehensive, for they knew through legend that the civilisations which had preceded them in the Central American isthmus had met with sudden and unexplained destruction. The men who had built the great city of Teoti-

huacán, whose ruins stood and are standing thirty miles from Tenochtitlán, had gone and left no trace, so had the gifted Olmecs, the great, the classic Mayans, the Toltecs, a people of genius, the Miztecs, whose architecture astonishes in the valley of Oaxaca. They had been smitten down as it would be unbearable that human beings should be smitten down except as punishment for a grave sin. The Aztecs feared that they might commit such a sin themselves, from sheer ignorance. Their state of mind can be imagined if one conceives a turn of history whereby the British had known, not only their own Norman invasion and the fall of the Roman and Byzantine Empires, but had (before the sixteenth century) witnessed the obliteration of France, Germany, Spain and the Low Countries and found themselves the only surviving people in their area. So the priests scanned the skies for messages, while appealing to the gods in the name of reason by their saintly lives." West gives an alternate account of the disappearance of successive Mexican cultures on p. 141.

137 a lover of virtue: The subject of Montezuma's virtue is controversial. Hugh Thomas states in *Conquest: Montezuma, Cortés, and the Fall of Old Mexico* that "[Montezuma] seemed astute, wise, prudent . . . [and] courteous" (44). But later he modifies this assessment, calling Montezuma "an inflexible man" and a "butcher," whom sources in the *Florentine Codex* referred to as "'this evildoer,' [because] he terrified the world. 'In all the world, there was dread of him. When anyone offended him' a little, he slew him. Many he punished only for an imaginary evil" (406).

138 "where the air is": This appears to be a misquotation from *The Daily Life of the Aztecs*, where Soustelle writes that the Lord and Lady of Duality "lived at the summit of the world, in the thirteenth heaven, 'there where the air was very cold, delicate and iced'" (96).

138 Louis de Broglie: Louis-Victor, duc de Broglie (1892–1987), French physicist. He first propounded the theory of electron waves and then extended the theory of a wave-particle duality from light to matter.

139 fifty-two-year cycle: Correction. West wrote "fifty year cycle."

139 has its achievement. / Aztec religion was: Excision. "Our universe is obstinately coherent and lays down trails where the bird-dog, the mind, must pick up the scent." This sentence seems to conflict with what West wrote earlier, "Here we see the crucial hardship of Aztec religion: too obstinate a determination to make the universe consistent."

139 Professor Michael Polanyi: 1891–1976, scientist turned philosopher. A professor of chemistry at the University of Manchester, Polanyi devoted more and more of his attention to writing about the relationship between science, beliefs, and political culture.

139 Many Aztecs must: Modification. "Many Aztecs must have got trapped in such blind alleys of fact, considering now a migration of horned owls from a district where shortly afterwards the principal temple was struck

by lightning, an epidemic breaking out under skies which had recently been ornamented by an unusual number of solar halos."

140 a superior and vanished nation: Refers to the Toltecs.

141 "Come and be gathered": Revelation 19:17–18.

QUETZALCOATL

144 "all the pages of Quetzalcoatl": C. A. Burland, *The Gods of Mexico* (London: Eyre & Spottiswoode, 1967), 160.

MONTEZUMA

150 When the Spaniards came: Aztec sources, translated from Nahuatl by Bernardino de Sahagún, tell of an unprovoked massacre at Cholula. "Suddenly there were knifings, there were sword strokes, there was death. The Cholulans had suspected nothing. They faced the Spaniards without swords or shields. And so by treachery they were slain. They died like blind men, not knowing why." Bernardino de Sahagún, *Florentine Codex: General History of the Things of New Spain*, book 12 (Santa Fé: School of American Research and the University of Utah, 1975), 39–40.

TENOCHTITLÁN

154 "When we beheld": The corresponding passage in Maurice Keatinge's translation of Díaz's *True History of the Conquest of Mexico* (New York: Robert M. McBride, 1927) appears at p. 160.

154 *Amadís de Gaula:* Spanish-Portuguese romance supposed to have been composed in the thirteenth century and written down in the second half of the fifteenth. Amadís, an illegitimate child of royal parentage, is cast away in a box on a river, picked up by a Scottish knight, becomes the epitome of chivalry, and elopes with the daughter of the king of Great Britain. The Roman emperor, to whom she had been betrothed, makes war on Great Britain but is defeated by the forces of Amadís, who is forthwith reconciled with the king of Great Britain.

159 He came to the emperor: The corresponding passage in Maurice Keatinge's translation of the *True History* appears at p. 168.

160 "Malintzin, Mr. Marina": The closest approximation of this passage (and of the one following it) is found in J. M. Cohen's translation of Diaz's *True History* (London: Penguin Books, 1963), 222–24.

164 Once, long ago: This episode relates to the chapter "St. George's Eve: II" in *Black Lamb and Grey Falcon*.

165 sold for food: West did not develop the story of the conquest of Mexico beyond this point. A good account of the remaining course of events leading to the sack of Tenochtitlán by the Spaniards in August 1521 is found in Ronald Wright, *Stolen Continents: The Americas Through Indian Eyes Since 1492* (New York: Houghton Mifflin, 1992), 30–47.

RACE RELATIONS II

166 So we believed: This abrupt transition from the Spanish conquest to contemporary Mexican race relations follows one of West's notebook versions.

167 know the Forsytes: A reference to the Forsyte Saga, as described above.

167 This recalls Great Britain: Modification. "This recalls Great Britain, but the contempt for the vulgar aim of balancing the budget is as to the contempt for it in Mexico as British cooking is to Mexican (far hotter in the mouth); and indeed I cannot think how a state can get its figures properly prudent when it knows its population is going to multiply itself by six in a century."

168 violence in Mexico. / Yet I received: Excision of marginal annotation in West's handwriting. "I am one who sees violence when I visit strange places; people try to assassinate Presidents when I am about, one of the first times I went out for a walk in New York I saw a man shoot another in front of outside the."

168 term of six years: Correction. West wrote "seven years," but the term in office for Mexican presidents has been six years since at least 1934.

CUAUHTÉMOC

169 on a stone block: Modification. I have added the word "a."

169 On the pedestal: Excision. "On the pedestal is represented the scene of his torture, which is the blackest mark on the name of Cortés who gave Mexico to Spain."

169 The Spaniards said: A variant reading from another typescript is, "The Spaniards said he was sniped by an arrow, and the sniper was one of his Indian allies gone treacherous, but the Spanish chroniclers record this with a certain embarrassed vagueness."

DR. ATL I

172 He mentioned him: Marginal annotation on the typescript. Although this sentence was later crossed out by West, I have retained it here because it strengthens the personal link between herself and Dr. Atl.

173 young Mexican painter: Modification. I have supplied the word "painter." West wrote "he was simply a young Mexican disciple living in Paris."

173 Murillo: Bartolomé Esteban Murillo (1618?–82), Spanish religious painter of the Baroque school. His paintings are noted for their soft forms and sumptuous colours.

173 Truman Capote: 1924–84, American novelist, short-story writer, and playwright, author of *Breakfast at Tiffany's* and *In Cold Blood*. On November 28, 1966, Capote threw a gigantic masked ball in New York City's Plaza Hotel for several hundred guests, among them the most

distinguished artists, film stars, and thinkers of the time. West was in Mexico when the legendary party took place.

ELIE AND ELISÉE RECLUS

175 Elisée and Elie Reclus: Elisée Reclus (1830–1905) was a French geographer and anarchist who wrote the monumental *Nouvelle géographie universelle*, a work consisting of nineteen volumes and serving for decades as a standard work of reference in the discipline. He pioneered the subfield of human geography, studying the interactions between people and their environment. Elie Reclus (1827–1904) was a French anthropologist, educator, economist, and anarchist who tutored the four Fairfield sons from 1852 to 1856. *Les Primitifs* (1885), translated into English under the title *Primitive Folk: Studies in Comparative Ethnology* (1896), is generally considered his best work of anthropology.

175 Bakunin: Mikhail Bakunin (1814–76), Russian anarchist. An ultra-radical and outspoken atheist, he advocated terrorism in order to overthrow the power of church and state. His quarrel with Marx precipitated the crisis of the First International and split the European worker's movement into anarchist and Communist camps. *Statism and Anarchy* (1873) is Bakunin's most important work of political theory.

175 Prince Kropotkin: Peter Kropotkin (1842–1921), Russian anarchist. The son of a Russian prince, he renounced his heritage to become an influential anarchist theoriser. Several times imprisoned before he went into exile in London, Kropotkin is best known for his view that mutual aid rather than competition was the driving force in human society. His most influential books include *Memoirs of a Revolutionist* (1899) and *Mutual Aid* (1902).

177 Louis Napoleon: Louis Napoleon III (1803–73), Napoleon Bonaparte's nephew, who was elected president of France's Second Republic in 1848. In 1851 he expanded his power with a coup d'état. As emperor of France (1852–1870), he pushed an aggressive military agenda, expanding France's territory while introducing a programme of political liberalisation. In 1864, he installed Maximilian of Habsburg as Emperor of Mexico.

177–178 Tribes of Israel. / It is not: Excision. "They had in fact been introduced by a Hungarian Revolutionary who had crossed with the Reclus brothers from Havre on the same boat, himself having been just released from a prison cell in Budapest, to which he had been consigned for taking part in the Kossuth rising against the tyranny of Austria. The Hungarian had been in London before and was able to take them to one of the lodging-houses which welcomed political refugees, sometimes because the owners themselves belonged to one radical movement or another, and sometimes because such lodgers were undemanding as to food and comfort and only required that they be allowed to sit up to all hours and talk to their friends. He had then taken them to the social centre of refugee life, the British Museum Reading Room, where he had found an Irishman, whom he had come to know in the same place on his previous visit, because both were Hebrew scholars of academic standing."

179 John Nelson Darby: 1800–1882, Irish Protestant fundamentalist. His "Plymouth Brethren" rejected both the Anglican and the Catholic churches, both of which they deemed ruined by corruption and clericalism. Darby and his followers were orthodox Bible Christians with a strong social commitment to the poor. They also lived by eschatological beliefs and awaited the return of Christ.

179 Racinean: Jean Racine (1639–99), French playwright who wrote numerous tragedies, among them his masterpiece *Phèdre* (1677), which is patterned on Greek mythology. After initial collaboration with Molière, Racine played intrigues against his former mentor and they became enemies.

179 Molierean: Jean-Baptiste P. Molière (1622–73), French playwright who wrote comedies and satires, such as *The Imaginary Invalid* (1673) and *Tartuffe* (1664), in which he exposed contemporary social, political, and religious follies to ridicule.

180 It was obviously written: Elie's obituary was actually written by his older brother, Elisée, who died one year later. See *Les Frères Elis & Elisée Reclus: ou du Protestantisme à l'Anarchisme* (Paris: Les Amis d'Elisée Reclus, 1964).

180 Verlaine: Paul Verlaine (1844–96), French lyric poet. One of the so-called Decadents, Verlaine had a homosexual relationship with Arthur Rimbaud, but later shot and wounded him during a violent quarrel. Verlaine's "Art poétique" was the forerunner of the symbolist school of French poetry, and his book of criticism *Les Poètes maudits* (1884), is a classical study of the six most famous poets of his time, including Baudelaire, Mallarmé, and Rimbaud.

181 For several years: The original text, written in French by Elisée Reclus, reads, "Introduit dans une famille irlandaise de moeurs plus libres, Elie eut, pendant quelques années, à Dublin et à Londres, a conduire les études de quatre jenes gens qui lui firent certainement honneur et don't l'un surtout, Digby Fairfield, mort encore jeune dans les Indes, dépassait de beaucoup la moyenne de sa génération par la noblesse du caractère et la clarté de l'intelligenge." *Les Frères Elis & Elisée Reclus*, 177.

182 socialist thinker Saint-Simon: Henri de Saint-Simon (1760–1825), French social theorist. Saint-Simon was a technocrat who believed that economic policy should be based on scientific principles. He was also a de-

voutly religious man, and his political ideas became the prototype for Christian socialism.

182 industrial and commercial projects: Correction. I have supplied the word "projects." West's manuscript reads "giving long term credits for industrial and commercial credits."

182 Université Nouvelle in Brussels, / where his brother: Excision. "Nouvelle Université in Brussels, where education was frankly propagandist on the side of the Left, where his brother."

182 Blanqui, the great apostle: Auguste Blanqui (1805–81), French revolutionary who believed that a temporary dictatorship of the working classes was needed to eradicate the old order. He was imprisoned for a total of thirty-three years of his life. After his death, his disciples carried on his worker's movement.

182 Victor Noir: French journalist (1848–70), also known as Yvan Salmon. He was shot to death by Pierre Bonaparte, nephew of Napoleon III. Noir, who was asked to be witness at a duel between Pierre Bonaparte and a fellow journalist, had a brief preduel conversation with Bonaparte, then was shot at point-blank range. It is unknown what prompted this action, but Bonaparte was acquitted of Noir's murder, a verdict that raised a storm of protest.

183 the aggressive impulse: Modification. I have supplied the word "impulse." West wrote "and also of the aggressive which they were suppressing."

183 the glowing sunsets: Modification. I have changed the word "sunset" to "sunsets."

DR. ATL II

185 Courbet: Gustave Courbet (1819–77), French landscape painter and naturalistic portrayer of everyday life. His disdain for authority was notorious; he opened his own pavilion at the 1855 Paris World Exposition when the jury turned down his work.

185 Puvis de Chavannes: Pierre Puvis de Chavannes (1824–98), French painter and muralist. He created large canvas paintings which were hung in public buildings in Paris. His paintings usually depict mythical scenes and allegorical subjects.

185 John Ruskin: 1819–1900, the preeminent English art critic of the nineteenth century, whose *Modern Painters* (1843–60) became a benchmark of art history. He was also a populariser of architectural aesthetics.

185 development of Proust: Marcel Proust (1871–1922), French novelist whose *A la recherche du temps perdu* (1913–27, trans. *In Search of Lost Time*), a vast anatomy of memory and desire set in turn-of-the-century France, influenced generations of modern writers, including Rebecca West.

186 Everybody still laughed: Excision. "Everybody still laughed at him, but he was so rich that he was able to carry out enterprises in spite of the laughing, and in fact he was always able to get things going."

186 supreme artist, Velasco: José María Velasco (1840–1912): Mexican landscape painter.

186 Parra: Felix Parra (1845–1919), Mexican painter who was fascinated by pre-Columbian culture.

186 Gauguin: Paul Gauguin (1848–1903), French painter and sculptor and a driving force behind the French impressionist movement in the 1880s. He eventually broke with impressionism and moved to Tahiti, in 1891, where he embarked on his now iconic series of paintings depicting native Tahitians, mostly women, whose underlying primitivism influenced the development of cubism.

186 Zuloaga: Ignacio Zuloaga (1870–1945), Spanish painter. Although he lived most of his life in Paris, his subjects remained Spanish. He is noted for his richly coloured renderings of Basque peasants, gypsies, and bullfighters, painted against a sombre background.

186 Goitia: Francisco Goitia (1882–1960), a fiercely realistic painter famous for his unsentimental depiction of marginalised members of Mexican society. Among his best-known pictures are *Viejo en el muladar* and *Tata Jesucristo*.

186 Goyaesque: Francisco de Goya (1746–1828), Spanish painter and printmaker who was appointed court painter for Charles III and Charles IV. In spite of royal patronage, Goya kept on producing such provocative works as *Naked Maya*, a practice that eventually landed him in trouble with the Inquisition.

187 There is something: Excision. "There is something of this secondary suffering in Goitia's great picture of Indians keeping their All Soul's Day, "The Day of the Dead," "Tata Jesucristo," which is to be found in the Philadelphia Art Gallery."

187 Käthe Kollwitz: 1867–1945, German graphic artist and sculptor. Considered the last great representative of German expressionism, Kollwitz's etchings, drawings, lithographs, and woodcuts explore the lives of the urban poor. In depicting their misery, Kollwitz used an honest, starkly physical approach.

187 centenary celebration of the revolt: A reference to Father Miguel Hidalgo's unsuccessful insurgency of 1810, which had mobilised Mexico's urban and rural poor. It was the beginning of a powerful pro-independence movement in Mexico.

187 the dictator Díaz: Porfirio Díaz (1830–1915), Mexican president from 1877 to 1880 and again from 1884 to 1911. Díaz ruled Mexico with an iron hand, opened the country to foreign investors, and encouraged in-

dustrial development. To end his dictatorial rule, opposition groups started the Mexican Revolution in 1910.

187 Corot: Camille Corot (1796–1875), French landscape painter whose handling of light and colour, especially in small sketches that he later amplified on larger canvasses, left an imprint on the development of impressionism.

187 Daumier: Honoré Daumier (1808–79), French painter and caricaturist with a keen eye for the less salubrious aspects of contemporary life. He painted his subjects in a vigorous, sketchy manner, and his caricatures make bitingly satirical comments on French political affairs.

187 Manet: Edouard Manet (1832–83), French painter and printmaker. When the guardians of proper aesthetic taste, the members of the "Salon" in Paris, refused to exhibit his works, Manet formed a circle of avant-garde artists who later became the impressionists.

187 the sculptor Dalou: Jules Dalou (1838–1902), French sculptor whose involvement in the Paris Commune forced him to flee the country in 1871. During his exile in London he obtained a teaching position at the Royal College of Art and began to influence the development of English sculpture. After his return to France in 1879, he accepted commissions for public busts and monuments. Dalou's grand *Monument to the Working Class* remained unfinished at his death.

187 André Gill: 1840–85, French caricaturist, illustrator, and member of Paris's bohemian artistic community of the 1870s.

188 Seurat, Signac: Georges Seurat (1859–91) and Paul Signac (1863–1935), French painters who collaborated in the development of pointillism and attempted to apply scientific principles to the techniques of impressionism.

188 Flora Tristan: 1803–84, French socialist feminist who came from a working-class household and rose to prominence by speaking out for divorce and against restrictive gender roles. She later became a vocal champion of the proletariat, but she always exhorted working-class men to emancipate their women first in order to achieve their social and economic goals.

188 Camille Pissarro: West-Indian French painter (1830–1903). He moved to France at age twenty-five and distinguished himself as one of the foremost impressionist landscapists.

189 atheist-socialist-religious movement / and commissioned many: Excision. "atheist socialist religious movement called <Comtist?> and commissioned many." If the uncertain word is "Comtist," West is referring to a movement based on teachings of the French sociologist August Comte.

189 gave the country: Modification. I have substituted the words "the coun-

try," where West wrote "Mexico was about to celebrate the centenary of the revolution which gave Mexico its independence from Spain."

191 firm of Tiffany: Glassmaker Louis Comfort Tiffany (1848–1933), American painter, craftsman, and designer. Tiffany was trained as a painter in Paris and began to work with stained glass in 1875. He founded a glassmaking factory in Queens and produced large stained-glass compositions which greatly influenced the formation of the Art Nouveau style.

191 Swann taking Odette de Crecy: Refers to the tormented love of Swann, a Parisian Jew, for the sensuous courtesan Odette de Crecy at the centre of *Swann's Way*, the first instalment of Marcel Proust's *In Search of Lost Time*.

192 Edith Wharton: 1862–1937, American novelist and short-story writer. Wharton, who grew up as a member of New York City's upper class, explored the interaction of people from different social backgrounds and their often tragic fates in a society ruled by money and status.

192 "God dwells in light": I Timothy vi, 16.

192–193 It recognised that Providence: Modification. "It recognised that Providence set earth and sky ablaze, often to the delight of men's eyes, but sometimes to end all delight and close all eyes, and that all the victims of this fire, by comparison with its huge, hot, indiscriminate guilt, are innocent, and that this is the work of God, so either He does not exist, or this fire also is worshipful."

REVOLUTION

194 But their faces: Excision. "But hope as they might that it were otherwise, their faces were bright with hope."

194 Octavio Paz: Correction. West wrote "Mario Praz," but she was almost certainly mistaken. Mario Praz (1896–1982) was an Italian critic, editor, and translator. Octavio Paz (1914–98), on the other hand, was the preeminent Mexican poet and essayist of his generation. Paz, who served as Mexico's ambassador to India from 1962 to 1968, was renowned for his essays, notably the highly influential "Labyrinth of Solitude" (1950), in which he clarifies Mexico's relationship to its past. He was awarded the Nobel Prize for literature in 1990.

194 Montaigne: Michel de Montaigne (1533–92), French moralist and writer who perfected the essay as a rhetorical vessel for the exposition of critical thought and the evaluation of experience. His *Essays* (1580, 1588, 1595) are penetrating, sceptical, and self-reflexive explorations of the human predicament, ranging from philosophical problems to political institutions to local customs and opinions.

195 genetic chance is: Correction. I have supplied the word "is." West wrote "it can be guessed how large the genetic chance that a number of Spaniards."

195 liberal called Madero: Francisco Madero (1873–1913) was elected president of Mexico in 1911 and was assassinated by his rival Victoriano Huerta in 1913.

196 Henry Lane Wilson: 1856–1932, American diplomat. An inveterate alcoholic, apostle of dollar diplomacy, and conspirator in Mexico's internal affairs, Wilson is sometimes considered the worst ambassador the United States has ever sent abroad.

196 native of Indiana: Modification. I have supplied the name of the state, which West left blank.

196 1896 presidential campaign: Modification. I have added the word "presidential" for clarification. West wrote, "he had worked for McKinley in the 1896 campaign."

197 by name Huerta: Victoriano Huerta (1854–1916), Mexican president whose repressive dictatorship lasted only one year (1913–14). After his defeat by American-supported rebels in 1914, he fled to Spain but returned to the United States, where he was arrested and later died in custody.

198 "On the day": Henry Lane Wilson, *Diplomatic Episodes in Mexico, Belgium, and Chile* (Garden City, N.Y.: Doubleday, 1927), 284.

198 "Profoundly as the violent death": Ibid., 286.

DR. ATL III

199 the young Epstein: Jacob Epstein (1880–1959), British-American sculptor. Many of his allegorical sculptures depicting men and women in the nude were too demonstratively naturalistic for the taste of his contemporaries.

199 Aleister Crowley: 1875–1947, English writer and apostle of the occult. Crowley toured the world in search of what he termed "magick" and secret knowledge. He advocated the use of sorcery as a means of gaining higher self-knowledge.

200 Martov was engaged: L. Martov (1873–1923), Russian revolutionary. Together with Lenin he cofounded the Saint Petersburg Union of Struggle for the Liberation of the Working Class in 1895. Later he joined Lenin in exile in Switzerland. Originally a Menshevik, Martov converted to Bolshevism after the Russian Revolution of 1917.

201 Alexander Berkman: 1870–1936, Russian anarchist. He immigrated to the United States and met Emma Goldman in New York, where they collaborated in anarchist agitation. From 1892 to 1906 Berkman sat in a Pennsylvania prison for the attempted murder of the steel magnate Henry C. Frick. After his release he continued his anarchist activities in San Francisco. In 1919 both Berkman and Goldman were deported to Russia, where they were appalled by the Bolshevik dictatorship. Berkman found his last exile in France.

201 Lenin in Lausanne: Modification. I have supplied the words "in Lausanne" for clarity. West consulted Bernard S. Myers, *Mexican Painting in Our Time* (New York: Oxford University Press, 1956), for biographical information on Dr. Atl. Myers states that "Dr. Atl left Mexico again to study volcanology in Naples. In Lausanne he talked politics with Lenin and, together with a young socialist newspaper man named Benito Mussolini, put out an anticlerical paper in Switzerland" (12).

201 Henry More: 1614–87, English philosopher. He started out as a Cartesian and taught Isaac Newton, but then turned increasingly toward mysticism. More, who was a famous member of the Cambridge Platonist School, is the author of *Philosophical Poems* (1647) and *Divine Dialogues* (1668).

201–202 interview with Lenin: Modification. I have supplied the words "with Lenin" for clarity. West wrote, "why it was that after an interview, which he was told was a great privilege."

BENITO MUSSOLINI

203 Angelica Balabanov: Also spelled Balabanoff (1877–1963), Russian revolutionary who cofounded the Bolshevik Movement of Zimmerwald, which included Lenin, and became secretary of the Second International.

204 "Not to be an anarchist": West was quoting loosely from Balabanoff's memoir. The passage runs as follows in the book: "Not to have been either a Socialist or an Anarchist in Romagna would have meant to swim against the tide. For a worker to have been anything but a radical in that province might have required courage." Angelica Balabanoff, *My Life as a Rebel* (1938; repr. New York: Greenwood, 1968), 45.

205 Lloyd George: David Lloyd George (1863–1945), British prime minister and head of the Labour Party; one of the longest-sitting members of Parliament (fifty-five years). His social policies helped to lay the foundations for the modern welfare state.

205 "I will give God": Balabanoff, *My Life as a Rebel*, 49.

205 "Why can't fate be innocent?": Modification. "But can't fate be innocent?"

206 free of Spain in 1821: Correction. I have supplied the correct date. West wrote "1810," obviously referring to the insurgency led by Father Miguel Hidalgo (1752–1811) just before his death. Hidalgo mobilised New Spain's working and peasant classes to fight for land redistribution and better working conditions. The movement, which swiftly spread throughout Mexico, was defeated in 1811 by Mexico's regular army, but it laid the groundwork for the next rebellion, in 1820, which was more successful. At that time Colonel Agustín de Iturbide (1783–1824) effectively ended Spain's colonial rule. Mexico's Declaration of Independence dates from September 28, 1821.

206 Moreover, by its: Modification. "Moreover the Catholic Church makes anti-clericals in all countries where there is a simple view of sex, where the male makes the same uncalled for and unfunctional fuss over the exercise of his sexual powers as the bull, by its insistence on the celibacy of the clergy."

DR. ATL IV

207 There was Carranza: Venustiano Carranza (1859–1920), Mexican president, 1917–20. Carranza did not fulfil the promises of social reform contained in the constitution of 1917, causing his presidency to be undermined by the unrest and revolt stirred up by the more radical Mexican populists Pancho Villa and Emiliano Zapata. He is held responsible for Zapata's assassination and was himself murdered while fleeing an armed rebellion.

207 Pancho Villa: 1878–1923, Mexican guerrilla leader. Villa, who was an orphan, had to run from the law as an adolescent after murdering a local landowner who had assaulted his sister. He later became an advocate of radical land reforms and joined forces with Madero against Porfirio Díaz. He next contributed to the overthrow of Victoriano Huerta, but Huerta's successor, the moderate Carranza, did not appreciate Villa's and Zapata's extremism, and they had to go into hiding. Villa was pardoned after Carranza's overthrow in 1920 but was assassinated three years later.

207 There was Zapata: Emiliano Zapata (1879–1919), Mexican revolutionary and champion of the rural poor. An orphan like Villa, Zapata organised a small force of insurgents to fight on the side of Madero. When Madero's land reforms proceeded too slowly, Zapata took matters into his own hands and saw to it that land belonging to large haciendas was given to the Indians as *ejidos*, or traditional communal farms. While carrying out his unauthorised land reforms, he was ambushed and killed by forces loyal to Carranza.

207 There was Obregón: Álvaro Obregón (1880–1928), president of Mexico, 1920–24. A political moderate, Obregón was largely responsible for the liberal constitution of 1917 and took a leading role in the revolt to depose the increasingly reactionary Carranza.

208 Industrial Workers of the World / organised the miners: Excision. West wrote "Industrial Workers of the World had organised the miners." I have deleted the sentence's redundant second occurrence of "had."

208 miners and industrial labourers: Modification. I have supplied the word "labourers," in place of the original's "workers," to avoid repetition.

208 There was Orozco: José Clemente Orozco (1883–1949), Mexican painter. Orozco used his paintbrush to make social commentary and took many of his subjects from slums and brothels. His naturalistic radicalism caused him to be persecuted by consecutive Mexican governments, and

he spent several years as an exile in the United States. Under President Cárdenas, he was allowed to return to Mexico and carried out several large murals, one of them in the Palacio de Bellas Artes.

208 There was Siqueiros: David Alfaro Siqueiros (1896–1975), Mexican painter and revolutionary. A militant Marxist, Siqueiros fought in Mexico's revolutionary wars and was sent to Europe on a scholarship from Venustiano Carranza. Together with Diego Rivera and José Clemente Orozco he forms the triumvirate of great Mexican muralists. He was arrested for his role in the 1940s assassination attempt on Leon Trotsky. Later he chose self-imposed exile but eventually returned to Mexico and became the first president of the Mexican Academy of Arts.

208 stability and tradition: West's account of Dr. Atl stops here. The following synopsis of his remaining career is from Bernard Myers, *Mexican Painting in Our Time*, 25–26.

"As the new director of the Department of Fine Arts, Dr. Atl made a systematic study of the popular arts of Mexico, adding his name to those of Roberto Montenegro, Manuel Rodríguez Lozano (who was to make a specialty of folk sculpture), Jorge Enciso, and many others—some of whom absorbed the influences from this material into their own art. In his official capacity Atl also chose the first walls for the painters to work on. He himself did a rather hasty series of murals in San Pedro y San Pablo, which, like the early 1920 job by Montenegro and Guerrero, soon deteriorated very badly. The archindividualist in a group of individualists, Atl worked in a personal wax-crayon technique known as 'Atl colour,' which, although effective in his innumerable easel landscapes of volcanoes, had no permanence when applied to walls. Having done this much for the Revolution and the art movement, Dr. Atl chose to drop out of the picture. During the 'twenties and 'thirties he wandered all over the world, continuing his studies of volcanoes and prolific writings. (His claim to have lived for six months inside the crater of Popocatépetl is not so unlikely as it may seem.) During World War II, disillusioned as was Vasconcelos with the direction of the Revolution, this former associate of Mussolini turned to fascism, publishing books and articles in support of that point of view. In 1943, when the Paricutín volcano erupted, Dr. Atl immediately hastened there and, to the gratification of the poor farmer whose fields had been destroyed, bought him out. On this site Atl produced 130 drawings, 11 paintings, and an enormous book dealing with the volcano. This material is now in the possession of the National Institute of Fine Arts."

Index